DAY *of* DESTINY

Other works by John Mini

Magic Steve Monogatari
(The Epic Tale of Magic Steve)

The Concorus CD-Rom
An Interactive Musical and Visual CD-Rom for
Self-Development and Healing.

Producer of the Musical/Multimedia Performance Group
Vulcan's Child. Vibrational Medicine Music CDs
by **Vulcan's Child** are:

Environment
Healing
Resolve
Transition
Shining Path

DAY *of* DESTINY

Where will you be August 13, 1999?

JOHN MINI

Trans-Hyperborean Institute of Science
Publishing

Special thanks to Michael David Ward for the background cover art, space picture entitled: *Earth Rising*. Visit his on-line studio at: http://www.mdwuniverse.com

Cover design entitled: *The Big Synthesis* and text illustrations by Jennifer Dumm. *The Big Synthesis* is available as a poster.

Title page is the *"Ilhuitlapoalamoxtli"* or Aztec Calendar Stone. Resides at the Museo Nacional de Antropologia, Mexico City Tenochtitlan.

For information write to:
Trans-Hyperborean Institute of Science
P.O. Box 2344, Sausalito, California 94966 USA
Phone: (415) 331-0230 Fax: (415) 331-0231
Book website: http://DayofDestiny.com
Publisher website: http://t-hyp.com
email: destiny@t-hyp.com

If you are unable to find this book in your local bookstore, you may order it from the publisher. Quantity discounts for organizations are available. Call 1-(800) 485-8095.

First Printing September 1998
Second Printing April 1999

10 9 8 7 6 5 4 3 2 1

Library of Congress Cataloging-in-Publication Data
Mini, John
    Day of Destiny : Where will you be August 13, 1999? A Message to You Across Time from the Land of Shaman Kings / by John Mini
        p. 352
Includes bibliography and index
ISBN: 0-9657825-8-1
1. Aztec Sun Calendar
2. Aztec Dance
3. Spirituality and Shamanism
4. Indigenous Healing Practices
5. Mexica
6. Quantum Physics

LC# 98-86547

Printed on acid-free paper in Canada

*To everyone everywhere who knows
there's something more.*

<u>Day of Destiny</u> is the product of the sincere efforts and inspirations of many people. Special thanks go to:

You, for reading this book.

Jennifer Dumm, for her constant patience, untiring efforts and superb graphic design.

Kleo Mini, whose revolutionary spirit of giving has helped the entire world.

Judy Dumm, for her sincere openness and assistance.

Assumpta Curry, for graphic and moral support.

Melba Beals, for psychic editing and cheerleading.

Alex and Patti Apostolides, for help with "whoms" and Mexicanisms.

Daniel Free, for always looking into the heart of all things.

Carolyn Means, for her expansive willingness to tread beyond.

Jill Alofs, for her spirit and determination.

Craig Fraser, for his exceptional pluck and dedication.

Edward Maesen, for his technical support and penetrating mind.

Rochelle Willox, whose future contains the Great Seed of Being.

Anne Mini, for help with imponderable questions of grammar.

Dr. Lai Yat Ki, for opening the doors of the Great Tao.

Dr. Richard Tan, for his pioneering efforts and open-hearted, creative attitude in the world of Chi.

Gail Schwartz and Kimberly Chaquiso, for their constant love, inspiration and courage in facing the unknown.

D. Boon, for his inspiration and encouragement from the other side.

Susan Verby, for her interest, enthusiasm and great networking.

Krsanna Duran, for her patience and inclusiveness.

Trudy Kelsey, for her sincere criticisms and unconditional support.

Kathy Pappageorge, for her purity of heart and abundant *agape*.

Rene Lopez, an Aztec who has always known.

Gene Ossorgin, for his wonderful ongoing inspirations in the world of music.

Finally, and most importantly, to all those who, for political and other reasons, can't be named.

Thank you.

Table of Contents

Your Journey

Countdown

Appendices

References

Bibliography

Index

Warning/Disclaimer

The purpose of this book is to educate and entertain. The author and Trans-Hyperborean Institute of Science shall have neither liability nor responsibility to any person or entity with respect to any loss or damage caused, or alleged to be caused, directly or indirectly, by the information contained in this book.

The information written is based on the personal experiences, observations and research of the author, who is not a medical doctor. The practices and techniques described are not to be used as an alternative to professional medical treatment. The book does not attempt to give any medical diagnosis, treatment, or suggestion in relation to any human disease, pain, injury, deformity, or physical condition. If you have a mental illness or disorder, a medical doctor or psychologist should be consulted before you start the exercises.

Anyone who undertakes these exercises does so entirely at his or her own risk. Pregnant women, people with high blood pressure, heart disease, or a generally weak condition should consult a physician before practicing any of the exercises.

If you do not wish to be bound by the above, you may return this book to the publisher for a full refund.

PASSING THE FIRE

Passing the Fire

There are many good reasons to learn about Aztec culture. One is that it's just plain fascinating. Another is that it's timely. It could save your life. Here's why: the Aztecs were a people who appreciated and understood the timing of natural cycles. They believed humanity is going to face an immense challenge and a decision point on August 13, 1999.

The purpose of this book will be fulfilled if you get a wake up call regarding the date of August 13, 1999.

This isn't your typical churn and burn, shake and bake, die and fry, roast and toast book of predictions about our future. It's not a prophecy of disaster. Day of Destiny is a story of let's see what happens and how we can be involved. It's about choices and action. Most prophecy books primarily focus on how we're going to die. In these pages, we're going to focus on specific ways to help you live your life more fully.

The material here isn't prophecy any more than it's prophecy to look at a road map. A map can show you how to get to where you want to go. It can help you on your journey. This book will help you understand how the Aztecs mapped the qualities and textures of time as accurately and exquisitely as we map the qualities of space today.

The story you're about to read isn't a two dimensional, extra heavily starched underwear official academic interpretation. It isn't archaeological or sociological speculation, but it's archaeologically and sociologically valid. Archaeology interprets events and artifacts from the past. This information isn't of the past. It lives right now.

There are plenty of books that can tell you about the various histories of Mexico. Others can relate to you many wonderful legends and Mexican folkloric tales. What you'll find in these pages is different. It isn't meant to replace or to be used instead of the others. Read this book along with the other ones. It will enhance your perspective on the story of Mexico.

The story of Mexico is the story of our world. It's a story we've been scared to tell because it's so close to home in so many ways. Until very recently, we haven't even had the vocabulary to tell it. This story lives in us every day and in every moment. It calls out to us from the deep silence of our ancestry. It grips an ancient, instinctual part of our being that knows things aren't quite as they seem, but can't say exactly *how*. It creates an unusual feeling, like a dream you can almost remember, but not quite.

What are we trying to remember?

This book will take you on a journey. This journey may be one of the most deeply interesting and eye opening experiences you'll ever have. Through these pages, you'll follow a subtle thread of understanding into the exotic world of the Aztecs.

One of the best ways to study Aztec culture is by learning about the Aztec Sun Calendar. The Calendar teaches and encourages you to engage with your life from multiple points of orientation, or how to operate from a number of truths at the same time. It teaches you about *synthesis*.

Our word synthesis comes from a Greek word meaning to put together.* In general usage, synthesis means to put together parts to form a whole. Reading this book will train you how to think and perceive in synthesis. By the time you've finished reading it, you'll be able to look at the Aztec Sun Calendar, and our world, in a state of synthesis.

As you read through these pages and do the exercises, you'll learn to look at the Calendar with a sense of awe, respect and wonder. This reverence isn't just for the Calendar. It's for the incredible

---

* Synthesis is the complementary opposite of analysis. It's the action of proceeding in thought from causes to effects, or from laws or principles to their consequences. In chemistry, it's the formation of a compound by the combination of its elements. In physics, it's the production of white or other compound light by combination of its constituent colors, or of a complex musical sound by combination of its component simple tones. In the classical philosophy of Immanuel Kant, it's the action of understanding by combining and unifying the isolated data of sensation into a cognizable whole.

majesty of the universe we live in. By the time you reach the conclusion of <u>Day of Destiny</u>, you'll have a practical tool that can help you organize and make sense of all the apparently separate details in your life. You'll have the opportunity to look at our world from a very different perspective. You'll understand how our modern society came to be the way it is today, and a lot more. You'll have a key to unlock your personal destiny.

The material presented to you here was handed down from an oral tradition. Oral tradition requires you to use all your senses. It trains your imagination. It's a truly engaging interactivity where you create meaning, image and energy in your mind and body as you participate. You co-create each moment as it happens.

A transmission of energy passes from teacher to student in an oral teaching. It's not a conceptual thing. You could read a hundred or a million books and still not get it. Oral tradition transfers a subtle essence, like fire, from one person to another. It creates a unique bond of living substance.

The lessons in this book were taught one on one. They were learned in funny, grueling and sometimes bizarre situations. They were scribbled on napkins in grunge filled *pulque* (POOL-kay) bars in the slums of Mexico City Tenochtitlan. They were sweated out dancing sacred dances barefoot for long hard hours on oil-soaked cement and dirt floors in the mountains of southern Mexico. They were absorbed in the vastness of nature. They were gleaned deep underground in the silent hearts of unexplored pyramids buried eons ago by a long forgotten race. They were punched out on pocket calculators, wandering through open air markets, slipping on vegetable scum and dodging pickpockets. They were tested in the loving cruelty of the crucible of ritual wisdom, often in the context of massive practical jokes that could take days, weeks, months and even years to reveal their staggering multilayered punch lines. Adventures like these don't make you an academic shining star. You live them through a deeply personal process you can experience only for yourself.

Reading this book is a powerful initiation. Many wonders of the natural world will begin to open up and reveal themselves to you as you go through it. Your capacities for integrated thinking will resurface after being dormant for centuries. You'll develop clarity and power. Your dream world will begin to blend with your waking state, and your subconscious mind will come up to meet your conscious mind as you read <u>Day of Destiny</u> through to the end. You may feel sleepy as you go through this process. It's natural. The sleepiness comes from your brain and nervous system learning how to integrate and expand their range of motion while you're awake. If you don't understand something when you first read it, relax. The understanding will come to you in dreams.

A living tradition is going to be revealed to you as you read through these pages. This tradition lives and breathes inside you. It lives in all of us because it forms precisely and exactly the structures of our perceptions and processes. This tradition is a dynamic culture of life. It can't be lost, because it transcends all cultures and times. Every living creature, including you, embodies this tradition by virtue of being alive.

This is the story of Mexico. It's a story that connects us all through a vast and beautiful web of conflict and freedom. It's a story that, once you get what it's about, will help you put your world together in ways you never thought possible. It's a story of how you can, how we can, survive.

THE CALL

August 13, 1999

Have you heard? There's a revolution in Mexico. The old regime is gone. It's not that it was good or bad, it's just over. The failing Mexican government is scrambling wildly for international assistance. The ultra wealthy are moving their money into offshore bank accounts. Federal police even search tourists for contraband weapons. National guardsmen grip clear plexiglas riot shields, pocking the streets of Mexico City Tenochtitlan.

Tenochtitlan?

The capital of Mexico isn't called Mexico City any more. It's Mexico City *Tenochtitlan* (Tenohsh- like the ocean, TEET-lahn). And it's not pronounced Mexico or even *Mehico* any more. It's Meh-SHEE-koh. *Mexica* (Meh-SHEE-kah) is the appropriate name of the collective union of indigenous nations in central Mexico. Our word *Mexico* comes from the word Mexica.

There's a saying in Mexico City Tenochtitlan, "The only people in the city who eat three meals a day are the Panda bears and the priests." The people of Mexico have just barely survived since the arrival of the Spanish Conquistadores in 1519. It's been almost five hundred years now, and the Mexicans are coming into a new turn in the spiral of history.

When you come up out of the subway onto the *Zòcalo*, the main plaza in Mexico City Tenochtitlan, you hear a sound that wakes up something in your bones. It kindles an ancient ancestral fire in your blood. You hear the deep rumbling bass drums of the Mexica. This rhythmic pulse takes you back to a time when the air in Mexico was some of the purest on Earth. It transports you to a place where people once had dignity, respect and honor for themselves and nature.

The drums you hear are being played by people dancing sacred Aztec dances. Male and female dancers twirl and shake their rattles, imbuing all present with a deep feeling of sacred otherworldly communion. They're dancing on the very ground where, not so long ago, hundreds of thousands of their ancestors were burned at the stake for practicing their indigenous spirituality.

There, in the very center of the largest city in the world, poised motionless in the unmoving eye of the storm, is the date inscribed at the top of the *Ilhuitlapoalamoxtli* (Eel-hweet-lah-poh-ah-lah-MOSH-tlee), also known as the Aztec Sun Calendar. That date is August 13, 1999.

The highlighted glyph at the top of the Aztec Sun Calendar indicates August 13, 1999.

There's tension. Everyone breathlessly awaits what's going to happen on August 13, 1999. The people of Mexico feel and remember. They look to the hieroglyphic remains of the ancient stone calendar and a legend that has passed in secret for hundreds of years.

As the legend goes, the Mexica predicted the exact day of the fall of the Aztec empire, and the rise of a new empire. That's only one of the reasons why the true history of the Aztecs has been hidden, destroyed and shrouded in mystery since the time of the first Spanish invasion.

Something very important is happening in Mexico right now. Whatever it is, it seems to have a strange and intangible connection with the events going on in the rest of our world. Let's take a look at the current condition of our planet. Pop yourself into the big picture for a moment: You'll find economic collapse and insurrection in Indonesia. The moral and financial bankruptcy of Japan threaten its very existence as a modern nation. The "Asian Crisis" turned the future of our world at right angles to the way we thought it was heading even a few months ago. Countries governed by the criminally insane, like communist China, India and France, routinely explode nuclear devices without concern or regard to world wide fall-out patterns. There's racial blending and cleansing as Eastern and Western Europe reunite. Africa gropes in its struggle for identity and sovereignty as nearly half of its population grapples with the AIDS virus. The clarification, refinement and expansion of Islam, the fastest growing religion in the world, opens and closes doors to the Middle East at the same time. The chronic degeneration of the United States has allowed its government to become so corrupt, divided and incoherent, we can confidently say it has no government. It's turning into a society that refers to its children as a generation of super-predators as it allows ignorance, greed and sarcasm to slowly kill the American dream.

We're living in a time when even the most stable sociopolitical structures are dissolving before our eyes. International tension is growing like a tidal wave. Our demographic bottleneck is choking us in a psychological riddle no one's been able to solve.

This is the modern world. It's a world where people are afraid to say hello or smile any more. The mass media present fiction as reality and reality as fiction. It's getting harder and harder to tell what's real from what's not real.

Is it your imagination, or do you really see fear in people's eyes? What's creating the tone of bitterness in the deep muscles of their faces? Have you noticed an unexplainable wave of apathy, depression and lack of essential integrity in those around you? What could be causing it?

We're living in a time of growing chaos. The right impulse at just the right time could launch a cascade of events that may decide the fate of the Earth. You don't have to be an Einstein to figure it out. The old world is a house of cards waiting to be blown away.

The Call

The Mexican revolution has a unique and contemporary spirit. Part of it is composed of the long time oppressed indigenous people of Mexico, who are doing their best to create decent lives for themselves. There's also something deeper, more profound and persuasive happening. This isn't just another pre-failed, empty and painful intellectual revolution we've seen so many times before. This is new. It's more inclusive and creative. You can see it in the eyes of Mexican children everywhere. You can feel its roots reach back into the dawn of time. Its cellular memory contains a knowingness of the connections, of the oneness of all things, of all people, and of all history with this moment.

Revolutionary meetings in rural Mexico are an interesting cultural mix. You'll find local indigenous people, Mexican intellectuals, and other individuals from all around the world. How did such a diverse crowd gather together in one place to help one another out? Through the Internet.

Because of the Internet, small minority groups now can communicate directly with other people anywhere on the planet for the first time ever. Revolutions don't have geographical boundaries any more. Even if the people of a particular geographical location are repressed or exploited to the point of helplessness, as they are in rural Mexico, there are thousands of helping hands from Europe, Asia and the United States waiting to be of assistance.

The Mexican revolution is connecting and blending with the world revolution. It's bigger than any force of fear or one-sided political projection. People all over the planet are participating in a new kind of active and empowered democracy. There are no workers or oppressors battling in this revolution. There's a more essential wisdom coming forth out of the dialogue. It's creating a transcendental knowing and a liberation of who we all are.

The revolution in Mexico is different than anything we've ever experienced before. It has a sense of great caring and maturity. People are helping one another. They're bursting with compassion. There's even a revolutionary sense of compassion for the members of the Spanish blooded ex-ruling class. These are the descendants of the Conquistadores, whose dozens of generations of social, cultural and religious inbreeding have rendered them so morally and intellectually challenged, one wonders where they'll go and what they'll do next.

The Mexican revolution is more than a revolution to gain basic necessities for all. It's a revolution that's striving upward for possibilities. It's breaking through the glass ceilings of antiquated, lifeless human thought and birthing a new global indigenous child. It's a revolution that's taking place inside you and all of us right now. It includes our deepest primal yearnings for peace and safety. It's building itself from the dreams and aspirations of how we would most want our small planet to be. The events in Mexico are happening in an ancient and fascinating historical and cultural context that integrates us with our ancestral psychology, the forces of nature and the wonders of the cosmos.

We're at a rare and precious moment in history. Even in the face of all authority, people everywhere are beginning to do what they know is right rather than just doing what they're told. Revolutions are everywhere. There are revolutions in physics, medicine, religion, world trade and global communications. We're experiencing a fusion of science, philosophy, technology, economics, politics and culture. If you examine our modern world closely, you'll find revolutions just about everywhere. It's getting progressively harder to deny. We're in the middle of a world wide revolution.

We've reached a point where our global social problems have become systemic. We can't surgically remove individuals from public office to save the whole any more. It seems like every aspect of every government has become corrupt to the core. Most people are aware of it, at least on some level, even if their good intentions and beliefs tell them otherwise.

We can no longer irradiate major portions of the global population in massive group chemotherapy sessions. We need dynamic solutions to our world crisis. We need to support the profound vital principle of our world society so life may continue to thrive. We need to regenerate and revivify ourselves. We need a global revolution.

All indications point to a definite bursting forth of individual rights and sovereignty all over our planet. It's easy to see how this force is working itself out over the course of history and invisibly guides each of our lives. It's an impulse that helps us every day. It comes to us from many different points at the same time, in small ways we usually don't put together until after it happens. This impulse is holistic. It has an infinite number of sources and centers of activity. Each person you meet connects with it somehow and does her or his part to guide you into its flow.

The impulse is a living organism of change and progress. It adaptively evolves itself to changing situations, and achieves what is impossible to achieve by all human laws. Who could have predicted the many strange events we're seeing more and more of in the news these days? Who could have foretold the convergence of forces bringing us all together in ways we never imagined before?

The impulse is not of the mundane world. It can't be dismissed or simply explained away. The impulse lives over and above our conventional reasoning and influences the apparently random circumstances we meet with every day. It brings us together toward some mysterious and beautiful goal. Entire cultures have devoted themselves to holding the impulse back. Inevitably, the more they repress it, the more explosively it releases itself.

The impulse is an overarching and magnetic will. When you connect with it, you gain a sense of inevitable success. It brings you together at the right time and the right place with the right people to accomplish your task, whatever it is.

When the very Earth we live on cries out in full conjunction with the planets, and even the exploding supernovae beckon to you from the infinity of space in affirmation that the time has come and the time is now, you know the impulse is with you. When it touches you, your heart suddenly bursts into flame. You feel joined with something unalterable. You become unshakable. Unstoppable. This is the Call.

A Closer Look at
August 13, 1999

As the legend goes, August 13, 1999 is the date the Mexica will rise from the ashes of their broken condition to create a new Aztec empire. Could something even more inclusive happen? Could we all rise together in a greater synthesis of humanity from the ashes of our collective broken and scattered condition?

If only the story were so simple. Classical interpretations of the Aztec Sun Calendar also mean our world could be destroyed by *movement*, or earthquakes, on August 13, 1999 if we don't attain a global consciousness of peace, love, understanding, and harmony with the kingdom of nature by that time.*

What did the Mexica mean by "the world?" Did they mean Mexico City Tenochtitlan? The country of Mexico? The entire American continent? The world as we understand it? What was the world as the ancient Aztecs understood it?

Did they mean destruction will really come on that day, or do we have until that day to get ourselves together? Could they have meant destruction of the old world, or even old ways of thinking or consciousness? And what does movement really mean?

There's a lot of archaeological speculation concerning the different symbols on the Aztec Sun Calendar. There's no single, linear, simple definition for any of its elements. Rigid definitions violate the essential principles the Calendar teaches us. All of its meanings are relative. They depend on context. Each glyph has multiple layers of interdependent values. This is why it's a good idea to always refer

---

* The indigenous world view implicates our actions as a part of the chain of events in natural phenomena. Our influence on the weather and our interactive connections with the Earth have been key issues for human beings since the earliest of times. For example, the Emperors of ancient China were held personally responsible for natural disasters. Cataclysms were believed to reflect weak points in the Emperor's character.

Fig. 1

to the big fold-out picture of the Calendar at the end of this book as you study its parts.

Although the Aztec Sun Calendar appears to be very complex, it's made from a number of simple elements. More than anything, the Calendar is about *motion*, or *movement*. The glyph for movement is called *Ollin* (Oh-LEEN), and forms the center of the Calendar. (Fig. 1) It's made from the face of the Sun, whose name is *Tonatiuh* (Toh-NAH-tyoo), his hands, and the symbols of the four Nahui (NAH-wee), or *Ages of the Suns*. They are:

Nahui Ocelotl (NAH-wee Oh-seh-LOH-tl), the *Sun of Jaguars*

Nahui Ehecatl (NAH-wee Eh-HEH-kah-tl), the *Sun of Wind*

Nahui Quiahuitl (NAH-wee Kee-ah-HWEE-tl), the *Sun of Rain*

and *Nahui Atl* (NAH-wee AH-tl), the *Sun of Water*

Taken together as the symbol of Ollin, these elements indicate that motion, movement, and change are central to our world, which is ruled by the fifth Sun, *Nahui Ollin* (NAH-wee Oh-LEEN), the *Sun of Motion, or Movement*.

Tonatiuh wears a jade necklace, tipped by eagle feathers, and a large jewel, which is one of five jewels surrounding him in the center of the Calendar. Above his head is the tip of the *Solar Dart*. The center of the Calendar can be seen as a Solar Dart, or ray of light. It's also sometimes described as the *Solar Eagle*. (Fig. 2)

Fig. 2

The center of the Calendar is also shared by the four directional symbols:

Tlauilcopa (Tlow-weel-KOH-pah), the East

Mictlampa (Meek-TLAHM-pah), the North

Cihuatlampa (See-wah-TLAHM-pah), the West

and *Ce Quiahuitl* (Seh-Kee-ah-WEE-tl), the South.

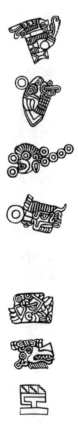

The entire center of the Aztec Sun Calendar is surrounded by the *Ring of Solar Archetypes*. In order, they are:

Cipactli (Zee-PAHK-tlee), or Crocodile

Ehecatl (Eh-HEH-kah-tl), or Wind

Calli (Kah-llee), or House

Cuetzpalin (Kwehtz-PAH-leen), or Lizard

Coatl (KOH-atl), or Snake

Miquitztli (Mee-KEETZ-tlee), or Death

 Mazatl (Mah-zah-tl), or Deer

 Tochtli (Tohsh-tlee), or Rabbit

 Atl (Ahtl), or Water

 Itzcuintli (Eetz-KWEENT-lee), or Dog

 Ozomatli (Oh-zoh-MAH-tlee), or Monkey

 Malinalli (Mah-lee-NAH-llee), or Herb

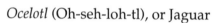 *Acatl* (AH-kah-tl), or Cane

 Ocelotl (Oh-seh-loh-tl), or Jaguar

 Cuauhtli (Koo-AUH-tlee), or Eagle

 Cozcacuauhtli (Kohsh-kah-koo-AUH-tlee), or Vulture

 Ollin (Oh-LEEN), or Motion

 Tecpatl (Tehk-pah-tl), or Flint

 Quiahuitl (Kee-ah-HWEE-tl), or Rain

 and *Xochitl* (Shoh-chee-tl), or Flower.

The Solar Archetypes are surrounded by the *Ring of Fives*. It's divided into four sections by the four *Masculine Solar Rays*, indicating the four cardinal directions.

The Ring of Fives is surrounded by the *Ring of Eagle Feathers*. It's divided into four sections by the four *Feminine Solar Rays*, illustrating the directions, or relationships between the four cardinal directions.

The Ring of Eagle Feathers is surrounded by the *Ring of Polarity*, which is ornamented by *Luminous Pearls*, *Portals*, and *Towers*.

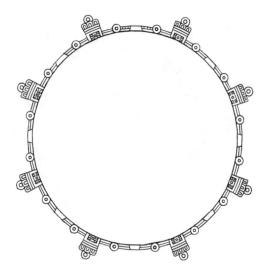

The Ring of Polarity is surrounded by the *Ring of Sacrifice*, which is made by drops of blood.

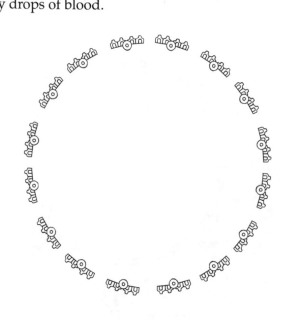

The Ring of Sacrifice is surrounded by the *Ring of Fire*. Each of its flames is divided into the four points of the *New Fire*, and the four points of the *Old Fire*.

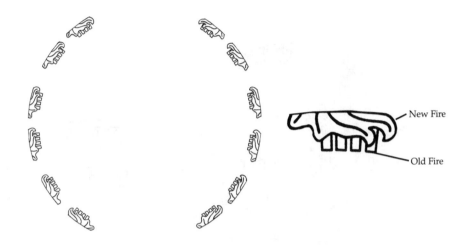

The Ring of Fire emanates from the two *Xiucoatl* (Shyoo-KOH-ahtl), or *Fire Serpents*. Each of them has a head, an eleven sectioned body, and four paper fans on its lower torso.

The glyph at the top of the Aztec Sun Calendar is called *13 Cane*. It has many interpretations. One of them is August 13, 1999. 13 Cane has a number of associations that cluster together to form its complex meaning.

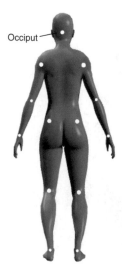

Occiput

Fig. 3

Cane means hollowness, emptiness and rigidity. Nothingness is at the core of matter. Three dimensional space has a hollow structure.

Cane, or *Reed*, also refers to origin. The *Place of Reeds* is the place of origin for the Mexica, and in many indigenous legends around the world. Alpha and Omega, origin and endpoint are crucial seed concepts for the ancient cultures.

There are 13 major joints in your body. (Fig. 3) Your joints are physical pivots of change, freedom and motion. The ancient alchemical practices of the Mexica regard the 13 joints as *energy gates* that can be tuned, strengthened and refined. The Mexica placed the 13th joint at the *occiput*. The skull over the crossed bones and the number 13 on the *Jolly Roger*, or pirate's flag, is a vestige of this esoteric symbol. (Fig. 4) One of its meanings is completion, or the attainment of a goal.

Fig. 4

13 Cane is located in the visual center of the brain. (Fig. 5) People who explore the world of natural energy call 13 Cane the *Alta Major Center*. The ancients taught that this area relates to divine inspiration.

Fig. 5

Six is a model of efficiency in two dimensional space. You can fit exactly six circles around a seventh central circle in a plane. (Fig. 6) Thirteen is a model of efficiency in three dimensional space, where twelve spheres exactly fit around a central thirteenth sphere in the most efficient packing arrangement. (Fig. 7) Thirteen is a basic structural unit in nature. It means the attracting center around which elements focus and collect.

13 refers to the sky, and to Heavenly paradise. It indicates the 13 Heavens of Aztec cosmology.

Fig. 6

13 is the number of the Sun along with the twelve constellations. (Fig. 8)

There are 13 lunar cycles in one solar year. (Fig. 9) Our Moon travels 13 degrees per day across the sky.

Fig. 7

Fig. 8

Fig. 9 13 Lunar Months of 28 days = 364 days in one year.

Fig. 10

Fig. 11

Fig. 12

Fig. 13

Fig. 14

13 relates to the renewal of the sacred Aztec ritual fire every Mexican century of fifty-two years. The Mexica believed in August 13, 1999 so strongly, they ritually demolished and destroyed their entire civilization every fifty-two years as a dress rehearsal.*

13 is an octave of semitones on the musical scale. It brings us through the door to a new octave. (Fig. 10)

13 Cane is the end of an old cycle, and the beginning of a new cycle in the Calendar's ring of 20 Solar Archetypes. (Fig. 11) This meaning is reemphasized by the placement of 13 Cane at the top of the Calendar, with the eighth Solar Ray, and the tip of the Solar Dart aligning with its center. This alignment threads between the first Solar Archetype, Cipactli, or Crocodile, and the last Solar Archetype, Xochitl, or Flower. (Fig. 12)

13 Cane is the quiet, still, hollow center of events. It's the calm, peaceful eye of the storm. It's the spindle of a *vortex*. (Fig. 13)

13 Cane sits at the delicate point of balance on a pair of scales. It indicates a time of exquisite responsiveness, and tells us we can choose, influence and impact what will happen on August 13, 1999. (Fig. 14)

Overall, 13 Cane carries the notions of movement, freedom, change, simplification, the sky, Heaven, visions, inspiration, emptying, completion, returning to origin, centrality, choice, possibility and the beginning of a new cycle. Does it seem like the Mexica are conveying a hopeful, encouraging and positive message to us across time? August 13, 1999 could be a very significant day for humanity.

* (13x4=26x2=52) You'll learn in later chapters how there are intimate connections in nature between the process of doubling and change. You'll also discover how doubly-doubling holds a very special position in the creation of life and the art of the Mexica.

The August 13, 1999 forecast flies in the face of everything we know about predictability and probability. In a system with as many variables as the ecosystem of planet Earth, there's no way we know of to make a prediction of such all-encompassing magnitude. The equation is just too complex. According to our current level of mathematical predictive science, no one could make a forecast of such accuracy.

But what if someone did?

Listen to the Mexica

The Mexica had a profound understanding of the nature of space-time. If they said something big might happen on August 13, 1999, we might want to listen to what they have to say and prepare ourselves to take action.

We tend to appreciate other cultures most when we can define them in terms of our own vocabulary and cultural concepts. In the spirit of adaptation, the lessons in this book will be presented to you in our own modern terminology. You'll be able to apply what you learn to your life more easily this way.

Besides, it's only been in the last few years modern science has progressed to a level where we can even begin to appreciate the cultural and scientific achievements of the Mexica.

There's something very interesting going on here with the Aztec Sun Calendar. It's worthy of our serious attention and sincere investigation. As you'll learn in the chapters to come, it appears as if the Mexica attained at least our current level of scientific understanding. Yet their perceptions of the world and the technology they developed were very different from ours. As time goes on, maybe we'll learn just how advanced they were.

Our New Age Forefathers

Fig. 15

Fig. 16

The dual aspects of the great seal of the United States contain many elements of the Aztec Sun Calendar.

Fig. 17
The Solar Eagle

Revolution. Esoteric symbolism. It all sounds like a bunch of New Age hocus pocus.

Not to the American forefathers. The Masonic patriarchs of Europe and the United States must have been a bunch of sensitive new age guys. What were they thinking when they put a Mexican pyramid on the back of the dollar bill?

Egyptian pyramids have pointy tops. Mexican pyramids have flattened tops. The pyramid on the back of the dollar bill is Mexican, not Egyptian (Fig. 15). The pyramid has thirteen steps leading up to its flattened top. Look closely at the base of the pyramid. Isn't that a *nopal* cactus? Seen any of those in Egypt lately?

The great seal of the United States is a twin or double seal. The great seal abounds in thirteens, and many other prominent symbols from the Aztec Sun Calendar. Note the thirteen stars above the Eagle. (Fig. 16) The eagle is a symbol of the Sun for the Mexica culture. (Fig. 17)

One of the earliest non-Spanish explorers of Mexico was Alexander von Humboldt, who was a Masonic brother of Thomas Jefferson. Jefferson and von Humboldt visited together in 1804 after Humboldt's epic adventure into

Mexico. Did they concoct some kind of plan? Did Humboldt inspire Jefferson with tales of his adventures?

Whether it's by design or by chance, every state of the United States that was once a part of Mexico now has a *Latino* population majority. Most of these people come from Mexico. Mexico's not so far away after all, is it? The Latinos who live in these areas can now throw off the mental prison of minority thinking. They can involve themselves in and influence politics in the United States. And they might just do it.

There's a popular song in Mexico right now called <u>Viva Mexico, Viva America</u>. Are the Mexicans aware of something the people of the United States are still reluctant to admit?

Masonic and indigenous principles formed the theoretical basis of the United States government. Equality is a Masonic inspiration. Democracy was an idea the American forefathers borrowed from the Native Americans.

This line of questioning may seem frivolous, but it's also important. We all share an ancient connection history has erased from our memories.

Here's an exercise to help you appreciate modern Mexico:

Perhaps the best way to learn about and enjoy the world of modern Mexico is through the music of *Pedro Infante*. Nothing can really compare with the delight and joy of Mr. Infante's music and the true inspiration he's been to the Mexican people for decades. It's challenging for non-Mexicans to understand what a great hero Pedro Infante is to the Mexicans, but when you listen to his music, something wonderful will happen inside your heart. Go to a Latino record store. Ask for music by Pedro Infante. Watch for the special look in their eyes as you say his name. Buy something and listen to it. Imagine what kind of a world view could have created this music.

The Way We Were

The more thoroughly you investigate the different cultures of the world, the more conclusively you'll find we all come from the same root culture somewhere in ancient prehistory. This is the basis of the *diffusionist* theory in archeology. Nearly everywhere you go on our planet, you can find evidence of the same *indigenous sciences*. If you go back far enough, you'll even discover we all spoke the same language. The science of *Paleolinguistics* is showing us how all the major languages of the world really do come from a single root language buried deep in history. For example, the word for God in Greek, is very similar to the word for God in *Nahuatl* (NAH-wah-tl), the native tongue of the Central Mexican highlands, and language of the Mexica. The Greek word for God is *Theo*, and in Nahuatl it's *Teotl*. There are many examples of these cross-linguistic connections in very remote areas of the world. According to our current notions of history, these connections can't exist. But they do.

The cultural treasures of every tradition belong to all people of the world. Once upon a time, we shared a common culture. If we don't choose to believe it, our alternative is even more surreal. Does it seem likely that indigenous cultures all over our planet spontaneously and independently came up with nearly identical reality paradigms and sciences?

Sun God Tablet, Babylonian stela, courtesy of the British Museum.
(Negative no. E2057)

The same symbol for the Sun God appears in
very remote parts of the world. Here are two
examples, one from ancient Babylon, and the
other from Tenochtitlan.

Mexica Sun Disk with glyphs of the four Ages of
the Suns in the corners. Peabody Museum of
Natural History, Yale University, New Haven.

INQUISITION

The Aztecs

The Aztecs aren't an extinct group of people who lived somewhere in the remote past. Millions of Aztecs are alive and well today. If you're reading this book, you may be an Aztec, or part Aztec.

Quick: what flashes in your mind when you think "Aztec?" It's curious the Aztecs, or the Mexica, of today don't exhibit many of the characteristics portrayed so long ago by the Catholic historians. In fact, you'll find the Mexica you meet today are quite the opposite of that picture. They're fundamentally kind. Their kindness has a unique depth that's unlike anything else in this world.

The Aztecs aren't a dead and forgotten culture, land or race. It's not appropriate to speak of them in the past tense. How would you feel if people habitually referred to you and your family as if you were gone forever? It would get to you after awhile.

Yet if the Aztecs were such an advanced culture, what happened to them? Where are they today? Where's the evidence of their great technology and civilization?

The Mexica have a rich and multilayered past. The people you'll meet in Mexico today are descended from the few survivors of one of the cruelest and most extensive genocides in human history. The Mexica were a culture who were violently, and almost completely, wiped off the face of the Earth. If we want to understand the events happening in Mexico today, and the real significance of August 13, 1999, we need to know what happened to the Mexica.

History

Here's the paradox: we need to talk about history, but we can't talk about history. What we've called history is just stories preserved and told to us by the winners of wars. We rarely get to hear from the people who lose.

Much of history is based on the following principle: if a lie is told for long enough, and if it's strongly reinforced, eventually anybody who knew it was a lie will be gone. Then the lie will be perceived as truth. Mexican history defines this principle through and through.

Modern notions of history in the West are grossly Eurocentric. We usually attribute things like important discoveries to the time and place a European finally figures something out, even if it happens hundreds of years after someone in the indigenous world initially made the discovery. Historians do their part to pass on the myths and lies we call history. What are the sources historians rely on?

Most often, the sources of information historians consider reliable are the ones written down by Europeans. Accounts of indigenous people themselves are often completely discredited and discounted. Living oral tradition is disrespected and disregarded. Historians say it's unreliable. Meanwhile, we remain satisfied with our own insipid story. It's full of gaping holes. It's boring, incomplete and misses the point. But it's ours.

The history of the Mexica we've been taught is standing on toothpicks. There are no first hand indigenous accounts to be found. All we have is a handful of fragmentary papers. Historians believe these few scraps of paper might be copies of parts and pieces of third hand stories about life at the end of the Aztec empire. Each of these accounts was told and then transcribed years after the events were supposed to have happened.

What's passed on to us as Aztec history is a senseless and unexamined regurgitation of what could be the stories told by these few people a long long time ago. Does this seem a little tenuous? Is it sound academic practice to base our entire sense of the Mexica on these accounts?

There's one more small detail. The information in these documents was obtained under the threat of brutal torture and dismemberment. Much of the historical material relates to sacred ritual practices the people questioned couldn't have known much, if anything, about. Those who did understand the rituals of the Mexica wouldn't have divulged this knowledge under any circumstances, especially for something as mundane as physical pain. We might also want to reconsider the supposed indigenous accounts of "native historians," who clearly wished to demonstrate their new found Catholic zeal, such as Fernando De Alva Ixtlilxochitl, who was a descendant of the sworn enemies of the Aztecs. Do you suppose his historical opinions could be biased in any way? The chances of the information in these accounts being accurate in any way is infinitely small. The probability is much greater that it's completely false.

Why? Because the historical accounts of pre-Christian America we learned in school were brought to us by the truly objective and completely disinterested Catholic church. Most of these stories come to us from three or four friars known as the "good" priests. (To distinguish them from..?) These friars collected information for the church for a number of years after the Spanish Conquest.

Oh, and by the way, we don't have their original manuscripts. Every shred and scrap of original information was "disappeared" by the church centuries ago. The documents that supposedly survived are highly questionable. Between the threat of torture, translation challenges and major cultural and conceptual barriers, how much of the truth could really come across?

In both Europe and America, the church forbade the possession of any first hand accounts of what was going on in Mexico during the time of the Conquest. Anyone who was found with unauthorized books containing information regarding what was happening in Mexico was given the death penalty.[1]

*Historians who specialize in this time period call this extreme censorship the "Catholic free press."

When church authorities discovered any written material that didn't tell the story exactly the way they wanted it told, they simply vanished it and its author at the same time. All records of post-conquest Mexico were mysteriously "lost." The only writings allowed for public viewing were those that supported and glorified the church. Most of the church sponsored commentaries published in Europe were written by people who had never even been to America.

Except for a very small handful of exceptions who were kept under strict surveillance, non-Spaniards weren't allowed into Mexico for over three hundred years. That's a long time to rewrite history.

What happened to the Mexica? The Catholic church created the bloodiest, most horrific organized disaster in human history. Almost nothing was left by the time the church was done. No one who might have been able to recreate any coherent details of the massacre would have opened their mouths about it if they survived. If they had spoken out in any way, they would have been executed. Their families and friends would have been raped and tortured in ways that would fascinate and disgust our modern imaginations. For this reason, much of the history and tradition of the Mexica had to be passed on orally and secretly.

The Spanish Conquest reduced the population of Mexico by nine tenths in three to five years.[2] We're not talking about a few scattered tribes' people here. From what we can gather together out of the historical sources, we know that Mexico had a population of millions of the most highly educated and refined people on Earth at that time.

The glyph for Tenochtitlan

The culture of the Mexica was much more highly advanced than we've been led to believe. At the time of the Conquest, Mexico City Tenochtitlan and its suburbs alone had a population of nearly two million people. This made it one of the most densely populated urban centers on Earth, in a period when the very largest European cities had maximum populations of 100,000.[3] The main market at Tlatelolco hosted over 60,000 shoppers per day.[4] The city was an ecological wonderland of permanently sustainable agriculture and wildlife. It was a paradise of graceful canals, gardens and temples. All Mexica children went to school, where they learned the language of nature. They studied science and the arts. Mexica medicine was developed to a level where they were performing brain surgery,[5] and had over 90,000 substances in their medical pharmacopoeia.[6] They had thriving artistic guilds, multinational corporations, and a complex but fair bureaucracy that required nearly a half-million sheets of paper per year to maintain.[7]

Yet above all, life there was sacred. They respected the Earth and each of its precious gifts.

Why do we know so little of the Aztec culture? Could it be because they were alive and thriving when the Spanish arrived in Mexico?

The holocaust in Mexico was similar in some ways to the Holy Inquisition in Europe, but it was much more thorough. Its purpose was to destroy every trace of the Mexica culture and civilization. All that was good, beautiful and pure in the new world was hunted down and destroyed to the point of near extinction. Genocide was carried out in the name of Christianity, with the Spanish claim being that the indigenous people had no souls.

There's no need to catalogue the horrors of the Mexican holocaust for you here. You can find them elsewhere if you're interested. Let's just say the Spanish didn't exactly create an atmosphere conducive to heartfelt sharing.

The Spanish had disease, superior weaponry and the ability to lie on their side. A number of historians have noted the Mexica were unable to lie. Lying smothers the heart and the life force. It creates a painful constriction in the chest to someone whose indigenous nature is intact. The indigenous heart, like the heart of a child, is innocent to evil. It can not understand evil, even when it's suffering.

The city of Tenochtitlan, metropolitan center of the
culture of the Mexica, fell on August 13, 1521.

This isn't a secret or forbidden history any more. To the church's credit, they no longer deny these events occurred. On the other hand, they don't go around publicizing what they've done and doing penance for it, either. The spread of Christianity wasn't all love and light. The Catholic church is still eating the fruits of the most extensive and well concealed mass murder of our age.

It's essential to acknowledge the magnitude of destruction the Spanish created in their conquest of the Americas. Why? Because the Conquistadores were the sons of the Inquisition, and the Inquisition is something that still affects us all.

Mexico wasn't the only place to feel the burning pain of the Inquisition. For example, as you sift through the cremated remains of the indigenous European culture, you'll discover how Europe used to be a forest land filled with the magic of nature. The indigenous Europeans had a deep reverence for nature and its wisdom. They worked with and learned from what were the great forests of Europe.

Somewhere from hundreds of thousands to millions of people (professional historical opinions vary in numbers), mostly women, were persecuted and tortured to death in the European holocaust known as the Holy Inquisition. People of knowledge were burned at the stake and serially executed for practicing the indigenous natural sciences of Europe. The church did everything in their power to eliminate all traces of the ancient ways.

At the height of the Inquisition, it seems as if practically any natural expression of self could set the Inquisitors after you. A telling example was in their attitude toward sexuality. While publicly disallowing sexual expression of any kind, many members of the church sported a fiendish and repressed sexuality they expressed only behind the closed doors of the church. Fanatics almost always have something they're trying to conceal. The self-reinforcing tendencies of secret societies can become extreme. They often act out in extreme behaviors.

All over the world, the church eliminated and erased whatever it could of the remains of the ancient global culture. For example, the Spanish completely exterminated the native population of the Caribbean, comprising over three million people, before they even set foot on the American continent. Similar stories come from every part of the world that was touched by the Catholic church, which built its wealth on the carcass of our plundered planet. Today, the church needs to ride the line between blame and accountability for what it's done.

The purpose here isn't to harp on the past or to dwell on the destruction. It's to heal and move on. It's simply to reveal that we need to acknowledge something before we can proceed with integrity.

We're the ones who need to understand and heal what happened in Mexico. Why? Because it's similar to a family problem. No one likes it. Everyone knows it's there, but no one wants to discuss it or work it out. It just sits there festering as it slowly drives everyone mad. As time goes on, it becomes progressively harder to talk about it. The pressure builds. It becomes more difficult to articulate real feelings. The problem continues to get worse until someone has the strength to break the silence.

The first stage in healing any trauma is to acknowledge what happened. If we really want to heal ourselves and our global wound, we need to honor what we've gone through and what we've lost. When we acknowledge the holocaust in Mexico, we create a space for sincere grieving. It's time to name this amorphous shadow. If we can complete history through acknowledgment, we'll be able to move forward out of our denial and shame to embrace a healthier future.

The Mexicans have remained nearly clueless about their real origins since the time of the Conquest. Today, many modern Mexicans of pure indigenous blood have no idea of their indigenous roots. They don't know what language their grandparents spoke. They don't understand how they've come from a group of indigenous people who lived in a special place in Mexico for thousands of years. They don't let themselves feel how their ancestors merged with nature. Modern Mexicans are strangers in their own country.

Here are some exercises to help you understand and heal the severance from our indigenous roots and culture:

- Rent and watch <u>Burning Times</u>, by the National Film Board of Canada.

- Do some soul searching. Imagine when and where your ancestors were indigenous people. Where did they live? What was their connection with that place? What were their lives like? Do any of these qualities continue to influence you now?

- Do you remember the feelings you had when you first learned how to lie? What was it like? How did you feel?

- Set aside some time for this exercise. Read Appendix 4, Chief Seattle's Reply. Go for a walk.

The Veil of Darkness

The Catholic church fought to keep the information regarding the civilization of Mexico in complete secrecy for nearly 500 years. As you can imagine, it's been especially important for them to repress and eradicate all traces of the legend of the Aztec civilization rising again on August 13, 1999.

To this day, the Catholic church distributes propaganda warning the people of Mexico not to practice their indigenous spirituality. What is the church afraid of? Does indigenous spirituality represent a serious threat to the Catholic religion?

Marshall McLuhan pointed out a very important and useful idea in his book <u>Understanding Media</u>. He said that in order to sell products, news needs to be bad. The world needs to appear in the media to be a really hostile and unhappy place. It makes the products they're advertising look better. Consumables are very comforting if we believe we live in a dangerous, violent, empty and meaningless world where it seems like everybody's out to get us.

The church pioneered this marketing technique in the psychology of their religion and the Conquest. As the centuries pressed on, the people who were influenced by the church adapted their psychology to its grim and paranoid outlook. As these people transferred this dark perspective to nearly every aspect of their lives, the church no longer needed to rigidly control and punish them. Eventually, people learned to control and punish themselves and everyone around them. The brainwashing was complete. The veil of darkness was firmly in place.

Over time, the Europeans extended their world view beyond

the boundaries of their own culture. Nonreligious Europeans even created the Darwinist philosophy to justify their actions in the global arena. Today, practically everything in our modern society comes from this survival of the fittest model. Everything from parenting norms, to our "schools," to our business and social practices legitimizes the dog eat dog world view.

Take a good look at nature. You'll find the most elegant mutual respect, cooperation and acknowledgment in every citizen of its society. When you really examine nature, you find symbiosis. Everything works together to promote life. Predators are rare. When you do find them, they don't always act like predators. They're usually just hanging out developing character.

We've projected our Darwinist model onto nature. It's a worst case scenario. It's hard to believe, but some individuals still see their world that way. We tend to get what we believe in. If we're obsessed with a fear-filled fantasy, we'll probably attract those kinds of things to ourselves in one way or another. If a group of people shares the same fear, hysteria happens.

The modern world has been acting out a mental illness on planet Earth. This projection comes complete with a God who will save you from the horrors of duality the church created. In contrast to this nightmarish creation, the church looks like a blissful alternative. It promotes a fight or flight survival situation, and it's right there ready to save you from it.

God doesn't need to scare or threaten anyone. Fearful people use these tactics. The teachings of Jesus stand on their own merits. His philosophy isn't embellished or enhanced in any way by a cult of clowns practicing international thuggery on a scale unprecedented by any other single group in human history.

Jesus was a revolutionary. His teachings carried his followers in a direction completely opposed to the prevailing doctrines of his day. Jesus spoke in parables. If you study these parables deeply enough, you can understand the connections his teachings have with indigenous spiritual practices.

The God of the Catholic church has nothing to do with the God who loved everybody and everything and abundantly provided for our world before the church existed. True spirituality was torn away from our ancestors by a few individuals. Religion was enforced through fear. Spirituality ceased to come from within.

Today, we're encased in a situation that epitomizes the modern paradox: if there's any single entity capable of delivering our world from its problems in a jiffy, it's the Catholic church. If not with religion, then with money. The Catholic church is one of the largest, wealthiest and most infiltrated multinational corporations on Earth. It could solve our environmental crisis with less than one week of the interest on its bank holdings alone. What exactly is the church saving up for?

Even the Catholic church isn't immune to the movements of history. It appears to be dying its own natural death in the modern world. Young people just aren't signing up to become priests any more. For the first time in history, the Eucharist is in danger of becoming extinct due to a lack of qualified priests. Some sociologists believe the decline in men going into the priesthood could be due to the social acceptability of being gay. Men no longer need to express their gay sexuality through the church. Now that free and open sexuality flourishes all over the free world, the church is no longer needed to provide a vehicle of escape.

The spiral of history is opening. Maybe we don't need the church any more. Maybe we're ready to take back our spirituality.

Here are some exercises to help you understand and heal your indigenous spirituality:

 Could the ancient science avert the Armageddon of the church's Bible and return our world to being a wonderful place to live? What would happen if we banished the illusion of the Heaven and Earth duality forever?

 Rent and watch <u>The Name of the Rose</u>.

 What are the things you most believe in? Who would you be if you didn't believe those things?

 If you had an indigenous spirituality of your own, what would it be?

The Cycles and Rhythms of History

History shows us cycles of oppression and liberation. For example, the Islamic Moors conquered Spain. Five hundred years later, the Spanish drove the Moors out of Spain back into Africa. The Spanish acquired an insatiable lust for war during this process. After they finished reclaiming their own country, they turned their savage jaws on conquest.

The Christians also were oppressed for hundreds of years. Then they rose to power, and turned their focus on conquest. Most people who have been repressed for long periods of time, once they're able to turn the cycle around, will do whatever they feel they need to do to ensure it won't happen again.

Historians tell a similar tale of the Mexica, but with an interesting and enlightening difference. Long oppressed, discriminated against, misunderstood and scorned by their contemporaries in the Valley of Mexico, they completely reversed their situation in a series of brilliant political, social and economic maneuvers to become the most powerful nation in Central America. However, the Mexica didn't impose their values and beliefs on the other people around them. Instead, they appreciated, incorporated and included the wisdom of other cultures into their own. They became powerful through synthesis. The magnanimous, respectful and inclusive attitude of the Mexica naturally led them to receive the Spanish with open arms, and bring them directly into the heart of their civilization. The rest is history.

As history marches on, there's been a global shift away from governments that benefit their people, to predatory governments that take from their people. This has mirrored the shift from spiritually based religions to the predatory modern religions that must expand and assimilate or destroy their victims.

Rhythmic cycles of repression and rebellion undulate through history. They rise and fall as the centuries slowly unwind. In the old days, oppression and liberation were limited to individual countries and small geographical locations. Our modern situation is very different. Now we're in a position where there's been a global oppression of both the indigenous and the industrial worlds for nearly five hundred years. It's natural to expect some kind of global liberation is ready to make its appearance.

That's why August 13, 1999 is about much more than Mexico regaining its independence and dignity. The spiral of history is much bigger on this turn. This time, it's big enough to include the entire planet.

Look at the cycles of history. What happened to the grand civilizations of Mexico? Where are they today? Examine the masterworks of the ancient Chinese. Compare them with modern communist Chinese society. What's the connection? Examine the glory of old Europe. Why has Europe been locked in a world looking backwards for hundreds of years? Where's the glory of ancient India? Where are the power, opulence and great wisdom of the Africa that was?

History is in motion. Statistically and historically, it's very likely the next revolution will change the whole world.

Here are some exercises to help you understand cycles and rhythms in history, our modern culture and your life:

🏵 Rent and watch <u>Koyaanasquatsi</u>.

🏵 What are the long term rhythmic cycles in your life? Are there repeating themes that seem to come up again and again? What's their rhythm?

🏵 Do something to break up the rhythm of your day today. Let yourself shift into a refreshing new rhythm.

COME TOGETHER

The Inquisition Today

Religious conquest still continues today in many forms. Indigenous repression is spreading as religious missionary groups infiltrate our globe. It's happening in places like the United States, where Native American children are kidnapped from their homes and taken to Christian schools. They're forbidden to speak their native language, tortured, ridiculed and systematically hypnotized into believing their indigenous heritage is wrong. Their hair is cut off and they're taught to hate themselves and all they came from. They're trained to turn against their own kind, which many of them do with great vengeance. Very few have the strength of spirit to resist.

The Inquisition is also still alive today in many nonreligious forms. Take a look around our world. Everywhere you go, you'll find the systematic removal of indigenous lifestyles and an imposition of the new world order. The conquest, repression and subjugation of indigenous people never ended. It's happening right now in places like Tibet. The communist Chinese, having destroyed their own religion, still exhibit the same behavior as the very institutions they claim to have destroyed. They've even done it to themselves. Consider the stunning tragedy of modern China and the destructiveness of its cultural revolution, in which the communists almost totally annihilated the Chinese indigenous sciences. This is especially odd, considering the Chinese spent thousands of years retaining and improving these sciences. They preserved the ancient sciences better than most other cultures because they escaped the ravages of the Catholic Conquest. Then they destroyed their culture with as much zeal as they had maintained it. Many modern communist Chinese people who survived the Cultural Revolution are still petrified to speak openly about matters of energy and the spirit.

If your own indigenous nature is repressed, you'll feel the desire to belittle, negate, punish and destroy it when you see it alive and well in others. The modern world invalidates indigenous cultures in the same way communist China invalidates the presence of Tibet. The entire philosophical foundation of the modern world stands in opposition to what the indigenous world represents. The indigenous world is one of permanently sustainable ecological and social harmony. The modern world is its complementary opposite.

Repressive behavior is extreme in places like modern China, but you don't need to go very far to find it. In fact, it's probably a lot closer to you than you'd like to believe. You've been through inquisitions and conquests in your own way, too. Remember? When in your life were you forced to take on someone else's beliefs, even when you knew they weren't true? We're often trained as children to do and believe what we're told, rather than what we know is right. Is it any wonder the heart of the modern world has gone to sleep for a while?

We face a silent Inquisition every day as the people around us judge everything we do. They constantly compare what we're doing to what they think we should be doing. If our actions don't match their expectations, they condemn and crucify us however they can.

It gets even more convoluted. We even do it to ourselves through the mechanism of guilt. We constantly compare what we're doing to what we think we should be doing. We even compare what we're doing to what we think other people think we should be doing. It's an endless cycle.

Fear backs up the silent Inquisition. There's a fear of litigation and of being outcast in the modern world. There's a fear of losing your job. There's a fear of slipping out of the popular mind set and being rejected. This fear has it roots in the persecution our ancestors felt in the crushing grip of the Holy Inquisition.

A tremendous amount of time and energy in modern life goes into evaluating whether or not you're *weird*. Being weird is the most terrifying, degrading and possibly life-threatening judgment that can be cast upon someone in our modern society.

Our word weird comes from an Old English root. It means the principle, power or agency by which events are predetermined. Weird means fate, destiny, to foresee and to control future events.

It's that which is destined or fated to happen to a particular person. It's a happening, event or occurrence.

In Middle English, weird meant to have the power to control fate or destiny. It meant partaking of or suggestive of the supernatural. Of a mysterious or unearthly character. Something uncanny. A strange or unusual appearance. Odd looking. Out of the ordinary. Strange. Unusual. Fantastic.[8]

It's OK to be weird.

Most of us still go deeply unconscious when we hear about the worldwide holocaust perpetrated by the Catholic church. This is because we still feel the pain our ancestors suffered. We're still afraid to speak out and express ourselves because of the centuries of cultural conditioning our ancestors went through. We go to sleep on the issue just like anyone who's suffered severe abuse.

Psychologists who do hypnotic regression work find nearly everybody has internal images and impressions of being tortured and killed by the Inquisition or at some other time by the church. The Inquisition has stamped a deep racial memory on our collective unconscious. It affects our psychology every day.

The Inquisition took away our profound connection with nature. It disowned our kinship with the animals, the trees and the air. It orphaned us of nature and our direct experience of God. The Inquisition created an hysterical frenzy that continues to this day. We've all felt the repercussions of the spiritual genocide wreaked upon our planet by the Catholic church. Whether you believe you're an indigenous person or not, no matter who you are or where you live, you've felt it. We've all been conquered.

The fear of being persecuted for our indigenous nature is usually strong enough to keep us completely repressed. We've internalized the repression of the Inquisition over the centuries, and now we repress ourselves. There's no longer any need to do it from the outside, because our brainwashing has become genetic.

There's a cultural spiritual experience all people of the world once shared. It was taken away a long, long time ago. We're all healing from this loss. We've been living with PTSS (Post Traumatic Stress Syndrome) since the Middle Ages. We've all been in shock for hundreds of years. We've been in shock for so long nobody has any idea what it would be like not to have it. If we really want to be free to be ourselves and do the things we came here to do, we must heal this historical wound. We need to heal this syndrome on a planetary level.

Here are some exercises to help you heal from being judged by those around you, and from judging yourself:

- ✽ Do something weird. Be aware of what comes up for you at each stage of the process.

- ✽ Go out of your way to appreciate and do something kind for a person who has been socially outcast for being weird. Be aware of what comes up for you at each stage of the process.

- ✽ Read Malidoma Some's <u>Of Water and the Spirit</u>.

Modern Life

It appears as if the worse our world situation gets, the more narrowly we focus on how great technology is. We worship the wonders of the modern world to the exclusion of what's going on all around us. But what would we think if someone we knew obsessed like that while her or his world was falling apart?

Everywhere you turn in the media you'll find the assertion that we're the first, the biggest, the best, and the most advanced civilization this planet has ever seen. It seems to be our most fundamental assumption. What if it isn't true? What if the Emperor has no clothes?

When people die in the hospital these days, we often hear they died from complications. There's an ironic and mystical grain of truth in this saying. Modern life has become unnecessarily complicated.

One of the purposes of modern life seems to be to keep us overwhelmed with daily minutiae. When we're running around every moment of the day and night, we rarely get a chance to ask ourselves the big questions that could put our lives back into perspective for us.

Have you left any space in your day for something important or meaningful to happen? Will you have the time and energy to let it into your life if you're too busy or tired to accept it? Do you ever ask yourself, answer and act on the fundamental questions of who you are and what you're doing here? Do the answers to these questions paint the picture of your life the way you want it to be? If you can't even ask yourself these important questions, how will you take the necessary actions to improve the quality of your life and the lives of those you love?

The modern world makes it easy to get completely engulfed in our everyday lives. We sometimes get stuck in mundane existence. Existing just isn't the same as living. It can get to the point where even the most magical and wondrous things seem dull, boring and lifeless.

It's easy to get too exhausted and embittered to reclaim yourself in the modern world. If you allow them to, day to day compromises can suck you dry. Sometimes it seems like responding with your heart is too painful if you feel there's nothing left to give. Without tremendous inner strength and support, even acknowledging you have a heart can bring the entire weight of life crushing down upon you.

If you aren't diligently self-respectful of your time and energy, the modern world can keep you too busy, distracted, sick or poor to do what you came here to do. This is especially true if you've become successful, or you're in the process of becoming successful by society's standards. In the environment of success, your issue can turn rapidly into one of being consumed by the very lifestyle you've sacrificed so much to create.

There's the "s" word. Would you have felt truly satisfied if we went through an entire discussion of the Aztec culture without delving into the arena of sacrifice?

Are you tired of sacrificing yourself? Many of us feel we can't sacrifice one more thing. We're sacrificed out as a society because we've sacrificed our true selves. We've sacrificed most, if not everything we know is right, on the altar of modernity.

We were sacrificed by our parents when we were children as they offered us up to the modern machine for processing. Some of our parents did it out of love, because they wanted the best for us. Other parents did it out of fear, others out of greed. Some parents didn't even think about it.

If you want to examine a case study in true human sacrifice, observe the lifestyle of anybody working for a modern corporation. Do you find it odd that many people living in our modern world gladly sacrifice their lives for causes that are completely devoid and bereft of any honor, dignity or valor? Where's the joy? Where's the sense of personal achievement in this macabre tribute to the banal?

We're living in an age of information pollution. It's called trivia. Frivolity and trivia can dilute our ability to embody our purpose. They confuse and encloud our coherency in a shroud of meaningless details. At the same time, we've created a vacuum of sacred knowledge in the modern world. We're experientially impoverished. Maybe this is why even the most successful modern lives have a genuinely toxic sense of failure in them.

Something smacks of a paradox when people in Los Angeles are bullet-proofing their cars with Kevlar. Our technological world has become a techno-illogical world. We're getting progressively numb. Everywhere you go in modern society, women are pissed. Isn't this an appropriate time to start asking why?

The rhetoric of the modern world becomes more hollow each day. A deep longing for nature and its vitality is rising in the technological cultures of planet Earth. It's time to rend the veil of darkness.

Here are some exercises to help you reclaim yourself from the trials of modern life:

- What in your life has any objective value? What do you want to incorporate into your life? What do you want to weed out?

- How can you get yourself out of the loop of being burned out on giving? Do whatever you have to do to reconnect with your purpose. What do you do to rejuvenate and reanimate yourself? Do it as often as possible. In its most positive sense, sacrifice is the willingness to compromise for a higher good. What are you giving? How are you giving back to the world for the things you're receiving?

- Where are you just existing in your life? Where are you really living? How can you bring more livingness into your daily life?

- Where's the joy in your life? What percentage of your time do you spend in that joy?

- True sacrifice is an act of respect. It's an investment that yields a balance or a return. What sacrifices are you making in your life? What kind of returns are you getting on your time and money investments? If you've been sacrificing a lot and you aren't seeing much in return, you might want to try a different approach.

An Incident on the Zòcalo

The Zòcalo, Mexico City Tenochtitlan. Sunday, January 4, 1998, approximately 10 PM.

It's an eerie scene, filled with the slow silence of a true disaster. About ten thousand people are milling around the Zòcalo on a warm post-holiday evening. Indigenous street vendors are selling all manner of gadgets and trinkets from their blankets on the cobblestone plaza. Children throw Styrofoam toy airplanes. Huge tufts of cotton candy float through the air. Ripe young Mexican teens catch the cotton candy on their tongues when it falls. Sometimes two youths jump for the same piece and they accidentally kiss.

The Mexica are dancing. Some of them perform healings with *copal* (koh-PAHL) incense from their ritual circle.

The last dance completes, and the circle is blessed. Drums are put away. The dancers slip on their shoes.

Suddenly, without warning, all the hundreds of indigenous people on the Zòcalo dive to the ground in unison and start scrambling for cover. It's like watching a flock of birds or a school of fish change directions all at once.

There were no visual or auditory cues whatsoever. Business as usual broke into a life or death struggle in a fraction of a second. The odd thing was, the non-indigenous people didn't even notice anything unusual was happening. Tourists lounged. Urban Mexicans went on their merry ways.

It was as if the two groups of people were living totally separate realities...

Come Together

One of the main issues we face in the modern world on a daily basis is ongoing multi-cultural synthesis. Our world population is blending together. We're uniting through the media and integrating as millions of indigenous people leave their native homelands in search of stimulation in the big cities. All over the planet, people are trading their citizenships with any particular nation for the benefits of a more global and universal life-style. Humanity is recombining as we nomadically and sensibly follow the flow of wealth and freedom around our Earth.

There's a massive influx of indigenous and tribal people pouring into the modern cities of the world right now. Many of these traditional people have unique and interesting talents. One of these skills is the ability to perceive subtle vibrations and energies. Many indigenous people can perceive these energies as easily as you can perceive the chair you're sitting on.

One of the main reasons our modern world has developed into what it has become is because we've repressed our indigenous natures and sensitivities for centuries. Modern society lives in a state of perceptual retardation when it comes to the world of natural energies. This density tragically separates us from our natural environment and those around us. As more and more indigenous people enter the mainstream of our lives, we face the very real challenge of being virtually blind in our personal, social and business interactions with them. Call it superstition if you like, but when and if these people become involved with your life in any way, their subjective reality is going to affect your objective reality.

People with intact indigenous natures have a very keen edge on you if you don't have the ability to perceive energy patterns as they do. Many indigenous people can read your subconscious like an open book. For a person with an intact indigenous nature, it's a simple matter to know the fears, desires, and soft spots of another, and build strategies accordingly.

There are much better reasons than simple competition to develop these natural skills for yourself. For example, when you begin to perceive your world in this way, you'll enter a magical wonderland of subtle energies. This is the common ground all indigenous people share. You'll open yourself to experiences you never even dreamed of, and discover a quality of life you always knew was possible, but never knew exactly how to attain it.

It's in your own best interests to begin to open up your indigenous nature. You can train yourself out of perceptual retardation. It will help you to be happier, healthier and more positively engaged with your world.

Since we're all coming together, and so quickly, it's best to learn about different cultural perceptions. Learning how other people perceive the world can help us lubricate the process of integration. Integration doesn't mean assimilation or homogeneity. It means mutual respect, communication and understanding in a relational field that accepts and welcomes diversity among its members.

It's also very practical. For example, how many languages do you need to speak if you live in a modern city? The more you know, the better off you'll be. You'll have more connections, and you'll also have a lot of fun.

When different cultures meet, it isn't all wine and roses. We learned that from the Inquisition. Many people today still hold beliefs that were forged in remote antiquity. Some of us were raised in culturally isolated environments, where our beliefs were never challenged or questioned in any way. Some people even believe they hold the unique and only truth, particularly around religious matters.

Here's the real truth: everyone believes his or her own truth. One person's beliefs conflict and contradict another's beliefs. So much for the truth.

Here are some exercises to help you understand about different kinds of perception:

 Read <u>Ishi.</u>

 Plato describes four levels of the mind in his <u>Republic</u>. They're typical mental attitudes and ways we tend to process information. These levels are:

> *Ignorance* - you don't know anything about anything, and you don't care.

> *Opinion* - You care, mostly about yourself.

> *Reason* - Your mind is more trained and capable of being used.

> *Intelligence* - Your mind can have true understanding, perspective, and depth.

> It doesn't matter which one of these levels you're coming from. We all demonstrate a mixture of these qualities. Wherever you're coming from, ignorance, opinion, reason or intelligence, own it. Where are you coming from?

 Practice each level of mind. Especially practice the ones you're absolutely sure you never embody. Even if you feel like you can't relate to a level, pretend. Get a working sense of each level of mind.

 One of the most liberating experiences you can have is realizing, accepting and acknowledging that you're just plain ignorant. Discover a new area of your ignorance daily for the next ten days. You don't have to do anything about it. Simply acknowledge your ignorance.

THE BIRTH
OF SCIENCE

Archaeology

Then there's the view of history presented to us by the archaeologists. It's as if you were looking at the world of the Mexica through a pinhole. Most archaeological perspectives are gross projections of a simplistic, Pollyanna world view onto the rich and subtle complexities of an indigenous culture. Sending a team of archaeologists into an ancient sacred site is like sending a group of chimpanzees into your local supermarket to do research. What do you think they'll find? They'll discover the bananas and have a heyday.

If you asked archaeologists to interpret the Bible, would you get Christianity? If the archaeologists tried their hands at the Buddhist scriptures, what would they create? What capacity or training do archaeologists really have to interpret and translate these teachings? What can we realistically expect of them? Why should they be up to the task of bringing the most profound synthesis of human thought through their brains onto paper for our humble understanding? Have you ever had lunch with an archaeologist? Five dollars and an hour of your time will radically restructure your opinion of history.

Maybe the indigenous world can't be reduced to simplified linear formulas and thought processes. What would happen if we turned somebody like Stephen Hawking loose on translating the antiquities of Mexico?

Human bones have been found, at archaeological sites in Central and South America, that have silver implantations in them. The bones have completely healed around these implantations. Modern surgeons have rediscovered this practice in the last few years, and now it's used as an ultramodern surgical technique to regenerate non-healing fractures and nerve tissue.

How does this kind of evidence change our orientation toward indigenous discoveries of the past? Does it completely overturn our preconceptions of the ancient world, or do we dismiss the evidence?

All too often, we form opinions based on what authorities tell us to think. Mass hypnosis tends to set in as soon as authorities stamp their official seal of interpretation on a subject. We instantly forget to investigate the issue more deeply.

Great monoliths straight out of 2001: A Space Odyssey get found in places where our current understanding of history says they can't be found. The archaeological bigwigs arrive, and the monoliths disappear. No one knows where or why. What's their investment in maintaining our belief in the same old story of history? You may want to consider keeping your mind as free as you can from official interpretations.

For the most part, archaeological writings reveal a vacuous ignorance of the indigenous mind. They demonstrate a complete lack of natural intelligence and connection with truth, and an absence of the self development required to understand these great teachings in any meaningful way.

But let's be kind. Let's be politically correct. Let's call these archaeological writings developmentally challenged.

There are many developmentally challenged translations of indigenous art, customs and ritual. There's very little archaeological writing authored by those who understand the nature of ritual magic and the world of energy. Indigenous cultures live in a magical world of nature. If you don't get nature, you don't get the indigenous mind.

Until recently, most archaeologists didn't seem to be very interested in discovering the perceptions of the indigenous world. It appears as if they just wanted to affirm the superiority of our own culture and impose it on anyone they could. Look at the language used in a typical archaeological text. You'll find words like "primitive," "barbarian," "uncivilized," and the favorite, "half-civilized."

Archaeology is a random process. It's creating a random picture. If you read a book the way the archaeologists are putting together the tale of the world, what kind of story would you create?

We live in a time of credentials. What were the credentials of Jesus, Mohammed, Buddha, Einstein, or any other human being who has gone down in history as someone who has changed the course of world events forever? One thing all of these great people had in common was their absolute lack of credentials. Credentials are the language spoken by the very clusters of parasitic decay these great bastions of humanity strove against. Credentials are the sticky web woven by a self created hierarchy. They deny true achievement and thrive on game playing and bureaucracy. None of the great people of history had their greatness handed to them on a silver platter by the society they lived in.

What credentials do archaeologists have even to set foot on sacred land? What credentials do they have to destroy architectural and burial sites that were meticulously designed to bring great harmony, good weather and ongoing prosperity to the people of that land? What credentials do they have to desecrate the dead? Wouldn't we consider destructive archaeology an act of war if another culture did the same things to our national monuments?

Exactly what credentials would an academic scholar need to interpret the remains of a culture that used a technology and a scientific vocabulary based on energy wave forms and hyper-dimensional geometries?

Fortunately, archaeological trends of the past are changing. For example, professionals who have broadened their field of study to include both archaeology and astronomy are investigating the sacred sites. It's no surprise that they're finding a wealth of astronomical data contained within the architecture. These *archaeoastronomers* were the first people to enlarge our understanding of the cultures of ancient Mexico.

Archaeological research is just like anything else. The more you know, and the more open you are to learning, the more you'll find. Mexico has over 20,000 discovered archaeological sites. Many, many more are yet to be found. America is still an undiscovered continent.

Ancient Architecture

While the Europeans were scuttling around in animal skins foraging for food, the Mexicans were designing and implementing civil and architectural structures for hundreds of thousands of people. These wondrous city-states were created to promote human, geological, atmospheric and even intergalactic harmony and balance. They were a demonstration of sustainable ecological living on an astounding scale.

The architecture of these ancient cities was designed to get you out of your small self and into the big world picture. They were constructed to teach you about universal relationships, and how you personally fit into the living patterns of nature. Can you imagine a healthier urban environment than that?

Most of the ruins of central Mexico haven't been excavated. Those being explored are still only partially uncovered. Archaeological research into the ancient sacred sites of Mexico didn't even begin until the early 1900s, and it didn't get into full swing until the 1950s. Very little of what's there has been discovered.

The remnants of thousands of pyramids are buried in Mexico at the centers of ancient sacred cities. Bit by bit, we're discovering a very different picture of ancient Mexico than the historians used to teach. Original archaeological works by Augustus le Plongeon and others began to reveal how the ground plans and architectural gridworks of the ancient cities and buildings in Mexico were built using the principles of a profound ancient science. The sacred sites contain encoded purposes at which we are just now beginning to guess.

These cities were built by very advanced technical engineers.

For example, The pyramid at Cholula, Mexico has the largest cubic content of any known structure in the world.[9]

The edifices in an ancient city are linked intimately with their surrounding environment. They're connected both spatially and over time to align the placement of the buildings with events occurring in the sky and on the Earth at long intervals. Placement and proper alignment are very important features in most ancient art. Taking this art out of its native environment is like trying to understand the meaning of a liver outside a living body. You might be able to come to some conclusions, but you won't really get what it's about until you can understand the entire dynamic system in its proper context. The exact placement of the art of the Mexica was a vital element in their function as scientific and magical tools.

Unfortunately, that wasn't generally understood or even recognized until recently. Much of the archaeological evidence that could round out our understanding of Mexican history lies buried in the vaults and basements of museums and historical societies all over the globe. Collectibles of looted artifacts get shuffled together as they're acquired by historians and archaeologists. The information contained in these priceless relics becomes scattered, irrelevant and meaningless when they're taken out of their environmental contexts.

Ancient architect priests used solid scientific principles to create natural electromagnetic wave phenomena. This helped them create ecological and economic abundance for their people. They used architecture to optimize the beneficial relationships with their environment, and to minimize the less advantageous ones.

Although the Catholic church outwardly condemned the pre-Christian sciences, it still used indigenous scientific principles in all its own magic, ritual and architecture. The church took over and implemented the indigenous European, and later the Central and South American technologies.

In North America, the effects came much later and in a different form. It wasn't the church, but the US military who took over the sacred grounds of the Native Americans. It's still unclear what, if any, indigenous technology was used in building the US military. All we know is the indigenous power spots were purposely captured and utilized for military purposes.

Much of the indigenous sciences were based on a profound understanding and practical application of the principles of geometry found in nature. We call it *sacred geometry*. If you have trouble believing the US military would make extensive use of the powers of sacred geometry, please recall the shape and the name of the big building in Washington, DC serving as their headquarters. These guys are serious about sacred geometry.

Back to Mexico. The church used the advanced technology of indigenous cultures to gain power over the people they subjugated. At the same time, they didn't allow the indigenous people to empower themselves with their own advanced sciences. When the church practiced the indigenous sciences, it was blessed ritual. When anyone else practiced them, it was witchcraft.

The conquerors destroyed the indigenous temples and scientific centers, and built their new churches and cathedrals on top of the ancient sacred sites. They did this in order to "steal the *Feng Shui*," or to capture the magical potency of these locations and all that had been done there before. This process didn't happen just with architecture. The church laid a claim on every human emotion of our ancestors. They copied and then copyrighted all indigenous ritual and made it their own. They used the technological, cultural and material wealth of conquered nations to create their religious empire. One of the simplest examples of this practice was to place the birth of Jesus, or Christmas, at the approximate date of the winter solstice. This was a time the Pagan cultures celebrated the return of light, or the return of the Sun from darkness. The church assimilated our ancestral psychology to captivate and manipulate our deep feelings.

The great cathedrals of Europe weren't built on faith alone. The architecture of these monuments embodies the timeless principles of the indigenous sciences in their design. The grandeur and beauty of the church was built on the ancient sciences. Masonic architects used indigenous geometrical principles to encrypt the ancient wisdom into some of the most famous buildings in the western world.

Many of the churches in Europe are *geomantically* oriented according to *ley lines*, or *electromagnetic Earth meridians*.[10] A meridian is a channel or flow of electromagnetic energy. All living creatures, including the Earth, have interconnecting systems of meridians. The monoliths of the ancient world functioned very much like our cell towers of today. They were geomagnetic acupuncture resonators. Acupuncture is one of the last vestiges of a science once used to create enormous regenerative architectural environments. The indigenous scientists used this technology so groups of people could live in optimal relationships with their surrounding landscape. Acupuncture has internalized this science for centuries, practicing it privately within our own bodies.

Archaeologists are quick to jump up and down when they find sacred priests buried in the remains of the pyramids in Mexico. They use this architectural practice to triumphantly wave the checkered flag of human sacrifice. Yet the foundations of most old European churches also contain cadavers who are aligned to geomagnetic nodes. Were they also sacrificial victims?

The Greeks and other ancient architects used to make the proportions of their temples and other important buildings similar to the proportions of the human body. The Bible even contains an interesting description of this process in *Isaiah 44:13*: "The carpenter stretcheth out his rule, he marketh it out with a line, he fitteth it with planes, he marketh it out with the compass, and maketh it after the figure of a man, according to the beauty of a man; that it may remain in the house."

Examine the architectural layout of practically any ancient Egyptian, Greek, Roman or Gothic building. You'll find both the floor plans and vertical faces are based on regular shapes inscribed within a circle, or a number of regular shapes inscribed within concentric circles. These circles are divided into 4, 8 or 16 equal parts. (Figs. 18, 19, 20)

This circle and its inscribed polygons form what is known as the *circle of orientation* in classical architecture. It was used to align the buildings with specific directions and local energy grid lines. The first markings traced on the ground at the construction site of a building were always the *north-south axis* and its *perpendicular*.

Fig. 18

Fig. 19

Fig. 20

A circle was then drawn and often divided into 5, 10 or 20 equal parts. This naturally begins to create relationships based on the *golden section*. You'll learn more about the golden section in coming chapters. It's the fundamental geometrical ratio of all life as we know it.

Tenochtitlan was divided into four quarters with five subdivisions (calpullis) each.

The famous geomancer John Michell tells us European churches were usually placed so a natural spring was positioned directly beneath its spires.[11] The ancients understood how the Moon's cycles influence the flow of electromagnetic energy in the Earth's meridians. This relationship physically relates to the way the Moon affects the tides. The Farmer's Almanac in Europe and the United States, and the Tong Shu in China both contain a wealth of information on this subject.

Indigenous people learned, cultivated, nurtured and benefited from the powers of nature. The sacred sites were used as places where geomagnetic and other energetic forces could interact with water. For example, the ancient Mexicans revered, respected and took care of their water. They knew how to keep it at or near its optimal living temperature, where it's able to stay strong. Water retains its vitality when it is properly cared for. It stays healthy, resists bacterial and other opportunistic growths, and has a number of other qualities that have gone unnoticed in the modern world.

The Mexica knew to keep their water away from the Sun, so

they irrigated their crops at night. They understood how even very minute fluctuations of water temperature can change its dynamic properties. They knew when sunlight shines on water, it slows the water down. The indigenous scientists say when water is exposed to sunlight, it curls up like a snake and goes to sleep.

Tonatiuh is the Sun

When you explore a Mexican sacred site, you'll find many serpent forms undulating in waves. You can also find carvings, sculptures and reliefs of seashells everywhere. Eduardo Matos Moctezuma tells us in his <u>Treasures of the Great Temple</u> that conches and other varieties of fresh and sea water shells were the most frequently discovered treasures in the *Great Temple* of the Mexica.[12] The ruins of the Great Temple complex are buried underneath the Zòcalo in Mexico City Tenochtitlan.

Stone sculpture of a conch from the Great Temple of the Mexica culture in Tenochtitlan. The conch is a symbol of sound, water, rain, fertility the logarithmic spiral and life.

You'll discover evidence of a fascination with and practical use of water and rain in the architecture of a sacred site. Water was gathered from the roofs of important buildings and springs. It was channeled through aqueducts and protected from the rays of the Sun. This water circulated into cisterns and larger systems of aqueducts to flow over and through the sacred areas and then out to irrigate crops in the fields.

Natural springs were highly revered in ancient Mexico. Their water was used for specific purposes relating to their mineral and electromagnetic qualities. When and how the spring flowed gave evidence of its character.

The Mexicans were masters of hydroengineering. They used confluences of water to create utopian cities beyond our most heightened grasp of beauty. One of these cities was *Teotihuacan* (Teh-oh-tee-WAH-kahn).

Stone rattlesnake from the the Great Temple of the Mexica. Resides in the Mueso del Templo Mayor, Mexico City Tenochtitlan.

In its day, Teotihuacan was much larger than imperial Rome. Today, it's probably the single most striking demonstration of the majesty and connectedness of an ancient city you'll find anywhere in the world.

Teotihuacan is a city of what the archaeologists used to call interesting coincidences. Interesting coincidences like the base dimensions of the Pyramid of the Sun are exactly one eighth of a minute of arc on the Earth's surface.[13]

Archaeological excavations removed some of the outer covering of the Pyramid of the Sun. Taking this small deviation of one to three feet into account, the Pyramid of the Sun at Teotihuacan and the great pyramid at Cheops in Egypt have the same base dimensions.[14]

It's also an interesting coincidence that both the Mexicans and the Egyptians designed the exact positions of their pyramids on the surface of the Earth into their architectural design in the same way. You can find the location of a pyramid by measuring the relationships between its angles.

Our pre-Christian ancestors didn't believe in a flat Earth. Peter Tompkins tells us in his impeccably researched <u>Mysteries of the Mexican Pyramids</u> the ancients didn't lay out their maps on a Cartesian grid. They used a *spherical* grid of triangles in the form of an *icosahedron*, the twenty sided *Platonic Solid*.*[15]

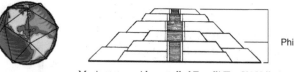

Mexican pyramids are called *Teocalli* (Teo-KAH-llee), God-structures, or energy houses.

There are many, many more interesting coincidences at Teotihuacan. For example, the mathematics of its architecture demonstrates the orbital shells of the planets in our solar system. They include the asteroid belt, and other planets we're able to see only with very high powered telescopes.[16] We've only discovered some of these planets and asteroids in the last few years.

It's also an interesting coincidence that the design of Teotihuacan embodies the physics of complex gravitational calculations only

---

*You can learn more about the *Platonic Solids* in Appendix 1, The Language of the Sorcerers.

just now being worked out by the top astrophysicists of our day.[17]

The ancients excelled in the sciences of geometry and *harmonics*. They used proportional measurements in their architecture to create *resonance phenomena*. Hugh Harleston, Jr. used a mathematical model based on proportional measurements to reveal some interesting coincidences in the architecture of Teotihuacan.*

Mr. Harleston discovered something curious. He found the proportional numbers of the relationships of the major buildings at Teotihuacan all add up to 9 : 162, 207, 216, 225, 369, 504, etc.

That was just for starters. Here are some of the other things he found:

100,000 times the base of the pyramid of Quetzalcòatl (Keht-zahl-KOH-ahtl) gives you the radius of the Earth. The levels of the steps on this pyramid yield proportions like the Tropic of Cancer, the location of the Earth's magnetic pole, the latitude of the pyramid itself and the Arctic Circle.

He found direct correspondences with the natural logarithm, the constant of the speed of light, the Hydrogen Constant and the 1.059 constant. (The 1.059 constant is a ratio that relates the characteristics and behavior of sound and light.)

The *pi* and *phi* ratios are built into both the structures of Teotihuacan themselves and the relationships between them. Phi is the foundation of the golden proportion.

The proportions of Teotihuacan reveal the mystical system of Plato (There's a great deal of Pythagorean based right triangle symbology at Teotihuacan), and the ancient Egyptian sacred

Nine was especially revered in precolombian Mexico. Nine is prominently featured in the Calendar because it creates the essence of numbers and the sequence of all numbers in a doubled-mirror reflection.

$$111111111 \times 111111111 = 12345678987654321$$

The magic of nine creates all the numbers in a doubled mirror reflection.

Another mirror reflection of nine is:

2X9=18	81=9X9
3X9=27	72=9X8
4X9=36	63=9X7
5X9=45	54=9X6

Fractional nines create an infinite repetition of all numbers.

1/9=.11111...
2/9=.22222...
3/9=.33333...
4/9=.44444...
5/9=.55555...
6/9=.66666...
7/9=.77777...
8/9=.88888...
9/9=1

Quetzalcòatl

---

* It doesn't matter what system of measure you use when you're using proportional measurements. The proportions come out the same in all systems.

numerical pantheon. There are many indications the Mexican astronomical system has connections with ancient Egyptian astronomy.

The sheer number of these correspondences, and the obvious intentionality of their use in the architecture of this city absolutely precludes that these could be chance phenomena.[18]

Overall, the layout of Teotihuacan clearly represents an incredible synthesis of universal physical constants on a scale model of the Earth. This Earth model nests within a scale model of our solar system. The solar system model nests within a scale model of the macro universe representing increasing levels of magnitude beyond our own solar system. And it's all elegantly presented to you in the mathematical and geometrical language of science.

Teotihuacan was a city designed to integrate human life with cosmic life force. It was built to tap into, harness and harmonize with the superhighways of energy that straddle the heavens.

You don't see a whole lot of that going on these days.

Think about it: we're lucky to live in a house or an apartment with a decent view that doesn't fall down in the rain. The Mexicans built entire cities hundreds of years ago that are still standing today. Can you imagine the effects of living in long term architecture designed to promote intergalactic harmony? What would it be like to live in a society which has that focus?

Here are some exercises to help you appreciate the value and benefit of regenerative architecture:

🦋 Rent and watch 2001: A Space Odyssey.

🦋 Calculate your relative position on the face of the Earth based on the geometry of the structure you live in.

🦋 Really examine the building you live in. Look at the materials it's built from and the intelligence of its design. How long do you predict our society will last based on the design of this structure?

🦋 If you were to look back at our culture archaeologically from a point of view of a thousand years from now, what kind of things would you conclude about our civilization?

The Mexica Mind

The daily reality of the Mexica was profoundly sacred, personal and experiential. It included both faith and science. They lived lives that were replete with meaning, honor, joy and connectedness.

Every child, woman and man in the Mexica culture understood and followed the intimate details of nature and its ecology. They knew how to care for their bodies by dancing, sweating everyday in the family Temazcalli (Teh-mahz-KAH-lli), or sweat lodge, and by consuming a very wide variety of foods and medicinal herbs.

They comprehended the physics of the universe and applied it to a peaceful and regenerative technology they used to enhance their lives and the health of their world. They used their pyramids, their knowledge of natural cycles and the properties of minerals and water to enhance their quality of life and rejuvenate themselves along with the seasons.

The Mexica respected and deeply communed with God in everyday life. They believed in and prayed to an omnipotent, omniscient creator God who they called *Tloque Nahuaque* (TLOH-kay-nah-WAH-kay) "The Lord of Everywhere," or *Ipalnemohuani* (Ee-pahl-neh-moh-HWAH-nee), "The one in whom we live and move and have our being." We don't find statues or other artwork depicting God in the relics of the Mexica. This is because they understood the qualities and attributes of God were inexpressible.

We do, however, hear and see quite a lot of the Aztec gods, who are of a different order from God. We can understand and appreciate the names, myths and legends of the gods only after very deep, subtle study and practice. Their descriptions are poetic symbols of natural forces. The Nahuatl word we've translated as God is *Teotl* (Teh-Ohtl). Teotl has many meanings. It means holy, divine or venerable. Another meaning of Teotl is energy.

The gods speak the symbolic language of nature. They integrate mathematics and poetry. The gods and goddesses are the constants of nature. They're the observable and unobservable motions of our universe, and the sources of the phenomena of our world. They're behind and inside the experiences we have every day. We find them in the great richness of human psychology.

The Aztec gods are energy beings. The Mexica deeply respected and revered them. The gods are our teachers and helpers. They're the guardians and masters of special places and times. We can contact and enter their worlds to explore and expand our potentials, possibilities and responsibilities.

The gods are natural energies. We can experience personal relationships with them. These relationships are different from the one we have with God.

The Mexica didn't practice adoration or idolatry. They practiced being grateful and thankful. They had respect and appreciation for nature and the natural world.

The Spanish weren't exactly known for the exalted state of their astronomical knowledge or their mastery of physics at the time of the Conquest. It seems as if the Spanish were incapable of complex, integrated thought when they arrived in Mexico. What the Conquistadores and missionaries couldn't understand, they sequestered to the realm of religion.

The Spanish just never got what this respect for nature was all about. They perceived the honor the Mexica showed for nature as idolatry. It's one thing to be appreciative and to venerate. It's another to worship.

The Mexica can show us how everything is alive. Their world view teaches about the many essential forces interacting to create our world. It describes a central, prime self-creating power that permeates all existence. The animistic spirit profoundly acknowledges and partakes of the creator God.

The Mexica expressed and communicated in *gestalts*. Gestalts are whole symbolic patterns that convey massive amounts of information at a glance. The Mexica understood how poetic symbols are the most efficient way to convey large amounts of complex information, because they convey multiple levels of meaning at the same time. Ancient Mexican art can take you right into this experience. Nuance always points to information in the art of the Mexica. For example, if you would expect an angle in a work of art to have a particular number of degrees, and it's off by a little bit, it isn't because they were being sloppy. It's because they were making a statement about something. In a typical Mexican statue every color, twist, turn and angle of its joints describe subtle networks of information. Martin Brennan takes you on a very detailed and scholarly exploration of this world in <u>The Hidden Maya</u>,[19] in which he explains how every detail of ancient Mexican art contains a universe of symbolic messages.

Like many pre-Christian cultures, the Mexica were exceptional geometers and mathematicians. They knew the mathematical and geometrical language of nature. The ancient Mexicans used the zero for hundreds of years before the Arabs gave it to the Europeans.

The Mexica had a highly developed astronomical science, and a vast capacity for abstract thought. Their perception of the world was that the entire cosmos is a vast living being.

They made extensive use of mirror reflection, symmetry and extremely abstruse mathematics to describe the behavior of physical phenomena. The Mexica described the universe this way because they understood the structure and dynamics of human perception with an astounding clarity we're just now beginning to appreciate.

There are many reasons why we know so little of the Aztec civilization. One of them is because the mathematical intricacies of their art are so complex, we haven't been able to figure out what we've found. The Mexica used the mathematics of infinite series to describe our world. Charles William Johnson explores a number of these abstract relationships in his <u>Science and Ancient Artwork</u>.[20]

The Mexica were masters of integrated thinking. They appreciated the elegant expression of interrelationships between many complex streams of thought. They enjoyed and respected images and ideas the linear mind can chew on for many years.

Mexica scientists somehow were able to calculate the exact dates of large earthquakes and other natural phenomena. They explored the geometries of interstellar relationships and understood how life energy flowed to Earth from the stars and the qualities of space itself. They mapped the flowing textures of spacetime, and looked into the infinity of the future and the past. They listened to the properties of cosmic rhythm and resonance as they focused on the date of August 13, 1999. They used their indigenous sciences to enhance the quality of life in ancient Mexico.

Much of the world the Mexica knew can no longer be known. The natural environment they loved and lived in has been destroyed.

It's easy for us to assume that nature is as nature was. In some ways this is true, and in some ways it's not. As we learn to perceive our world more holistically, we're learning how the power of nature and the power of the magic of old came from the beautiful interconnections of all life. Now this delicate fabric has been torn and polluted. Nature's power and our ability to use it have been tragically diminished.

Our simplistic modern perceptions of the ecosystem are similar to believing the health and well being of any single part of your body has nothing to do with the rest of your body. Everything in nature is connected. The more you assist and develop relationships and connections, the healthier, happier, and more prosperous you become. It's simple.

The Mexica learned from the unmolested power of nature. They understood about creative transformation. Among many other wonders, they genetically engineered a complex and diverse system of agriculture, a small fraction of which gave us much of the diet we still eat today.

Fortunately, the Mexica used straightforward and thoroughly rigorous techniques in their science. Their thinking was so clear we can pick up on their spectrum of thought, follow and continue it even today. As you read on, you'll follow a subtle thread of these thoughts into the magical world of the Mexica.

The Mexica were deeply involved with modeling and scientifically applying the structure of infinity. What does this really mean, and how can we understand it?

We define order by our ability to describe a situation with some kind of formula or equation. We've progressed from the *linear equations* of the Newtonian era to the *nonlinear equations* of our current sciences. Nonlinear equations can statistically describe the probable evolutions of *dynamic systems*.

Dynamic systems are the real world events of life. They're the structures and patterns of motion, or movement. They're the unpredictably complex relationships happening all around us all the time. Dynamic systems live on a pulsating boundary between order and chaos. Science has just begun to explore these nonlinear universes with the aid of sophisticated computer modeling techniques. The Mexica also understood and used nonlinear models in their science.

Scientists use nonlinear equations to make models of natural phenomena. They're teaching us how very minute changes in subtle influences can create enormous differences in the evolution of a dynamic system over time. This is because a nonlinear equation in science is one where slight changes in variables can create disproportionate, fundamental changes in the whole system.

The Aztec Sun Calendar is a nonlinear model. It describes how subtle factors can compile within a dynamic system until at some critical moment, the entire system abruptly crumbles into chaos.

Then an incredible transformation occurs. The system emerges from the furnace of chaos and reorders itself into a new kind of system.

When does this critical moment happen? We can't exactly say. We can't make the same kinds of predictions with nonlinear systems as we can with linear ones. The evolution of a dynamic system is unpredictable. It rides on the crest of the wave between order and chaos. It dips in from one side, then passes through the wave onto the other side.

Yet the Mexica believed this critical moment will happen on a global scale August 13, 1999.

The Mexica understood about probability. They knew enough to predict Cortes' arrival in Mexico to the day. When he landed his ships on the shores of Veracruz on Easter of 1519, the Mexica were there waiting for him. They'd been preparing for that day for centuries.

They also knew enough about probability to predict the fall of their own empire to the exact day. A track record like this might influence your decision whether to believe them about August 13, 1999.

We could logically criticize this point on the grounds of their collective belief. We could say that since the Mexica believed their empire was going to fall on August 13, 1521, it did. Then how exactly did their collective belief cause Cortes to sail across the ocean from Europe, land at that particular time and place, and do the things he did? Was he really that sensitive and obliging?

Regarding the fall of an empire, how much more completely do we subscribe to a similar vision through the constant repetition and indoctrination of biblical prophesy regarding our particular time in history?

Science and Religion

Modern science has constructed a world model in the last fifty years that's basically identical to the indigenous world view. It's just not as complete. If we continue to insist indigenous science is religion, it will have the unique distinction of being the only religion scientifically proven to be true. By the way, how scientifically verified is your reality?

Science has changed our appraisal of the indigenous world view forever. It has brought our understanding of the indigenous sciences outside the realm of our opinions. We can no longer dismiss the indigenous sciences as superstition. They never were. Does this mean we can begin to practice them again?

The life affirming ancient sciences used their regenerative technology to enhance and enrich life on Earth. They glorified the Creator through the creation. They tended and cared for the Earth for tens and possibly hundreds of thousands of years.

The life negating modern religions disrespect and revile life, the Earth, personal power and the development of wisdom. Within a mere 2000 years after the arrival of the modern religions, the entire Earth has fallen into a state of collapse. It would be wise at this point in history to create and revivify a number of life affirming spiritualities.

Real science and real spirituality are both quests for truth. When a truth is discovered, cultures and civilizations can come and go. Knowledge can be lost for generations, but truth remains. It can be discovered, discredited and destroyed again and again. As many times as it's thrown away, truth returns. Each time it comes back, it becomes a part of a larger whole.

That's why August 13, 1999 is about much more than a social revolution in Mexico. This time, the spiral of rediscovery of the ancient knowledge is big enough to include our entire planet.

The traditional religious path is one of faith alone. It doesn't require proof. It's not mental. Thomas Aquinas labored over this issue in his <u>Summa Theologica</u> for dozens of volumes and decades of sincere inquiry. By definition, faith rests outside the realm of science. Our word faith comes from the Latin root *fidere*, to trust. It means confidence. It's a belief proceeding from reliance on testimony or authority. Faith means belief in the truths of religion. It's a conviction operative on the character and will. Faith is the spiritual apprehension of divine truths. It's supernatural illumination, that which is believed and the power to produce belief or credit. It's the duty of fulfilling one's trust and the obligation of a promise or engagement. Faith is fidelity. Faith is loyalty.[21]

Faith is the realm of religion. Proof is the realm of science. Faith is a beautiful expression of human consciousness. So is science. The two co-evolve together.

In a sense, the church incubated science to become what it is today. If you wanted to prove or even bring forth any kind of new idea in the old days, you had to come up with an overwhelmingly convincing argument for your cause. Even the densest vestigial minds of the church couldn't possibly disagree with you. If your proof wasn't clear and simple enough, you'd be burned at the stake, or tortured to death in some other Christian fashion. These are the roots of our healthy skepticism and scientific attitudes of today.

A classic example of this process is the story of the famous scientist and astronomer Galileo Galilei. Galileo was a revolutionary. He spent the later part of his life trying to persuade his fellow Europeans the Earth revolved around the Sun, not the other way around.

Galileo's scientific arguments weren't quite persuasive enough, and he narrowly escaped being burned alive. Begging on his knees at the feet of his Inquisitors, he took back everything he ever proclaimed in the name of science. Galileo spent the rest of his life under arrest.

Science defined an *objective reality*. It's accessible to anyone at any time under any circumstances. It defined the ordinary and the mundane by eliminating *subjectivity*.

That all changed recently. Science was so objective, it became subjective. Modern science objectively proved our subjective perceptions can create measurable effects in the realm of quantum physics. This is one of the many dimensions of the famous *Heisenberg principle*.

Science also began to prove many other faces of the indigenous sciences, such as the objective existence of the four *Elements*. It discovered things like everything in our world is made of vibration, and life is a dynamic force electromagnetically connected with the Sun.

The boundaries of the animate and inanimate worlds have dissolved again. We can stop pretending everything around us isn't alive. It is.

The Process

If you really want to appreciate the works of the Mexica and the importance of August 13, 1999, we'll need to dive a little deeper into the bowels of science. Relax. It's fairly safe.

Real science is a little different from its stodgy cultural stereotype. It needs to revise constantly and revitalize itself. Science needs to bare its naked flesh to the light of new information. Every new generation of scientists strives for a newer, more evolved, and more comprehensive understanding of our world. This is the scientific impulse that drives our society forward and humanity closer together over time.

Many groups of professionals believe the theory they've built their world on is the supreme and defining statement of the way things are and always will be. This is usually true, for a while, until new information and insights come along. Then they get to learn if their structure is big enough to accommodate growth. Fundamental belief structures tend to become modified, outdated or less useful under the evidence of new discoveries. If a new theory is more coherent and useful than an old one, the old one becomes history.

Science would never progress without ongoing experiments to reveal differences between what is generally accepted and the fresh insights of recent discoveries. The famous British scientist Roger Bacon once said:

"He therefore who wishes to rejoice without doubt in regard to the truths underlying phenomena must know how to devote himself to experiment."

Experiments reveal exceptions. Studying exceptions leads to progress. We can always find exceptions to rules. This is what advances our theories toward their ultimate goal.

Science is an urge to progress. It's experience and experiment based. It battles the ever present dangers of simplistic thinking. Real science is the complete opposite of rigidity or dogma. It has a sense of daring and adventure in it. True science lacks the brown-nosed fear of the academic scholar.

Science is the process of scanning our universe in search of patterns. These patterns can help you navigate and make the best use of the things you find in your part of the world. Anything and everything in nature is composed of patterns. Each of them lives in a middle zone between both larger and smaller ones that spiral away into infinity. This is the core of the *fractal* concept in modern chaos science.

Patterns can be described by mathematics and geometry. Mathematics and geometry have developed into the universal language of science. This is because they're the best tools we've found to express accurately the relationships between things. If you can understand the qualities of relationships, you can identify patterns. You can get in touch with the forces at play in the world around you, and behave with intelligence.

No math can ever completely describe a living, dynamic system. Even the most beautiful and mathematically ideal theory won't fly until it's tested in the real world. Scientific process includes feedback systems that weed out its mistakes over time. An experiment tests an hypothesis about something. If it seems to hold true, we run it as truth until it doesn't run any more.

Math and geometry are somehow behind and/or intertwined among real world events. They create ideals and perfect forms. Nature hints at these forms, but rarely embodies them completely. Nature does its thing within ideal boundaries.

It's the way we deviate from a perfect mathematical form that makes us so beautiful, interesting and mysterious to behold. Albert Einstein once wrote:

"The most beautiful emotion we can experience is the mystical. It is the source of all true art and science. He to whom this emotion is a stranger, who can no longer wonder and stand in rapt awe, is as good as dead."[22]

Science will never banish mystery from our experience. Scientific inquiry widens and deepens our perception and appreciation of mystery. It reveals the substance of miracles. The more we explore, the more infinite our universe becomes.

Physics is a purely *quantitative* science. It uses numbers to describe things. If the theories developing out of modern science are correct, then you could begin studying anything in the universe, and wind up at the same place in the end. Ultimately, your search will arrive at a family or community of scientific, mathematical and geometrical principles. Science currently believes all phenomena construct themselves from and integrally relate to this community of principles. This is why physics is called the mother of the sciences.

The biological sciences have traditionally been more *qualitative* and descriptive in their approach. That's beginning to change. Recently, modern molecular biology has become more mathematically based through its use of *probability equations.** Probability means that judging by present evidence, something is likely to be true, to exist or to happen.

We always have to say probably when we're describing nature. Probabilities are the only way we can even attempt to describe complex living processes using mathematics. This is because everything in the natural world occurs in the context of many different relationships at the same time. Our world isn't as simple as we once believed it was. Influences appear and disappear. Subtle forces converge to become major forces. Everything dances with everything else. Science is beginning to describe our universe as a vast network of dynamic, interdependent relationships. We're slowly uncovering the scientific truths behind the *Gaia Principle*. Earth really is a living being.

There are many relationships we just can't see if we separate a whole into its parts. We're beginning to understand how there's a

---

* As a measurable quantity in science, *probability* is the amount of antecedent likelihood of a particular event, as measured by the relative frequency of occurrence of events of the same kind in the whole course of experience.[23]

structure to our mystical perception of the wholeness of things.

The old science believed it could comprehend and master our world by disassembling it and examining its parts. It analyzed and fragmented our world to understand it piece by piece.

The new science is about synthesis. It examines whole systems. This new appreciation of synthesis is helping some scientists to go back and ask some of the fundamental questions again. They're asking with fresh enthusiasm about many of the things we stopped questioning hundreds of years ago. Our ancestors stopped asking questions when they were given pat answers to some very important issues. Beware of pat answers. They're the bedfellows of official interpretations. Remember, every scientific revolution is championed by someone who questions the foundations of what's generally accepted.

Nature is connected. There's no isolation or separation. You and the insects and all the creatures of the land, sea and sky are touched by each and every star in space and a million other forces we may never be aware of. Yet we still try to define our experience only in terms of the things we think we already know.

The old science encouraged us to focus our powers of observation on one part of a system. Then we proceeded from our knowledge of that part to the rest of the whole picture. There are some glitches in this attitude. We may think we're observing everything that's going on in an experiment, but how do we really know? What about all the factors we don't yet perceive or understand? What happens if our viewpoint is biased or incomplete? It's very difficult to discern whether we're observing something that's really happening, or we're just observing our own process of observation. If our assumptions contain even the slightest blunder, it can compound itself as we apply what we think we know to the whole system. If our ideas are just a little bit off in the beginning, small errors can multiply themselves repeatedly over time to become very large ones.

The phenomena of our world are a complex web of interactive influences. If you isolate individual parts in your process of observation, you're no longer examining the same thing. You have to investigate the whole system if you want to say anything meaningful about it.

Yet whole system descriptions have their own challenges. The biggest one is they're usually too vague to be useful. How can we combine the practicality of analysis and bring it all together in synthesis at the same time? How can we get the best of both worlds?

We observe the essence of the whole as we study its parts.* The only challenge point here is we can never know to what extent we're observing, because we can never truly observe the whole. There's only one whole. We're all inside it.

Scientific process is coherent, potent, tangible thought. It has to be inclusive or it invalidates itself. The scientific community developed the art of analysis. Science excluded synthesis for centuries because it was just too challenging to describe the world accurately in terms of whole systems. This threw science into the depths of contradiction, because it's supposed to describe nature. Nature includes. It synthesizes.

Science has shown us time and again how nature combines many subtle forces to create large nonlinear phenomena. Nonlinear means unpredictable. Science has given us copious linear proof of the nonlinear nature of our world.

Linear thought has its value within certain boundaries. Right alongside your ability to reason, you also have an inborn capacity for nonlinear thought. The problem solving potential of this part of your mind is truly astounding. What's even more incredible is that your nonlinear thought processes can come into a kind of *resonance* with the natural world around you. As you learn more about the ancient sciences of the Mexica, you'll learn how you can blend with nature. Nature is a part of you and you're a part of it.

If you can learn to keep your linear thoughts in their place, they can truly help you. However, if you allow them to run rampant through areas where they have no validity, they can speed you down the road of distortion and unhappiness like the wind.

The progress of science is nonlinear. Many, if not most, major scientific breakthroughs come to us through a combination of accident, observation and disciplined action. For example, Alexander Fleming discovered *penicillin* by accident when he noticed a particular kind of mold killed some bacterial cultures in his lab. The scientific part came when he observed what happened, and then tried to figure out *how* it happened. He stuck to his task until he could reproduce the phenomenon at will.

Progress is nonlinear. It's rare when we can predict what's going to happen tomorrow based on what we understand today.

*This is why it's important always to refer to the big picture of the *whole calendar* at the back of this book as you study its individual parts.

Science is like a pyramid. It progresses in leaps that include past discoveries into a more all embracing and satisfying whole. Science synthesizes. It's becoming more holistic as it advances. We're finally learning how to think across disciplines and include more and more with simpler, more elegant theories.

The Aztec Sun Calendar is simplicity itself, yet it describes many of the important connections between natural phenomena. It trains you how to think in synthesis. This ability, and the ability to reference from one system to another, is becoming increasingly valuable in our modern world. Science now is discovering more clearly how real breakthroughs usually come from somewhere outside of any particular field of study.

Here are some exercises to help you appreciate synthesis:

- When was the last time you experienced the joy of mystery? What can you do to cultivate an appreciation for mystery and the unknown?

- What areas of life are your linear mind trying to explain or control? Could there be nonlinear solutions? What are they?

- Find or purchase something. It can be anything, as long as it has a form. In a suitably ritualistic manner, contemplate the nature of form as you smash the object to smithereens. Do your best to completely destroy it. Really get into it. When you're done, spend some time with the remains, if there are any. See if you can construct the original form again from the pieces. After that, try to make something new and completely different from the pieces.

- The famous Jazz musician Charles Mingus once said: "Anybody can make the simple complicated. Creativity is making the complicated simple." Whom do you know who makes the simple complicated? Whom do you know who makes the complicated simple?

Indigenous Science

Our modern culture both benefits and suffers from professional specialization. We choose our fields and go deeply into them, narrowing our focus to learn more and more about less and less until we know almost everything about practically nothing. The other tendency is to become a generalist, and learn less and less about more and more until we know nearly nothing about close to everything. Specialization creates a positive sense of personal power and accomplishment. It also creates playpens of ignorance. It can lead us to believe we know everything, even if we don't.

Our biggest technological breakthroughs now are coming from interdisciplinary approaches. Physicists are making quantitative advances in biology. Biologists are inventing new forms of computing. Computing experts are revealing the inner structures of physics.

When you take an interdisciplinary approach to research, you explore the relationships between things. Our next frontier is in the science of relationships. Relationships are the essence of relativity. They're also the basis of the ancient sciences.

Leading research confirms the indigenous world view with more certainty every day. For example, the use of multi-factored probability equations, quantum numbering systems, and the inclusion of irrational numbers into their logic and scientific methodology all definitely point to a high level of agreement between the scientific culture of the Mexica and the culture of modern science.

The indigenous sciences are nature based. They keep turning up everywhere as we explore our universe. No matter where we go, there they are. Nature's here to stay.

The indigenous sciences are a thread that connects all the pre-Christian cultures of the world. We see remnants of these connections in the works of Joseph Campbell and others who have traced the remote origins of oral traditions.

Pre-Christian was a long time before Christ. Cultures as late as the ancient Greeks strove to piece together scattered fragments of the ancient science. Much of this technology survived in areas of the world that were untouched by Christian history.

People in the ancient world used the indigenous sciences to invigorate, empower and enliven themselves. Indigenous ways kept people in tune with the wonderful world around them. The indigenous sciences weren't a secret until the church began torturing and killing people for practicing them. Common sense then led these practices into secrecy. The word for secret in Latin is *occult*. The church created the occult.

Science has repeatedly demonstrated the phenomena of *self-similarity* and resonance at work everywhere in the natural world. These are two of the most basic principles of the ancient sciences. How could we not agree with a science that uses these principles to their fullest potentials?

Relax. This isn't a pagan religion. This is science. Can we all get along now?

The assertion that the ancients were unscientific is an ignorant one. How do we define scientific? Archaeological literature stains itself with statements like "pre-scientific culture" or "They created without understanding why..." These kinds of evaluations are a psychological dismissal of the level of achievement attained in the ancient world.

The culture of the ancients was precisely scientific. Their technology was also holistically integrated, aesthetically pleasing, constructive and ecologically regenerative. If you were to look at today's picture realistically, you could more accurately say it's we who create without understanding.

Another academic revelation you'll run into is that the indigenous people of the world used their intuition to discover their sciences. The word intuition is commonly applied to somehow diminish the true accomplishments of those who came before us in ancient prehistory.

Intuition is a fuzzy term. When the idea of intuition is used in this context, it just means the scientists of today don't understand the process of how something came to be. This attitude of putting down the achievements of others covers over the shame and denial we have of our own modern perceptual retardation. Our technological society is environmentally and developmentally deprived on many levels. Normal, healthy people with intact indigenous natures can see, hear and feel energy fields. They're aware of vapor trails from the past and the future spiraling into and away from the here and now. The entire cornucopia of creative potentials and probabilities for any situation as they unfold moment by moment is just plain as day to an integrated person.

Have you developed these basic coordinations? Or would you consider yourself among the ranks of the perceptually challenged? There's hope. Read on.

People who are integrated with their indigenous natures and in touch with their environment might seem to have extraordinary superhuman powers to someone who hasn't yet connected with his or her indigenous nature. Your levels of awareness naturally become very refined when you live a lifestyle that's genuinely at one with the Earth and the rest of the cosmos. You can appreciate nuance and pick up on things. Connecting with your indigenous nature doesn't mean you run around with your eyes closed with the back of one hand on your forehead channeling wisdom from the great beyond. You just see, hear and feel things other people don't. It's not a big deal. Your indigenous nature has a practical, rooted, down to Earth quality. Many of the ancient achievements belong to the realm of common sense for people whose indigenous natures are thriving.

When you get right down to it, we can't prove in any way the ancients didn't discover the things they knew in exactly the same ways we do today. There's just no evidence left of the processes they used, because they were destroyed.

Then again, maybe the evidence is here and we just can't see it. The Spanish looted all the scientific and medical instruments of the Mexica. These tools were melted down into gold and silver bars and sent to Europe. What would an operating room look like to someone who was completely ignorant of medicine?

Those we now call the indigenous people of the Earth retain the vestiges and perhaps the essence of a once global culture of a magnitude we're just now beginning to realize. The Mexicans had an incredible level of technology. It was possibly more advanced than anything we can comprehend even today. The ancients didn't subjugate or attempt to control nature. They worked along with nature. They complemented and served it. The ancients understood about actions and their consequences in closed systems. They cared about each other, their children, and the world around them with great tenderness and intimacy.

The indigenous sciences are a synthesis of what divided minds call science, art and spirituality. Indigenous science is practical and experiential. It involves processes of self-exploration and connection. It's empirical and scientific. It observes and measures natural phenomena in very precise and specific ways. It isn't faith based. The two systems of faith and indigenous science can easily coexist. They do in rural Mexico and many other parts of the world today.

It's our cultural conditioning to believe without direct experience. The modern world too often dogmatically accepts the past conclusions of science as if they were a religion. For example, we're taught and believe the Sun emits alternating waves of electromagnetic energy through space. For the Mexica, this was an everyday experience they measured and quantified over time. Living life connected with the wonders of nature is so rich in nuance and quality. Modern life has little or nothing to compare with it.

Indigenous scientists make every effort to enhance and augment the vitality of the soil and water where they live. They use their knowledge to preserve and perpetually rejuvenate the mineral skin of the Earth. They understand how a permanently sustainable high quality of life depends on maintaining the best possible relationships between the soil and water in their environment.

Indigenous scientists examine sequences of apparently separate events over time. They search for correspondences or coincidences connecting these events. They seek underlying principles. They look for patterns.

The factors of consciousness and perception are important variables in the differential equations of indigenous scientists. You alter some parts of nature when you observe them. Others disappear entirely when your focused mind and attention try to fix themselves on them. The very act of your focusing hides parts of the world from your observation. If you want to observe and interact with these qualities in nature, it takes a gentle and complete shift of your perception. It's a lot like those computer pictures where you need to change the focus of your eyes to see what they're really about. Sometimes if you focus too intensely on what you want, your intensity can push away the thing you're wanting. Working with the energy of nature is very subtle.

Indigenous scientists look for the principle of *analogy*.* An analogy occurs whenever a shape, figure or design contains a proportion or a series of related proportions that reproduce themselves in a way that creates those same shapes again.

The ancient scientists discovered systems of proportions. They used the principles of tone, interval and harmonics as extensions of their geometry. They knew how frequency reveals coherency in time the same way structure and pattern reveal coherency in space.

Geometry and number relationships were the keystone of the indigenous sciences. The quest of our modern science is revealing a world built on the exact same principles. In fact, the basis of our scientific proof often rests in our very ability to reduce observational data down to differential equations. These equations are geometric proportions and number relationships.

The famous mathematician Bertrand Russell once said of this relationship of the very new and the very old: "Perhaps the oddest thing about modern science is its return to Pythagoreanism."

Let's bring this idea even closer. We could easily say the greatest minds of the modern world have been those who could perceive indigenously. Go deeply into the music of Bach. Appreciate the art of M. C. Escher. Plumb the depths of Einstein's mathematical understanding. You'll find that each of them was able to understand and describe the holistic interconnections between the myriad phenomena of our universe. They found patterns, thought in metaphors and used the tools of analogy. They sought out similarities between events and examined structure. They strove to penetrate into the permanence that underlies the ocean of change.

If the entire universe really is one living being, then all the sciences are just parts of a grand cosmic physiology. There's no question all life shares an amazing unity. This is what Aristotle called an "Intuitive perception of similarity," and Theodore Andrea Cook described as "an overpowering evidence of continuity," and "a fitting between all things."[24]

Big details connect with little details. Complexity builds itself from simple processes repeating themselves over and over again. Randomness flows into pattern. Pattern flows into randomness.

Analogy means a proportion, or an agreement of ratios. It means an equivalency or a likeness of relationships. A similarity. It's the resemblance of relationships and attributes as the ground of reasoning. Analogy is a similarity of formative or constructive processes. It's a resemblance of form or function.[25]

We can't predict random events, but we can predict patterns of *oscillations*. An oscillation is a swinging to and fro, like a pendulum. Anything that goes back and forth between two points is oscillating. Any vibration is an oscillation. Oscillation can also mean a fluctuation between two opinions, principles or purposes.

If we know how geological and atmospheric conditions relate to other cyclic events, like sunspot cycles, we can forecast these changes with high degree of accuracy. Some phenomena in nature have a high statistical reliability in their behavior. They're consistent enough to determine their outcomes for all practical purposes. A culture as ancient and obviously advanced as the ancient Mexicans' could easily have collected and interpreted data such as these. There are many ways the Mexica could have calculated the date of August 13, 1999.

If mathematics is what distinguishes the hard sciences from mysticism, then the Mexica possessed a very high level of science. They used probability computations, convergent equations, Pascal's triangle, and a number of other statistical tools. Reliable statistical evidence appears when a sample size gets to be large enough. The larger the sample size, the more reliable the statistics are going to be. Sometimes, the choice of type or quality is more important than the sheer quantity of sample size. The ancient Mexicans refined this science to a high art.*

The modern belief is the Mexica didn't have technology. This means either the current historical theory is dead wrong, or their achievements are the best argument you're ever likely to find for the use of the intuition.

It's time to reappraise our dismissal of the Mexica.

Here are some exercises to help you develop flexibility in your perceptions:

- Buy a set of Tangrams at a toy store. Play with them. Tangrams are a supreme way to test the flexibility of your mind and to help train you to see in patterns.

- Pick a Tangram puzzle to work with. If you can't figure it out, and are ready to give up, try this experiment: have a friend look at the solution to the puzzle while you stare at the puzzle in a relaxed way. Watch what happens.

* For a more in-depth view of this subject, please refer to Appendix 1, Language of the Sorcerers.

Art and Nature

Cortes' initial letters to King Charles V described the Mexica as a culture of the highest level of advancement and achievement. That opinion mysteriously changed over time. The Mexica came to be portrayed in the later Spanish writings as some kind of a barbaric, devil worshipping cult. Back in Europe, Voltaire and many others believed the Spanish were withholding the truth about the Aztecs to cover up and justify the Mexican holocaust. Even Cortes himself admitted he never saw a human sacrifice in Mexico.[26]

There were a number of Satanic cults in existence around that time. One of them was the cult of science.

The early fifteen hundreds weren't exactly the golden age of science or an excellent time to be a scientist. Leonardo da Vinci finished *The Last Supper* in the same year the Italian friar Savonarola was tortured to death and publicly burned for disobeying the decrees of Pope Alexander VI. Leonardo worked secretly to avoid the Inquisition and the church's savage oppression of personal freedom. He encrypted all his research into a secret code so no one could understand it if it was found.

He wrote in that same year, "My arguments are derived solely from experiment, which is the source of all evidence, the one and only mother of true science. It is useless to conduct an argument by mere quotation from authorities; that does not prove cleverness; it only suggests good memory."

Leonardo da Vinci was a revolutionary. His work flowed in a direction that completely opposed the doctrines of his day. If Leonardo's writings had been known at the time he was alive, he would have been burned at the stake.

The people who would have persecuted Leonardo were the same ones who condemned and executed the Mexica. They're the same people who wrote the history we were taught in school, and the ones who pillaged Mexico at the time of the Conquest. Does it make any sense to believe the history they wrote?

The great classical artists weren't great because they simply copied what they saw in nature. The true masters studied nature in its depths. They blended with it, understood it, and could impart nature's essence to us through their art. Leonardo expressed this point very succinctly when he wrote:
"If you do not rest upon the good foundation of nature, you will labor with little honor and less profit."
and:
"Human ingenuity may make various inventions, but it will never devise any inventions more beautiful, nor more simple, nor more to the purpose than Nature does; because in her inventions nothing is wanting and nothing is superfluous."

The ancient Mexica scientists absolutely fit these descriptions. They embodied them to a degree that challenges us to redefine our own yardstick of judgment.

Dante, Durer, Goethe and da Vinci were all pioneers. They worked in the borderland of human knowledge to rediscover the unity of art and the natural world. If you examine the works of any of these great masters, you'll find they knew how to create harmonious interplays of ratios and proportions. They balanced each part with the other parts and the whole.

Any genuine work of art has an underlying, coordinating principle contained somewhere within it. The Aztec Sun Calendar shows us multiple hierarchies of coordinating principles. In fact, it's all about coordinating principles.

Great art uses the symbolic language of numerical and geometrical relationships. Highly developed artists guide your experience of their art. They take you on a journey of perception that winds directly and indirectly through subtle deviations from a basic numerical and geometrical structure. It's both the structure and breaking free from the structure that surprise and delight you when you appreciate a true work of art. Structure contains symbolic messages. Moving away from structure also conveys information. If you know what to look for, a single piece of art can take you on an adventure that can last for many years.

The indigenous mind is a holistic mind. Holistic science embraces multiple interrelationships of the part to the whole. Modern researchers are finding many of the ancient codices can be read in several different directions to reveal various data encryptions. When you read them going up they have one meaning. Read them going down, and they have another meaning. You can read some of the ancient texts diagonally, backwards, and as mirror images of themselves to reveal many dimensions of poetic nuance. Integrated minds create integrated art. The Mexica created masterpieces of holistic thought.

One of these masterpieces was the Aztec Sun Calendar.

Time Capsules

The Mexica didn't create great art just for themselves. They made it for us. They were like parents today who create "time capsules" for their babies. When the babies grow up, they get to open the time capsules. Inside, they find and enjoy the great love and wisdom their parents left for them.

Why did the Mexica do that for us?

They knew the Earth was going to fall into a time of great darkness, corruption, destruction and perhaps eventual transformation. This refers to what happened from the moment the Spanish landed on the shores of Ixachilan (Ee-shah-chee-lahn), or America, to the time we're living in now, and possibly everything we're about to go through.

The Mexica considered us to be their great great great great great grandchildren. They loved us as indigenous parents love their children. They wanted to give us a condensed and complete version of all the things we would need to survive and meet the challenges of August 13, 1999.

The Mexica wanted to carry their message to us across time. They created objects they knew would endure for hundreds of years into the future. They carved their messages in stone, encoding and encrypting their entire science into a symbolic form as a memory tool. They wanted to preserve their natural wisdom for us so it could be revealed when we most need it.

If our Mexican grandparents hadn't encrypted their information for us onto stone, the Spanish Conquistadores would have destroyed it. The Spanish did their best to demolish and "disappear" every scrap of evidence that could indicate the culture of the Mexica ever existed. At least that was their plan.

One of the greatest miracles in all history is that the Aztec Sun Calendar survived the Mexican holocaust. We may never know the true story of how and why it was spared.

It's not as if the Spanish didn't try to get rid of it. They made a number of attempts. They stripped it of its delicately positioned jewels and fine gold ornamentation. They buried it, threw it in the lake, and buried it again. But it just kept on showing up.

The Aztec Sun Calendar was created for us. We're the ones alive right now who are going to live through August 13, 1999. The Mexica formed a bridge between their time and ours. They wanted to help us through this time with their wise, gentle, guiding hands.

You can find relics of stone everywhere in Mexico. The information has survived the destruction. The time to decode it is now.

Opening the Gateway

Something in the air is just waiting to happen. It's calling out to you in the voices of your ancestors. If you dare to taste their world, you can meet them and listen to their message. You can go on a journey to reclaim a most precious gift that was taken away from them a very long time ago.

This journey will take you on a path many people of forgotten ages used to take. It's the same path your ancestors traveled in the pre-Christian era. You can take it, too. It's your birthright.

Will you respond to the Call? Do you have the spirit and individuality it takes to go your own way? Are you ready to take back your power? Are you willing to experience true community? Would you merge with the infinite heart of the universe if you had the opportunity?

> It's time to retrieve the rich mystery of your life
> and heal all that's been wounded.
> You can get help on your journey.
> Your ancestors will support you,
> because it's the right thing to do.
> Nature will support you,
> because it's the right thing to do.
> The Creator will support you,
> because it's the right thing to do.
> If you're ready to take your journey, read on.

Preparations
For Your Journey

Prepare to Meet Your Ancestors

You're about to enter into a world that sometimes, when you least expect it, makes no rational or even intuitive sense. It's helpful to be familiar with the territory before you enter.

This next section will train you mentally, emotionally and physically to prepare for your journey.

Enter on your journey with sincerity in your heart. You're going to see your own reflection. Be prepared.

Another Look at the Calendar

The map for your journey will be the Aztec Sun Calendar. We'll be focusing mostly on the direct physical and scientific aspects of the Calendar within these pages. The obvious and the more esoteric spiritual and philosophical implications of this material are free to arise spontaneously within you in their own natural terminology.

This chapter will include a brief overview of the Calendar. The other chapters in this section will go into more depth and detail regarding some of its key concepts. This process will prepare you to study and understand the Calendar as a whole, and begin to train you how to think in synthesis.

There have been many attempts to decipher the meanings of the Aztec Sun Calendar. You can find numerous books on its time and astronomical aspects. They're all interesting.

On the simplest level, it's correct to call this magnificent work of art a calendar, because it describes the processes of motion and change in our universe. Our universe and everything in it are moving through time. Some portions of the Calendar relate to the passage of time, but not in a linear, unidirectional sense as we perceive and describe it. Nor does it treat time as a subject that's somehow separate from the rest of everything. The Aztec Sun Calendar incorporates a number of different kinds of calendars into its design that interface and cross reference one another. In this sense, the Calendar is *holistic*, because it looks at a subject from multiple perspectives at the same time. The changing relationships of these calendars illustrate the relative motions of the planets in our solar system. They also demonstrate the effects these heavenly bodies and their motions have on us here on Earth. The interaction of the calendars portrays the spiral dance of local, interplanetary and even intergalactic events that play significant roles in our lives.

The Mexica were interested in relationships. One set of relationships they thought was significant was the Mexican century. A Mexican century lasts 52 years. This is not an arbitrary number. The Mexica understood how the phenomena in our universe come from the interactive relationships of two forces. They call these two forces *Nagual* (nah-wahl) and *Tonal* (toh-nahl), indicated on the Calendar by the two opposing Xiucoatl. (Fig. 21) Nagual and Tonal are a pair. The Mexica perceived many of the events in our world as complementary pairs.

Fig. 21
The Xiucoatl can demonstrate the primal polarity of Nagual and Tonal.

Mexican centuries come in complementary pairs. Every two centuries of 52 years makes a 104 year cycle. (Fig. 22) Their relationship provides an excellent example of the complex interweaving of the Calendar's design. This cycle completes when the Venusian, Solar, Terrestrial and Ritual calendars converge, align and renew themselves every 104 years.[1]

Fig. 22

The two century pair is just a portion of a 1248 year cycle. This cycle consists of 12 century pairs of 104 years of 365 days. (Fig. 23) During that time Venus makes as many returns as there are days in a 780 day cycle of Mars. At the same time, Mars makes as many returns as the 584 days in a cycle of Venus.

This process of observing the many elements of the Calendar from shifting perspectives is a key to understanding the subtle genius of its intricacies. We participate with the Calendar as it reveals its encoded information. It teaches us how to delicately alter nuances of our perception.

The astronomical and astrological dimensions of the Calendar could fill many volumes. Yet the very concept of time and the representation of time as a linear or even a circular process

Fig. 23
The Flames on the Xiucoatl's backs represent the twelve century pairs.

is misleading. The Aztec Sun Calendar connects us with an ever-present here and now. It shows how we're exposed to and participate in the unfolding of multiple energy fields and patterns within an infinite moment. Each of these fields has its own unique qualities and resonances. Our impressions of the continuity of these changes create our perception of time.

We also believe in cycles and resonances of time in the modern world. The way we celebrate holidays is a good example of how we believe a day in one year can have a resonance with the "same" day in a completely different year.

Time might seem to be linear if you perceive your world as a singular experience, as most modern people do. Many indigenous people live in multiple realities simultaneously. Living in several worlds at once leads to a different experience of time.

Each culture has its own sense of the qualities of time. Mexican time is world famous. The Mexica lived in an *inclusive* sense of time. They understood how each of its portions affects all others. Time is holistic, holographic, connected and includes all potentials.

Time is circular and it isn't. It's like playing a piano keyboard from left to right, up through the octaves. You hear the same notes over and over again, but at ascending frequencies.

Time mirrors the psychology of events. You encounter self-similar situations with different faces again and again, until you change your internal environment. Then the situations also spontaneously change.

The Mexica lived in a hyper-dimensional perception of time. The events we see unfolding over time had a quality for them that was understood in its wholeness. Time for them was a cycling, spiraling motion. It has an eternal quality to it. We can enter into this sense of time during the trance states of *ritual*.

Fig. 24 The original ten dimensions of our universe

The Calendar describes an original ten-dimensional universe. Four of these ten dimensions have temporarily crystallized to become our universe of today. (Fig. 24) This is the same model presented to us by the *superstring* theory of modern physics.

Scientists can draw abstract maps to describe the state of any multidimensional system. The Calendar is a cross-sectional representation of our multidimensional universe from the beginning, and possibly through to the end. The Aztec Sun Calendar is much more than a calendar. It's a spacetime calculator. (Fig. 25)

The Mexica used symbols like the Sun Calendar as calculators and computers. Its multiple geometries plumb the depths of number theory. The Calendar is similar to many of the ancient classics, because it can put a whole body of knowledge together for you. Once you know the science behind it, the Calendar becomes a fountainhead of information.

The structure of the Aztec Sun Calendar describes the gossamer thread reality builds itself around. It embodies the processes of perception itself. Its natural patterns blend your outer and inner worlds into a subjective/objective cascade of oneness. As you learn to work with the Calendar in this way, you'll discover that it's about many things, and how they all fit together. Here's an overview of some of its relationships:

The Calendar is a spherical energy wave. It's a luminous egg that demonstrates equanimity and evenness of consciousness. (Fig. 26) It teaches you about communication and sacrifice. (Fig. 27)

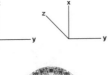

Fig. 25 The Calendar is a multidimensional model of our universe.

Fig. 27

Tonatiuh's tongue represents a vast conceptual matrix that includes the qualities of communication and sacrifice.

Fig. 26 The highlighted concentric circles define the equanimity of an expanding wave of energy.

Fig. 28 The Calendar is an anatomical map.

Fig. 29 The Calendar demonstrates energy fields.

Fig. 30 The Calendar illustrates correspondences between the iris and other parts of the body.

Fig. 31 The Calendar describes the genesis of our universe.

The Calendar is a detailed map of the human physical body with many anatomical counterpoints. It's an extraordinary medical textbook that includes a chart of your personal biology from the moment of your conception onward through your life. (Fig. 28)

It's a diagram of energetic fields that speaks of the relationships between radiations from space, the electromagnetic field of the Earth, your own energetic biofields, chakras, acupuncture meridians and other more subtle physiological systems. (Fig. 29) It's a model of the integrity of a healthy, well-developed human being.

The Calendar is an iris chart. (Fig. 30) It has holographic correspondences that extend through your whole body and into the world around you. It permeates your past, present and the probabilities for your future.

The Calendar is a cosmological blueprint that demonstrates the creation of our universe in the language of physics. (Fig. 31) It describes the genesis of stars and the structure of space-time.

It demonstrates the essentially sexual/polar nature of nature, (Fig. 32) the act of creation, (Fig. 33) and the creative use of sound and the spoken word. (Fig. 34)

Fig. 32 The Calendar teaches about polarity.

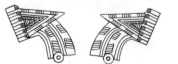

Fig. 33 The Calendar shows the process of creation

Fig. 34 The use of sound, vibration, voice and speech in the Calendar.

The Aztec Sun Calendar points to harmonic levels of expression of the cosmic impulse. The Sun at the center of the Calendar mirrors the whole of creation in multiple *golden mean* and *octave* relationships.

The Calendar demonstrates the amazing fractal symmetry of large, small and intermediate scales in the natural world, and shows you how patterns appear to generate themselves from inside other patterns. It teaches you how to shrink and enlarge your field of observation to find the same pictures and designs repeating themselves over and over again. (Fig. 35)

Fig. 35
The Calendar has a self-similar fractal structure.

The Calendar is a brilliant model of a *strange attractor*. A strange attractor is a locus in space-time that events tend to occur around. You'll learn in coming chapters how August 13, 1999 may be a strange attractor in time. (Fig. 36)

There are those who would argue almost anything could be demonstrated through the mathematics of the Aztec Sun Calendar. This doesn't invalidate it in any way. To the contrary. The mathematics profoundly illustrates its truth and versatility. If a modern scientist came up with a mathematical structure we could apply to nearly everything in our world, she or he would be featured in every science textbook until the end of time. The properties of number and geometry establish the universal validity of science. Is it logical to use the same argument to validate our own science and invalidate the science of another culture?

Fig. 36
August 13, 1999 may be a strange attractor in time.

The Calendar is a synthesis of geometric forms. It teaches us both general principles and intense specifics regarding the geometrical and numerical relationships in the world around us. (Fig. 37)

The Mexica had a profound understanding of the structure of spacetime in the cosmic, human and microscopic worlds. They knew the

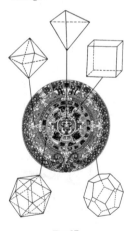

Fig. 37

Relationships between the five Platonic Solids and the Calendar are explained in Appendix 1, the Language of the Sorcerers.

principles of organic growth and beauty, and appreciated nature's puzzle of forms, patterns and processes.

A puzzle is nonlinear. You build it piece by piece, discovering portions or sections at a time, until you finally assemble the whole. This process mirrors the process of your becoming, which is the journey you'll take through the rest of this book.

Your Indigenous Nature

The complexity and intensity of the modern world are much too vast and complex to understand or control with your surface mind. Relax and trust your indigenous nature. Let it take care of you. Allow it to guide you to the right place at the right time. Create space in your life to become best friends with your indigenous nature. It understands and integrates your life with the whole global picture. It's at one, moment by moment, with all the infinite variables in the universe.

Your indigenous self always does the right thing at the right time, although it may not always seem like that to you in any particular situation. This is because your indigenous self is always connected with all events outside of time. It connects your conscious mind and your subconscious mind with the rhythmic pulse of all things.

You'd be surprised at how many people shy away from discovering their inner worlds and their indigenous natures. Many of them say they're afraid they'll go crazy if they start exploring themselves in this way.

Could that mean they're already crazy, and they're just running away from it?

Listen. If you have this kind of fear of your deep self, it's very important to do exercises like the ones in this book. The more strongly you repress your indigenous nature, the stronger the explosion you're building up inside yourself.

You can work constructively with your indigenous nature. It will help your creative energies go where they really want to go. Vitality is the currency of your indigenous self. It lives in a magical world of dynamic energy flows and patterns. Your energy wants to be creative. It wants to connect and be spontaneous with nature and the world around you. It wants to be free.

There's no fighting it. Your indigenous nature will triumph one day, one way or another. It's up to you to go with it happily, or kicking and screaming. If your indigenous nature is buried inside you like a seed deep within a rock, that seed has the power to split the rock in two. Go with it.

Something inside you wants to wake up and live. It's your powerful and infinite indigenous nature. If you try to control or repress it in any way, a deep and empty depression can overtake you. It's not easy to explain exactly where this depression comes from. It might not be directly related to any single event from your past. In fact, it might not be associated with anything in your past at all.

A huge proportion of people in the modern world drug themselves into oblivion with mood altering medications that murder the spirit and remove the natural impulse to action. Your spirit wants you to be the hero you knew you would be when you were a child. If you're depressed, it's probably because your spirit wants you to do something with your life. Depression happens when your true nature doesn't express itself along with others around you in a healthy environment. Depression is an appropriate and natural response to the modern world. It can be cured only by taking positive action to manifest and express your true nature.

Integrating with your indigenous nature infuses you with the power of history. When you tap into what it is you really want to be doing, you begin to feel an indescribable joy and power. There's a rightness in it. Synchronicities multiply as new doorways to a brighter future open for you. It's as if the entire universe is backing you up to do the things you want to do. You take the first step alone. After you take it, others will join you. Try it.

Cultivating your indigenous nature carries you beyond the boundaries of an imposed morality. You don't need to battle yourself with an internal doctrine. When you restore your indigenous nature, the consequences of your actions become physically palpable to you. You spontaneously know the right thing to do, and you do that and nothing else, because it's real to you. It resonates with your living spirit. There's no process you need to go through to make it happen, because an intense and passionate relationship develops with your conscience as you become one with your indigenous nature. The endless inner battles of decisions and indecisiveness end, and you simply flow with what you know is right.

The indigenous nature you share with all human beings can rescue you from trivial cultural disputes and disagreements. On an indigenous level, we all meet in a place of mutual respect and acknowledgment of one another's gifts. We enjoy being with one another as we experiment and create together.

When you're learning about your indigenous nature, it's helpful to begin to explore the idea of *connection* rather than interpretation. For example, your heart connects with and is actually a part of the Sun in the sky. (Fig. 38) Your heart is a part of the Sun the same way your hand is a part of your body. The linear mind often takes indigenous concepts and fragments them into its own set of rules. To use the same example, a linear mind would tend to interpret, or impose itself on the beautiful relationship between your heart and the Sun by knowing it all, and telling you your heart somehow represents the Sun instead of actually being a part of it.

Develop an awareness of your mind's tendency to give you pat answers. These answers can tragically separate you from the important essence of your connections with the universe.

A reactive mind goes one step further. It immediately says, "prove it", even before the rest of your being gets a chance to try the idea on and experiment with it. Indigenous perception naturally retreats from the harsh belligerence of a reactive mind.

Indigenous perception is aware of connections where a non-indigenous perception

Fig. 38
Heart and Sun

doesn't see anything at all. For example, babies and animals often actively engage with what we perceive to be empty space. They sometimes meet with things there that delight them or fill them with horror.

Indigenous mind is infinite perspective. It likes synthesis. Modern mind likes analysis. The indigenous world can coexist with the worlds of modern faith and science. They're complementary systems that can express different parts of you.

Here are some exercises to help you connect with your indigenous self:

📓 Do you remember the wonderful times in your childhood when you could see right through everything? Do you remember the things you did to turn off your perceptions?

📓 Nature returns when you appreciate it. Appreciate nature every day. Wherever you live, there's nature somewhere. Find it. Connect with it. Appreciate it. Be aware of your sensations and impressions as you appreciate nature.

📓 As you appreciate nature, allow it to appreciate you back. Let go and let nature appreciate you. Be aware of your sensations and impressions as you practice.

📓 *Now is a good time to begin practicing the exercises in Appendix 2.*

General Principles

The names and faces you'll meet on your journey may not appear familiar to you at first. It's OK. Allow yourself to go beyond surface appearances and into a true understanding of their principles. You and your ancestors lived in harmony with each of these concepts somewhere in your past.

You may feel fear, rage, or a number of other emotional responses as you learn this material. This is natural. Remember, you're unearthing energies that have been buried for centuries. They were probably hidden away in states of deep terror and confusion. This submergence took place when your ancestors did whatever they had to do to survive the Inquisition. It also happened to you personally in many ways as you were growing up. Be patient. Go through the book slowly. Allow yourself to digest it.

Heart

Fig 39

Everything comes together at the heart.

The Mexica are a culture of synthesis. They bring everything together at the heart. (Fig. 39)

You'll want to remember to take your heart along when you go on your journey. If you lost it somewhere, or you can't seem to find it, relax. You'll probably find it on the way.

Even the heftiest super computers can't model the complex weaving of the many fractal electric impulses moving through your heart. For many indigenous cultures, the heart is the seat of the mind. You can think with your heart. It's different from thinking with your head or other parts of your anatomy.

The Calendar teaches you how your heart is the central principle of your being. Your heart is a middle path between knowledge and power. (Fig. 40) It's a balance point. If you ever feel lost, alone, or afraid on your journey, return to your heart. It will know what to do.

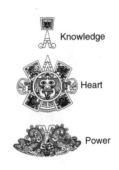

Knowledge

Heart

Power

Fig. 40 Your heart is the central principle of your being.

Here are some exercises to help you follow your heart:

⚘ Listen to your heart. What does it say to you? Begin to a dialogue with your heart. Maintain it.

⚘ Cultivate an awareness around the area of your heart and the middle of your chest. You don't need to do anything with it. Simply be aware of the sensations you feel there. What are they like? Practice this awareness in the different situations you meet with each day. Learn to sense the subtle vibrations of your heart.

Tonatiuh, the Sun, is the heart of our solar system.

Death

The Mexica respected and honored death. By acknowledging death on a daily basis, by ritualizing and regarding its presence and power, they externalized abundant life.

The skull and death you see so frequently in Mexican art can mean change, silence, or a return. There's a transformation that happens between life and death, and death and life. In your everyday world, death can be life and life can be death. Be watchful and attentive of the subtle tendency each one has to turn into the other.

Indigenous people profoundly respect the influence the dead have on our lives. Whatever belief system you come from, there's just no denying the dead affect us on some level. Their influence may be due to persistent memories. It may be due to our imaginations. It also may be due to something more active on the part of the dead themselves.

Our modern world has become thoroughly obsessed with death. Modern children learn how death is the only occasion where people gather together in sincerity, stop business as usual and deeply contemplate forces greater than themselves.

Even our most primal sexual desires have decayed into a death experience with the arrival of AIDS and Super AIDS.

Our daily denial of death is externalizing it on a massive scale. Have you noticed how completely death permeates modern media and entertainment? We're being forced to expose and examine the dying aspects of ourselves and our society. The dying aspect of the modern world lives caught between ignorance and opinion.

The most constructive way to deal with death is to face it. Are you living your life as if you're going to be alive for a thousand years? Face your death each day. What are the things you want to do before you die? Do them now. Take action. Respect your life. Why compromise one more minute? Resolve everything you need to resolve right now.

The Mexica had an attitude they called *oquichehualiztli* (oh-kwee-chay-hwah-LEE-tslee). It means to fully engage yourself in battle with absolute vigor and all your energy. It means action, and proactively confronting yourself and your world with valor, integrity and power. Whatever you do, do it with oquichehualiztli.

Go for your true life by simply acknowledging what needs to die, and what wants to live. There is no death. There's only returning to nature again and again.

Here's an exercise to help you acknowledge death and constructively deal with it:

> 🦋 What in your life needs to die? How can you help it to die and move on?

The Tzompantli (tzohm-PAHN-tlee) or "wall of skulls." From the Great Temple in Mexico City Tenochtitlan.

Serpents

The serpent is the life-force in your spine. It breaks out of the egg of your pelvis and undulates through the hole in your occiput, the location of 13 Cane.

Serpents embody the motion of water. Water means motion. Snakes mean motion. Water motion is snake motion. Serpents are everything that comes to us from the sky.

Many indigenous cultures revere the serpent as a bearer of intelligence, knowledge and wisdom. The indigenous world respects the snake as a living symbol of the essence of movement, power, sagacity, and connection with the Earth. The serpent is divine wisdom.

The modern image of the serpent has been turned around to represent evil. Why? Because it can teach you how to develop yourself, attain freedom, mobility and transformation.

The serpent brings you spiritual power. It's a mistake to debase your understanding of the serpent with modern psychological interpretations and superficial dogmas. The serpent is deeper than all that. It goes much further than any amount of emotional and rational debate can take you.

The serpent is the motion of time. Its head moves through this moment, and its memories trail behind. It illustrates how you are free in each moment to act as you please. As soon as you take an action, its consequences snake outward, communicate with your future and rearrange potentials and probabilities.

Serpent motion is vortex motion squashed onto a planar surface. Imagine yourself walking up the threads of a giant screw. As you walk, let that screw become flatter and flatter until it becomes a plane. Now you have serpent motion.

Coatl, the serpent, is the wave motion of all oscillations. It's the essence of *vibration*. It's life-force. It's power. It's your spiral winding from the smallest subatomic impulse through your entire life over time, to the motion of the colossal galaxies and even space itself.

Serpent motion is vortex motion squashed onto a planar surface.

Here are some serpent exercises:

- ✺ In *Matthew 10:16*, Jesus tells his disciples to "Be wise as serpents and harmless as doves." What did he mean?

- ✺ Begin to observe the motions of flowing water in the world around you. Let the motions of water teach you.

Bird wings screw through the air as they flap. You can find the driving force of the spiral form of the screw either physiologically, or in the forms of motion in many areas of nature.

Serpents are the essence of vibrations.

Your alternating footsteps trace the path of a snake's motion. The insteps of your feet outline the spirally arched curves of each node.

Xiucoatl

The Xiucoatl are the Fire Serpents. They're the light and heat of the Sun. They swan dive into our reality from higher planes of existence as a complementary pair. Each relates to the other dynamically and spherically.

The Xiucoatl teach you that no matter who you are, at least once in your life, you need to decide to hurl yourself at a goal, completely risking all.

The Xiucoatl are the intertwined serpents of order and chaos. Each one unpredictably becomes the other. (Fig. 41) They're the living relationship of tension and release, and the exceptional life that can integrate the vital, creative razor's edge between chaos and order. The Xiucoatl are the relationship of the rational and the irrational. They're the manifestation of complementary opposites, and the perpetually changing, complex patterns of motion and probability in our world.

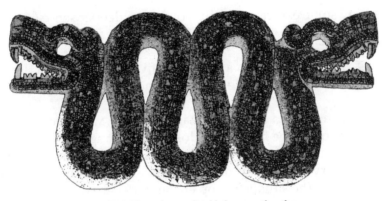

Fig. 41 Each Xiucoatl unpredictably becomes the other.

The Xiucoatl are the wave particle duality expounded by modern science that describes our universe as collections of *particles* or as cascades of *waves*. Both models are true at the same time. Subatomic particles, like light itself, partake of both particle and wave qualities.

Our particle model states every electron connects with an infinity of *virtual* electrons and positrons. They oscillate into and out of our universe in a perpetual dance.

Our wave model states that infinities of *quantum fields* create interdimensional ripples and patterns which shape matter. *Wave functions** are the mathematical maps of quantum systems.

Wave and particle nature are a complementary pair. The more deeply you go into one side of their equation, the closer you get to the other side.

---

* A Wave function is an equation that shows you the behaviors of a quantum system.

The Xiucoatl are the relationship of memory and active intelligence. They warn you of the danger of slipping into memory and reminiscence rather than actively experiencing the here and now.

The Xiucoatl are the essential sexual interplay that's the unifying impulse in a polar reality. They're the relationship of the two halves of your nervous system and the united duality of your form and perception.

The Xiucoatl are Tonal and Nagual.

Here are some exercises to help you gain a deeper sense of complementary opposites:

- Watch yourself in a mirror for five minutes. What do you see? Whom do you see? Practice every day.

- If you had a complementary opposite, what would he or she be like? Write down everything you can about him or her. Then draw his or her picture. Imagine every detail of his or her life. Imagine what he or she would do in the situations you encounter every day. What would happen if the two of you met?

- Repeat the same exercise as above, this time writing and drawing with the hand you don't normally use to write and draw with. For example, if you're right-handed, use your left hand in this exercise. If you are left-handed, use your right hand instead.

  How does changing your handedness affect your awareness in doing this exercise? How does it affect your perception of your complementary opposite?

Tonal and Nagual

Our world is born through a playful tension of polarities and cycles. We're presented with dynamic dualism. This is the great tantric dance of Nagual and Tonal.

Tonal and Nagual are relative terms. They're similar to *Yin* and *Yang* in Asian philosophy. Tonal and Nagual indicate a relationship of one thing with another.

Nagual also refers to a person of immense spiritual development. Nagual can be your spirit. This is the spirit that fills you in magical, powerful moments. It's the spirit you gain progressive access to, and it gains progressive access to you, over the course of your personal evolution in life.

Communicating with your Nagual is an essential part of existence. It's a basic need. It's a cleansing, purifying and rejuvenating experience that is the foundation and, in many respects, the goal of the indigenous way of life. It's so important, we can say it would be very challenging to have fullness, health and happiness without it. Once you taste your Nagual, even if it's only for a flash of a second, you'll probably go to extended measures to continue experiencing it as often as you can.

The longing to unify with Nagual may be the root of many, if not all, addictions.

The desire to relate with your Nagual is a very beneficial one. It creates a radical shifting of your consciousness and imbues you with the greatest and most permanent parts of yourself.

The purpose of discussing Tonal and Nagual isn't to passively observe the long term fluctuations of these forces in nature and in your life. The real point is to actively apply the principles of *balance* to every situation you encounter. This practice will prevent you from slipping into the pitfalls of duality.

Tonal and Nagual are qualities of energy. They can teach you how to use information proactively, and can help you through periods of apparent division and schism. They can train you to use your experiences to cultivate intelligent insight. Insight will help you make the best use of your opportunities to strengthen your life force through your positive actions in life.

Tonal and Nagual can train you how to perceive complementary pairs. Your perception creates a *neutrality*, or third element, that comprehends the unity of apparent opposites.

Your perception forms a dynamic triangle, shown by the equilateral triangle on Tonatiuh's helmet.

Here are some exercises to help you grasp the essence of Tonal and Nagual:

🏵 Find ten complementary pairs a day for the next forty days. Write them down. Find new examples each day.

🏵 If you were going to master balance in your life, where would you begin?

🏵 Stare at this circle as you soften your mental and visual focus. Two circles will appear on the page. Adjust your levels of focus to practice separating and blending the two circles by making the dots at the center move apart and come together. Practice this exercise whenever you feel you're needing to have a creative mental breakthrough.

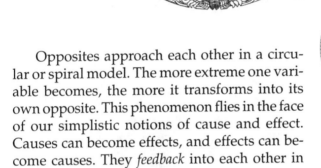

Feedback and Balance

Opposites approach each other in a circular or spiral model. The more extreme one variable becomes, the more it transforms into its own opposite. This phenomenon flies in the face of our simplistic notions of cause and effect. Causes can become effects, and effects can become causes. They *feedback* into each other in closed *control loops*.

The nonlinear systems in nature feedback into themselves. They multiply over and over again.

Balance happens naturally in the big picture. In the smaller picture of life, we often find *positive feedback cycles*. This means whatever

Negative feedback loops regulate and balance themselves.

Positive feedback loops amplify themselves exponentially.

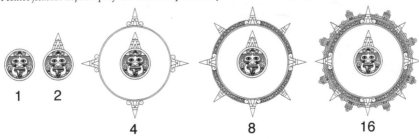

1   2   4   8   16

is happening tends to happen more and more until it reaches an extreme. At this point, the situation suddenly changes into its opposite. This is where many of the classical recommendations for *moderation* come from. They mean you probably don't want to send all your energy flying down the black or white hole of excessive behavior. Your energy will only transform into its opposite.

Positive feedback cycles can also work in your favor. It takes great discipline and acuity to use the principles of positive feedback to create balance in your everyday life. This is the foundation of doing simple meditations and affirmations. For example, if you want appreciation, you can cultivate it by appreciating the world around you. Remember, events tend to become more and more of what they already are. If you plant a small seed and focus on it, you can help it grow. You can feedback anything you want into the world. Plant your seeds wisely.

You're an amazing array of feedback loops. You use many different feedback systems to maintain homeostasis. These loops mediate between your inner and outer worlds. All your internal regulating systems are feedback loops.

Ollin

$$E = mc^2$$

Fig. 42

Albert Einstein's famous equation E=mc2 means that energy is mass at the relative velocity of the speed of light squared.

Ollin is movement. It's the dance of relative motion we're all engaged in. Movement is the essence of life.

Nature's forms show you how energy flows over time. Structure is the history of a moving process. Dynamic, living energy in motion creates the shapes of our world. Our universe is one continuous integrated process in motion.

Ollin is the central figure of the Aztec Sun Calendar. It illustrates how motion is at the center of all phenomena. Ollin teaches you about movement and transformation. It demonstrates how mass and energy dance each other into being. (Fig. 42)

Ollin teaches you to pay attention to appropriate forms of movement. It's about natural balance, posture and poise. It reminds you how everything happens over time through motion.

Ollin indicates the conversion of negative to positive and positive to negative. It's the process of change, and the cyclic alternation of Nagual and Tonal. Ollin is the dance of chaos and order. (Fig. 43)

Ollin's eye is half open and half closed. (Fig. 44) This means it's looking half into this world and half into another world. Ollin is the rela-

Fig. 43

Ollin indicates a dynamic shifting of polarity.

Fig. 44

Ollin's eye is half open and half closed.

Ollin is the relationship of your brain to the rest of your body.

The wings of Ollin are the four elements of *Fire, Air, Water* and *Earth*.

When stimulated your body sweats in Ollin-quadrants.

tionship of your conscious and subconscious mind. It relates to an attitude the Mexica have of unconditionally turning every situation into a positive experience.

There's an odd taboo against movement and motion in modern society. Movement unleashes your indigenous self to express through your body. When we're young, we're rigidly trained not to move in school. When you were a child, you were probably punished at one time or another for moving. We're educated not to have bodies. We're taught to accept and live in a conceptual reality, rather than reality.

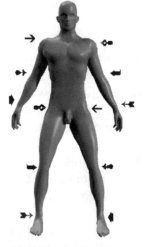

The Ollin principle works in your body with mathematical precision. It's one of the guiding principles of Asian Medicine.

Ollin is a *magnetic quadripole*. It indicates the quadripoles of radiations emanating from our Sun, and your body's mirror reflection of Yin and Yang energy meridians.

Dance

Every facet of Mexica life had deeply spiritual and philosophical qualities. The more completely a person demonstrated his or her spiritual essence in the world, the more highly regarded and respected he or she was in Mexica society. This outlook was expressed in the spiritually based Nahuatl language, and extended itself to social and even political proportions.

The Mexica were dancers. They danced because they believed in fully embodying their spirituality. Many indigenous cultures developed their own unique physical and spiritual disciplines. India has its Yoga. Tai Chi, Chi Gung and other forms of meditation developed throughout Asia. Many forms of ritual dance are practiced in Africa today as they once were in Europe. The sacred dances of the Mexica hold a very special position in the Yogic practices of the world.

The Mexica knew how to integrate the spiritual and physical into an incredible neurological ceremony. The movements, breathing patterns and intense visualization practices of their sacred dances are as advanced and refined as any of the most sophisticated spiritual systems in the world. These rhythms and movements are true national treasures. They're the gold the Conquistadores sought, but were completely unable to comprehend or appreciate.

Dancing the sacred dances imparts very precise rhythmic patterns into your nervous system. It tunes you in with deep essential levels of who you really are. When you begin to resonate with these rhythms, you can access states of being that go far beyond your ordinary reality. They can help you restructure and repattern your consciousness in very profound ways. Entire libraries of information, the ability to heal both yourself and others, and vast extrasensory experiences can open up for you.

We can heal ourselves and one another of anything. It's too bad group healings have been largely ignored by the alternative medicine movement. Maybe it's because of our modern culture's individualistic tendencies that encourage everybody to want the magic bullet for themselves. Meanwhile, one of the most powerful and purest forms of natural healing goes unnoticed.

Group healings are a foundational rock of our common heritage. Group dancing, praying and healings used to be common practice in many churches and religious groups until thirty or forty years ago. Believe in the power you have to heal yourself and those around you. It's real.

Sacred rhythms are a part of the natural world. They've been the center of indigenous cultures for many centuries. Indigenous people explore these rhythms to connect in a positive way with the world around and within them. They dance and drum together to unify themselves, their culture and their society with nature. You can do it, too.

This kind of dancing isn't about going naked and getting your yeah-yeahs out. What happens is much, much deeper than your yeah-yeahs. It helps you touch your true indigenous nature and become your virgin self.

Dancing in a group teaches you how to work together with others. It helps you develop an ability to communicate in profoundly subtle ways and discover how to blend with the moment. It awakens your ability to heal and support the other people around you. You go into flow with a universal impulse, and experience how your individuality breathes with the cosmic heartbeat.

You dance to love and respect your body, your spirit and the Earth. Dancing barefoot on the breast of the living Earth mother can connect and rejuvenate you as nothing else can.

The dance ritual goes in stages. When you start, you're in normal, ordinary waking mental activity. As you dance, you begin to become aware of what's floating around on the fringes of your awareness. All the things hanging around just outside the grasp of your conscious mind begin to swirl into clarity.

Your blood heats up and your breath gets into it. You enter areas your ordinary mind doesn't normally have access to, and you start understanding what motivates your daily behaviors.

The rhythm moves through you as you dance. Your body melts in motion as it plays the rhythm out through expanding waves of movement. Your heart pounds in syncopation with the beat and with the other people dancing around you.

Your gut relaxes. Memories flood in. You begin to dream. The structure of your reality loosens, your precognitive senses spiral open through infinite ripples of awareness, and you move backward and forward in time.

The rhythm continues. You sweat. You dance and sing like there's no tomorrow. Something much bigger than your mind takes over.

Suddenly, you enter the real world and merge into a very deep instinctual level of being. It's an essential, primal experience. At the same time it's all somehow impersonal and abstract. You dream about big things as you blend with the movements of the universe.

You become the rhythm and enter into a silent place. It's moving and motionless. This place isn't like any of the other levels. You can access all of them at the same time. Everything becomes one. It's equally personal and impersonal, individual and collective. All times, places and possibilities are one. Absolute freedom seamlessly blends with universal impulse.

The Earth hears you when you dance. It remembers you. This planet has good associations with the people who danced barefoot on the ground in the past. Earth remembers and supports those who care for and respect nature.

If you'd like to learn the Aztec sacred dances, go to the Zòcalo in Mexico City Tenochtitlan on any evening. There are many people there who would be very happy to teach you.

Rhythm

Any form corresponds to a set of proportions and respects a unique rhythm.

Viewed one dimensionally, rhythm is a series of dots.

Viewed two dimensionally, rhythm is a wave.

Every culture has its own rhythm. All people move to their own beat. You create your own unique and beautiful cadence in each moment. It's clear when you tap into it. We can spot people who are in their natural rhythm instantly. It's easy to tell, even from far away. They generate a certain feeling in the space around them. Their presence radiates when they walk into a room.

Rhythms and oscillations infuse every aspect of animal and vegetable life. Rhythm is in your heartbeat. It pulses through your respiration and internal muscular flows. Your nerves fire in patterns of rhythms. Rhythms are essential to every part of life. They're the mathematical and geometrical patterns of nature.

Hypnotists use rhythm to induce trance. Rhythm can take you into areas your conscious mind can't just will itself into. Rhythm is a password. It can guide you through gateways of perception.

Rhythm and *arithmetic* come from the same root word, *rhein*, meaning to flow. Rhythm is about time. It happens when the timing of different and perhaps otherwise unrelated events can be described by a formula, or a code. You can also create *virtual rhythm* if you believe a formula or code describes the events you're witnessing. In other words, you might perceive rhythm whether or not it's actually there, because your belief can give you an impression of rhythm. Rhythm springs up whenever you get a sense that some underlying proportion or proportions unite an experience you're having.

There's rhythm in the macrocosm, and rhythm in the microcosm. There are rhythms in our build up and release of creative energy. Our moods undergo rhythmic oscillations. We have biorhythms.

We're learning to perceive in rhythms, cycles, and oscillations. Rhythms of energy breathe into and out of matter. History repeats itself in rhythms.

Here are some exercises to help you tap into the rhythms in the world around you:

🏵 Listen for the rhythms that surround you in your everyday life. Are there some you enjoy more than others?

🏵 Check in with your natural rhythm when you first wake up in the morning, in the middle of the day, and at night just before you go to sleep. Listen to it. Feel it. Get a sense of how it wants to blend with your environment, and then simply flow into it. If you ever feel out of sorts for any reason in your day, come back to your natural rhythm. Let it heal you and take you into the pulse of life.

Viewed three dimensionally, rhythm is a pattern.

Viewed four dimensionally, rhythm is a self creating, evolving, devolving, rebirthing essence.

You can slow down any wave form to reveal many intertwining spirals of rhythms. This figure is a magnified sound wave.

Life is Motion

Fig. 45

The oscillations of a pendulum take place around a stable point. This point is August 13, 1999.

The Aztec Sun Calendar illustrates processes of motion and rhythm. *Attractors* are the mathematical maps scientists make to describe complex patterns of motion and rhythm. Attractors are shapes cocooned in motion. Motion always returns to its attractor.

Systems in motion come to different kinds of rest. An attractor can be a place a system winds up at the end of its cycle. It can also be a place a system rhythmically visits or approximates.

Think of a pendulum. Its oscillations happen around a single, stable point. The place it comes to rest is what scientists call a *fixed point attractor*. The Calendar models the motions of a simple pendulum by the back and forth opposing motions of the Xiucoatl. (Fig. 45) A pendulum is a model of motion in a flat, two dimensional plane.

Motion also exists in three dimensions. One way to describe an attractor in three dimensions is the way water moves. Water always flows to the point of least resistance. It seeks out and heads toward the lowest possible place in the landscape.

Imagine a mountain scene with hills and valleys. Water flows away from the hills and down into the valleys. The places water flows to are attractors. In the Calendar, the Xiucoatl embody the serpent motion of water. (Fig. 46) The path an attractor takes through a three dimensional landscape can be complex. If it gets to be very elaborate and convoluted, scientists call it a *fierce attractor*. (Fig. 47)

Fig. 46

The Xiucoatl illustrate the serpent motion of water.

The Calendar teaches us how life is motion. It shows us that rhythm is everywhere. It describes the oscillations of our world. Oscillation has a wonderful property: it tends to stabilize into a steady rate of vibration. It hits a home pace and comes into its own natural rhythm. Even if a vibration gets knocked out of whack by some outside event, it will want to come back to its natural rhythm. Scientists call this natural rhythm a *limit cycle attractor*. The Calendar demonstrates the motions of limit cycles by its many concentric rings. (Fig. 48)

Fig. 47

A Fierce Attractor

Many systems in nature like to find a home rhythm and stay there. The rising and falling of populations is a good example of limit cycle attractors, and how all systems reach a self limiting stage in their growth cycle. Insurance companies and casinos understand limit cycles. That's how they stay in business. They comprehend and benefit from the stable qualities of human behavior.

How can your free will, combined with all the random events in the world, along with everybody else's free will, yield predictable cycles of behavior? Go figure.

Fig. 48

The Calendar's concentric rings demonstrate limit cycle attractors.

Patterns of motion can get even more complex. When scientists want to model the relationships of two or more interacting forces, the resulting map of these relationships winds up looking like a donut. This relationship is called a *torus attractor*, also known as a *donut attractor*. (Fig. 49)

Fig. 49

The Xiucoatl are a three dimensional serpent donut attractor.

Fig. 50

Fig. 51

The Xiucoatl are the dynamic interplay between the rational and the irrational.

Fig. 52

A two system interaction is the simplest case scenario that will create a donut attractor. This is illustrated in the Calendar by the three dimensional serpent bodies of the Xiucoatl. Scientists can weave as many variables and systems as they want into a donut attractor. This is how they mathematically model complex situations like ecosystems.

Donut attractors represent degrees of freedom within a system. Its motions are described by *spirals* traveling around the surface of the donut. If the ratios of motions follow a whole number sequence, the spiral will join up with itself on the donut, and its cycle repeats. (Fig. 50)

If the relationships don't form a whole number ratio, they plunge themselves into the realm of what we call "irrational" numbers. An irrational number expresses itself as a decimal point with an infinite string of non-repeating numbers. An irrational spiral never joins up with itself again on the surface of the donut. (Fig. 51)

Systems in motion either run down to a fixed point attractor, roller coaster around on a fierce attractor, or slide into their natural rhythm on a limit cycle attractor. Multiple relationships find themselves rolling around on a donut attractor.

Are there any other, more complex forms of motion? What would happen if you took a donut attractor and exploded it? Exploded attractors are called *strange* attractors. (Fig. 52)

What would explode a donut attractor? *Resonance.** A donut attractor will explode at a point of resonance. Anything the resonance touches flies into a larger, vastly more complicated donut system. The sympathetic vibration

*Our word resonance comes from the Latin word *resonantia*. It means to echo. To resonate is to reinforce or prolong a particular vibration in one location by the use of a similar vibration in another location. Have you ever noticed when listening to music how certain pieces of furniture will vibrate during one part of a song? This is the principle of resonance in action.

of the resonance breaks up the donut attractor and scatters its points around in space. Whatever follows the path of the donut will jump around to find the closest point on the strange attractor. (Fig. 53)

Strange attractors model chaos. You can visualize the onset of chaos, or turbulence, as a donut attractor that's vibrating apart. Its crumbs are flying everywhere.

Chaos follows a definite rhythm. When any system begins feeding back into itself, it follows a distinct progression into and out of chaos. *Doubling*, or *bifurcation*, is the path from order to chaos and chaos to order.[2]

Here's how doubling happens: as the intensity of energy and information increases in a system, attractors begin to appear. The number of these emerging attractors doubles at specific intensities. As energy and information continue to multiply, the attractors double, then those attractors double, and so on. It's like the branching of a tree. (Fig. 54) This process of repeated doubling is the basis of the central portion of the Calendar. (Fig. 55)

After a critical number of doublings, chaos enters the system, and it changes into a completely non-predictable state of behavior. Chaos always hits after one of the doublings in this progression. Nobody can say exactly which one will stimulate the change. All we know is the change will occur along with one of the doublings in the progression of 1, 2, 4, 8, 16, 32, 64, etc.

Fig 53

13 Cane is a point of resonance on a strange attractor. It's a part of a larger, more complex dynamic system.

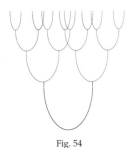

Fig. 54

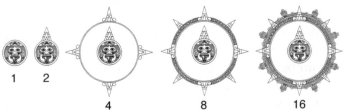

1 2 4 8 16

Fig. 55 The Aztec Sun Calendar demonstrates the process of doubling, or bifurcation.

Fig. 56

In a chaotic system, something is cocooned or hidden in the chaos that will rhythmically emerge over time as the chaos massages it into being.

Chaos reigns. Then magic happens. Rhythmic points of order germinate from some mysterious dimension within the turbulent heart of chaos. Ordered systems begin to appear and relate with one another in an ordered way. (Fig. 56) They form patterns of rhythms within the chaos.

You can find rhythm and order even in the midst of pure chaos. Any system that's sufficiently complex can break into chaos, no matter how ordered it seems to be. Stability nurtures the seeds of instability.

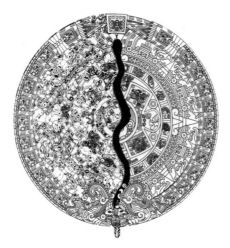

There's a rhythm that moves serpent-like between order and chaos.

The Calendar shows us that dynamic systems are sensitive precisely because of their complexity. Very small influences can create a huge impact on their development. Anything, no matter how subtle, can alter the course of a dynamic system to a profound degree. It just needs to be in the right place at the right time. If an influence is at a point of resonance on an attractor, it can radically shift the system's future.

Bifurcation, or doubling, is the pathway the invisible, subtle world uses to enter the everyday world in which you live and move and have your being. Chaos teaches you how the smallest parts connect with the whole. It shows you how seemingly insignificant factors can fundamentally influence and direct the whole shape of a dynamic system.

The Aztec Sun Calendar is a strange attractor model that shows the different stages of motion leading to chaos. It starts with a fixed point attractor, then it demonstrates limit cycle attractors, and then proceeds through a donut attractor stage. Finally, it goes through a period of bifurcations to become a strange attractor. Each stage indicates the same thing from a different perspective: we're going to hit a point of resonance on August 13, 1999. This resonance may allow us to profoundly influence our planet's future for the better.

Is August 13, 1999 a limit cycle attractor we haven't yet observed or understood? If so, the Mexica could have deduced this date from long observation.

If August 13, 1999 is a strange attractor, then the ancient Mexicans had a deep understanding of a nonlinear physics we're just beginning to explore ourselves.

Here are some exercises to help you appreciate the beauty of chaos:

- Pour a little milk into a cup of hot coffee. Watch what happens for five minutes.

- Watch clouds for thirty minutes a day for the next five days. How does cloud watching affect the rest of your day? How does it influence the way you perceive and engage with your world?

- Turbulence comes intermittently. It has a rhythm of its own. Listen to the sound of rain at night or the howling of the wind. Blend yourself with the turbulent rhythms of nature. Do they have a message or a meaning? What impressions do these rhythms give you?

Dynamic Systems

Ollin shows us how living systems dynamically cycle into and out of chaos. The Calendar demonstrates how order generates chaos and chaos generates order.

The ability to develop chaos is a feature of all natural, nonlinear systems. We need to learn to live with it. Chaos is why we can never make a definite statement about the future of a complex, living organic system.

Any prediction is just a probability. A prediction for any dynamic system will at best be as accurate as a weather report. Probability science and statistics provide some of the most basic planning processes we have at the heart of our modern world. They've taught us how the more closely we try to anticipate the future by investigating *known* variables, the more we learn just how powerful *unknown* variables are in determining final outcomes. It's impossible to give a 100 per cent iron clad guarantee on the future behavior of a dynamic system.

There are just too many factors to accurately predict the timing of a major world event like August 13, 1999. Yet the Mexica were especially focused on this specific day. For them, August 13, 1999 was hundreds of years in the future. How could they have calculated it? Why were they so interested?

The Mexica seem to have been much more concerned about the period of time we're living in than we appear to be. It doesn't take a rocket scientist to figure out that a world situation based on the concept of unlimited growth and expansion on all levels is going to wind up with its challenges eventually, and probably big ones. This conclusion is so obvious, it's impossible to believe we haven't even worked out a basic solution over the last thousand years. Instead, we've opted for the path of least resistance: the Darwinian feast.

The Aztec Sun Calendar is more about choices and probabilities than predetermined outcomes. Our future is unfolding moment by moment. It's implicitly connected with each choice we make. What will our collective choices be as we draw closer to August 13, 1999?

The weatherman can't predict exactly when a tornado, a volcano, or earthquake will happen. Does this negate the possibility of forecasting the events of August 13, 1999?

Modern chaos science, like the Aztec Sun Calendar, describes processes of motion and change and examines the dynamic systems of nature. It observes real world phenomena. Studying the motion of dynamic systems involves investigating how seemingly linear events explore and express their nonlinear potentials.

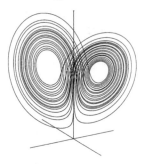

Fig. 57 The *Lorenz attractor* is a doubled complementary spiral. It's created from the complex relationships of three independent variables.

A dynamic system moves simply at first. It often goes into repetitive motions as it tests the water of its potentials. At some point, nobody can say exactly when, one bold part of the system begins to probe beyond the limitations of simplicity. It penetrates into a critical attractor zone. When it does, the whole system suddenly leaps into the zone along with it. It explodes in a flurry of non-predictable, radically new behaviors.

Sir Isaac Newton's equations for the laws of force work wonderfully for two bodies of mass interacting with each other. But Newton's equations become unsolvable as soon as you try to calculate the relationships of more than two bodies. The relationships of three or more differential equations generate chaos. All you can do is approximate their behavior. (Fig. 57 & 58)

When you make approximations, you create infinities of smaller and smaller terms in an

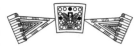

Fig. 58

These figures show that relationships of three or more differential equations generate chaos.

effort to describe what the system is doing. Small variations can create enormous nonlinear consequences in dynamic systems. When you add terms to nonlinear equations, the complexity of their possible outcomes increases exponentially. If dynamic systems have just barely detectable differences of origin, they can develop into vastly different structures over time.

As a result of these new understandings, we've discovered some major loopholes in the mathematical certainty we once felt we had about such basic things as the orbits of the planets in our solar system. We can say the planets will probably keep doing what they're doing, but we can no longer say they're going to be that way for sure.[3]

Instabilities can develop from inside the existing structure of any dynamic system. They appear as if from nowhere. Instabilities silently gestate within a secret place in the realm of numbers. When they're ready to be born, they spontaneously bubble into our reality. Instabilities can pop up in any system where large amounts of information are in flux. Big computer systems develop them all the time. We call them bugs.

Bugs are impossible to diagnose by taking a system apart piece by piece. They manifest out of probability waves. (Fig. 59) They don't happen for any single, isolated reason. They arise from a network of intangible factors. They're not there until they're there.

Fig. 59 The waveform aspect of the Calendar is probabilistic.
It's generated from multiple cascades of yes/no decisions.

Imagine the enormous complexity of a living being such as yourself. How many subtle influences are compounding moment by moment within and around you right now? How do you manage the infinity of variables in your world? You're a true hero to keep a rhythm of order flowing through your life. It's a miracle you continue to operate the system we recognize as you from day to day. (Fig. 60)

The chaos phenomenon points to the quantum nature of nature. Our world is locally unpredictable, but globally stable. In other words, you can't make a definite statement about any particular point in the system, but you can make a definite statement about the behavior of the whole system. Local behavior is *fuzzy*.

Chaos scientists have developed special systems of qualitative mathematics to model the movements of whole systems. (Fig. 61) They ask how systems behave over time. They search for patterns that develop as a system changes. *Fractal geometry* was developed to answer these kinds of questions.

Chaos has deterministic qualities and patterns to it. As we've seen, magic happens when chaos breaks out. Chaos has another magical quality. It's called *self-similarity*. (Fig. 62) Self-similarity means every part of a dynamic system in chaos mirrors the whole system in infinitely repeating patterns.

A *fractal curve* indicates there's some kind of recurring inner structure within the complexity of a form. Fractals are repetitions of order in descending and ascending *scales*. This means the same patterns show up at larger and smaller levels of size. Fractal patterns repeat themselves into infinity. They contain infinity in their finite structure. (Fig. 63)

Fractal geometry is an accurate way to measure and describe the seeming irregularities of form we find in the real world. Fractals precisely model complex dynamic systems. They also reveal a surprise: patterns of systemic chaos can be described by very simple, self generating equations. Fractals generate themselves from *iterative* equations. This is a fancy way of saying

Fig. 60 You integrate an infinity of variables and subtle factors into your life.

Fig. 61 If you want to analyze the qualities of a system, you need to observe how it changes over time. Ollin is the essence of scientific observation.

Fig. 62 Each Portal and Luminous Pearl indicate another whole dynamic universe contained within the Calendar.

Fig. 63 The Calendar's structure gives the impression of infinite length within a finite space. It illustrates the doubling and fractal qualities of nature.

a simple relationship repeatedly compounds on itself over time. Fractals generate their complex forms from very basic initial conditions. They graphically illustrate how and where a system changes over time. They show you how every level of a system connects, communicates with and empowers every other level.

When you feed rational numbers into iterative equations, their iterations generate pleasant, neatly ordered patterns. When you feed irrational numbers into these equations, they generate chaos patterns. Chaos and order arise from the essential numerical qualities of the ratios and proportions in the origin of a system. Once you understand this idea, you'll have a good grasp of the indigenous sciences.

The Calendar is a fractal. Could it be the Mandelbrot set? The Mandelbrot set demonstrates the qualities of numbers and their relationships with one another. It's a measure of how the rational meets the irrational on the *complex plane*. It's the shape of feedback. It describes the way a system chooses between its options.

The Aztec Sun Calendar and the Mandelbrot set have many correspondences. The Calendar inclusively dovetails chaos and order to create a whole picture. It demonstrates how the relationships between chaos and order create *fractal basin boundaries*.

Each section of the Mandelbrot set connects to the rest of the infinity of Mandelbrot forms by a thin mathematical filament in the area of 13 Cane. Mathematicians call this area the *inflection point*. The Calendar's graphic demonstration of attractors, doubling and self-similar phenomena are a testimony to its universality and efficiency as a cosmic map. It's a landmark of chaos science.

The self-similar nature of our universe also means our actions can influence the remotest galaxies, and vice versa. Chaos scientists call the complex interrelationships of all phenomena the *Butterfly Effect*. This relates to the possibility of a butterfly flapping its wings in one part of the world in just such a way that could stir up air currents to iterate into a hurricane in another part of the world.

Chaos scientists use iterative equations to model complex organic processes. They use fractals to model strange attractors because fractals and strange attractors share similar qualities.

Nature creates itself through iteration. It builds and feeds back on what's come before. Nature's equations are exquisitely sensitive to their initial, original conditions.

The Aztec Sun Calendar shows you how simple systems can mushroom into wild complexity. The places where complexity comes into a system are very important. Chaos scientists have found these places are *pressure points* where a system is highly sensitive to

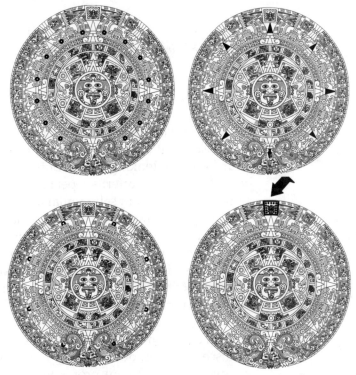

The places where complexity comes into a system are important pressure points that can magnify the effects of *nuance*. Dynamic systems become extremely sensitive at points of bifurcation, or doubling. Any input or subtle change in these places can radically alter the entire course of the system. Systems are also highly sensitive at or around places that relate to their *past* bifurcations.

incoming information or changes of any kind. They're critical moments and locations that can magnify the effects of nuance. If you introduce any change at one of these critical points, it can create effects that spiral completely out of proportion to anything you would expect from such a small amount of input. The Calendar indicates that August 13, 1999 is going to be one of these points on a global scale. This is why our actions on this date can have such a powerful effect on our entire planet.

Nature is self-similar from all points of view. Chaos mirrors itself at larger and smaller scales. Strange attractors are also self-similar. They reflect themselves as they double. This is how engineers can make small scale models of turbulent systems that tell them how larger systems are likely to behave. For example, a geologist can look at a small earthquake and make accurate estimations for the effects of a larger one. The physics of earthquakes are similar on different scales. Scales are like octaves of size.

Self-similarity is also how a good doctor can diagnose what's happening on the inside of your body by looking at the outside of your body. If the same patterns repeat themselves in a number of different self-similar areas, they're probably repeating at other levels inside you as well. This is why your whole life can respond and improve when you use holistic medicine. You're a self-similar pattern of the strange attractor of your life. You reflect the entire universe in your being.

The Mexica may have used self-similar models based on the principals in the Calendar to discern and understand the importance of August 13, 1999. Today, professionals in all areas are using fractals to model everything from economics to electronics to biology. Fractals are the structure of a truly holistic revolution that's touching every aspect of our modern society. We're learning how to think holistically. We're becoming indigenous.

When a system begins to bifurcate, it's going to crumble into chaos, attain a radically new order, or both. Large systems can remain stable for eons until subtle feedback loops push the system to a new bifurcation point. The Aztec Sun Calendar shows how August 13, 1999, is a bifurcation point in time. It's a strange attractor.

When a system is about to bifurcate, it's in the process of choosing which new order it's going to shift into. The number of feedback loops in a living system as large as the Earth is infinite. We have an infinity of choices. As the flux of our energy and information increases, it's guiding the planet into moments of instability. These are the moments when Earth decides which new order it's going to go with.

Each decision creates a new path. It starts out very small and magnifies over time through feedback and iteration. When decisions lead to order, ordered structure feeds back and the system becomes increasingly ordered. If the decisions lead to chaos, chaos feeds back and either shatters the system or brings it to a new level of order. The irregular and irrational contain the rich chaos out of which new order is born.

August 13, 1999, is a bifurcation point in time.

Wave Phenomena

Turbulence is a strange attractor. The natural flows of wind and water are chaos in motion. They are, to use the technical word from modern physics, strange. (Fig. 64)

At first it seems trivial to investigate the motions of wind and water, because we see them every day. But since we see them every day, we don't see them at all. It takes a special effort to retrain yourself to go back into your daily world with fresh perceptions, to experience your world as a foreigner, as an alien, as a child.

Wave phenomena are omnipresent in our lives. It's a good idea to familiarize ourselves with their patterns and processes. (Fig. 65) Leading scientists and mathematicians have tried to elucidate the principles of wave phenomena for centuries. Although we understand much, there's still a lot we don't know.

Sometimes nonlinear relationships in nature can feedback with one another to create a *super-coherent* wave emergence called a *soliton wave*. Occasionally, a soliton wave precipitates out of the chaos of watery turbulence in the ocean. A soliton wave is a stable form. It can travel for thousands of miles while perfectly retaining its shape.

There are many examples of soliton waves

Water   Wind

Fig. 64

Turbulence begins as the complexities of the motions in a fluid begin to interact and compound with one another. Fluid dynamics model chaos. Since the motions of fluid and air perfectly model dynamic systems, the Mexica used the images of wind and water to model turbulence and chaos.

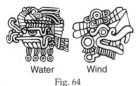

Sound   Electricity

Fig. 65

There are two wave models in modern physics: *Transverse waves* of electromagnetic radiation that can pass through empty space, and *longitudinal waves*, like sound, that require a medium through which to propagate.

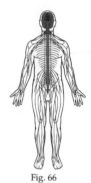

Fig. 66

The nervous system is a collection of soliton wave impulses.

in nature. One is in the electrical rhythms traveling around your nervous system. (Fig. 66) Your body hosts an enormous collection of soliton wave impulses communicating with and potentiating one another.[4]

Soliton waves are born when the energies of multiple wave forms couple and synergize. They ride the edge between too much impulse, which creates turbulence, and too little impulse, which results in dissipation. (Fig. 67)

Coherent waves are like birth contractions. They all need to work together to get the baby out. The inner part of the Calendar indicates what can happen when many individual forces converge and focus on a single point. These forces come together and harmonize into a very powerful wave. The waves of the Calendar emanate out from the center.

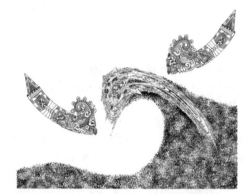

Fig. 67 The Xiucoatl indicate the convergence of two soliton waves to create a third superwave.

Nonlinear relationships of iterative and feedback control loops balance precisely as the soliton wave glides along toward its final destination. The soliton's integration of linearity and non-linearity creates super-coherency. It obeys a set of laws all its own. These laws are different in kind from any of the individual elements going into the system.

Soliton waves are an example of how the subtle forces in nature can combine to become an entirely different type of dynamic system. This new system is much greater than the sum of its parts.

Here's an exercise to help train you how to have fresh perceptions:

❀ Observe babies. How do they learn?

Tecpatl

Tecpatl is the word. It's the message, the light, the sound and the spark of creative inspiration. Tecpatl is sacrifice. It's the knife that can create or destroy. One of the more literal meanings of Tecpatl is the ritual obsidian knife blade of the Mexica, which creates a very powerful electric spark when it's struck.

Tecpatl is communication. Tonatiuh, the Sun, is giving you a message.* Tonatiuh's tongue is Tecpatl. Its very tip has many nuances of meaning. (Fig. 68) One aspect is the eye of God who constantly watches you. It's also the eye of death incessantly searching for you. (Fig. 69) A third meaning is flower, meaning the beauty and creativity of speech and sound. (Fig. 70)

You'll find a set of fangs at the other end of Tecpatl. (Fig. 71) They're the power to protect, and the ability to support your words with action. They're speaking with sincerity, integrity and authority. They're understanding. They're enjoyment.

How are you going to use your words?

Fig. 68
Tonatiuh's tongue is Tecpatl.

Fig. 69
Eye of Tecpatl.

Fig. 70
Xochitl/Flower

Fig. 71
Fangs of Tecpatl.

*Sticking your tongue out is how people say hello in many indigenous cultures. The tongue means *word* in Egyptian hieroglyphics, and it's the *flower of the heart* in traditional Asian medicine.

The Aztec Sun Calendar is a vibrational field.

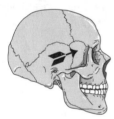

Tecpatl relates to synaesthesia. It's curious that the place we call the *temple* is located exactly between the eye and the ear.

Fig. 72
The Sun speaks with light.

Words have the power to begin and to end. They're your power to create sound. Sounds are forces that shape and direct your world. Every word you use is a magical incantation that directs energy.

The Aztec Sun Calendar shows how our universe is made of sound, or vibration. Many ancient traditions relate the ability to make sound with the act of creation. Sound is the fundamental creative force.

Western cultures believe our world is produced from sound. Modern science has revealed how everything in our world is made of vibration. We distinguish what's light and sound by our perceptions, which are subjective. They largely depend on our state of personal development.

The Sun speaks to us with light. Tecpatl speaks to us of *synaesthesia*. Synaesthesia means a sensation in one part of the body produced by stimulating another part. For example, when you experience synaesthesia, you can see sound, and hear light. Synaesthesia is a state of perception described in many religious and spiritual traditions. It indicates a very heightened state of awareness. Speaking in light is an ideal illustration of light-sound synaesthesia. The Biblical God creates our universe with speech, or sound. God's words "Let there be light..." are a perfect expression of Tecpatl. (Fig. 72) In the Bible, God would speak, rather than directly appear to human beings. The ancient Egyptians also spoke of the *Singing Sun* who creates through its "cry of light."

A number of modern religions prohibit making images to represent God. They understand how visual images give us only appearances. They demonstrate a surface reality.

Our modern world is a symbol based society. Symbols and icons can be substituted for reality. At this level, they're dangerous, because they can remove you from an experience based existence. Following empty images can lead to a deep and inarticulate sense of disappointment. It just doesn't satisfy. (Fig. 73)

Modern society in general has come to believe in vacant images. We've so completely become a visual culture that our abilities to listen and hear have atrophied. In his book <u>Nada Brahma, the World is Sound</u>, Joachim-Ernst Berendt points out how the deterioration of our sense of hearing has run parallel with the process of secularization in the modern world.[5]

It's paradoxical how we believe what we see, and discredit what we hear. The human range of hearing is ten times greater than the range of sight. You're wired for sound. The absurdity of visual proof has gone to extremes with the advent of modern image manipulation. Special effects in cinema, video facsimiles of anything you can imagine and more, and the sickening catastrophe of commercial television have all stripped our tolerance and trust in the visual.

We've got to begin to balance our perceptions. Today's children are exploding the trend from visual proof to *auditory* and *kinesthetic* confirmation. This sentiment is concisely expressed by the Rastafarian hero Bob Marley when he sings: "Who feels it knows it..." Listen to popular music. It's an entire vibrational experience. It surrounds, impacts and penetrates every part of you. The indigenous movement is an essential element in today's new music. It's part of the search for a deeper, more satisfying and universally connected reality. (Fig. 74)

Fig. 73

13 Cane can indicate the empty quality of images.

Fig. 74 The Calendar shows you how your ears grasp the heart of things. Tonatiuh relates to hearing and sound. It demonstrates the importance of active listening.

Wind
Fig. 75

Fig. 76

Resonance permeates
our world.

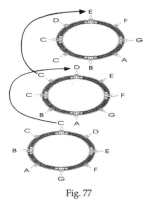

Fig. 77

If sound is a fundamental principle, then our universe should have a spiraling structure. Since everything in our universe is vibration, the number *two* is a fundamental physical constant. The ratio of 1:2, or 2:1 is the ratio and relationship of the *octave*. It's also the constant of the change of state, or transition into and out of chaos. The Calendar demonstrates spirals of octaves. The octave relationship is found many times throughout the Calendar design.

Sound is the creative element. Our world is sound. Matter is vibration. Sound is substance. Sound means whole, strong, healthy and robust. If you're sane and healthy, we say you're of sound mind and body. Sound also means to explore in the sense of sounding something out, or using a friend as a sounding board for an idea.

Sound relates to identity. In Opera, Jazz and to some extent Rock music, the players need to define a sound that's unquestionably theirs. They own it, or maybe it owns them. Their sound is an acoustic signature.

Sound is wind. (Fig. 75) It's ripples of wave forms moving through the air around you. Sound is spirals of octaves. If our world is made of sound, it means everything's influenced by an infinity of resonances. (Fig. 76) It suggests that vibrational field phenomena are fundamental laws, and we'll probably find quantum behavior just about everywhere we search. It indicates that we'll discover spiraling octaves of interconnected geometrical relationships all through nature.

The ancient Greek philosopher Herakleitos was right after all. His most famous saying, *"Panta rei,"* everything is in motion, turned out to be true. Einstein helped the modern world understand how everything in our universe is in relative motion. He explained how there are no fixed points in our universe. There are only changing points of reference. (Fig. 77)

A musical scale of relative *intervals* is therefore a brilliant way to describe the qualities and characteristics of our world. When you're mapping sound, relationships of the mathematical distances or proportions between notes are as important as the notes themselves. Melody is not in any single tone. It's in the intervals, or the relationships of the tones over time. It takes two or more notes to define an interval and a relationship. (Fig. 78) Many relationships interacting with one another are music. You can shift octaves, keys, and dance all over the universe and know exactly where you are as long as you understand about relative proportions.

The musical nature of nature is why many of the great astronomers of history were also musicians, and many of the great musicians of history were also astronomers. Ancient systems of astronomy and astrology expressed the relationships of planets musically as well as with visual models. In the ancient world, musical instruments were tuned to the planetary intervals. The strings and holes of instruments were even associated with particular planets.

Knowing the laws of resonance and harmony makes it possible to predict patterns in nature. Nature itself has a harmonic structure. It even shows a tendency to express in the major scale.[6] (Fig. 79)

The science of relating musical intervals is an incredibly esoteric language. Yet it doesn't take any special training to be affected by music. We all know how to interpret sound in our own way. We understand the relationships of tone and interval with parts of ourselves that go much deeper than conventional language. Deep memories and images can be evoked powerfully by music. Since tone, vibration and musical interval are essential expressions of ratio and proportion, they can speak directly to very deep levels of your being. Music has the ability to bridge the gap between the deep unconscious parts of you and what you are consciously aware of in the now.

The Calendar teaches how the laws of harmonics and octaves demonstrate a unity of structure in our universe. By recognizing this unity, we can translate and transpose relationships

An oscilloscopic picture of the octave relationship makes an infinity sign, or an eight.

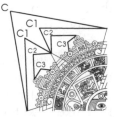

Each doubling of frequency maintains the same note, but at a higher octave. The same law holds true in reverse. Dividing frequencies by two, or halving them, produces the same tone in the next lower octave.

There are eight natural steps in an octave. Thirteen is an octave of *semitones* on the musical scale. Our evenly tempered scale creates an equiangular logarithmic spiral.

Fig. 78
The two tongues of the Xiucoatl define an *interval*.

Fig. 79 Female bodies tend to embody more minor proportions, and male bodies tend to embody more major proportions.

from any level of frequency into frequencies we can hear. We can convert anything into a musical model.

Rhythm and tone are in time what proportion is in space. Proportion can be translated into sound or rhythm, and vice versa. Anything with form has relationships of ratio and proportion. Music is the essence of ratio and proportion, so form can be mathematically transposed into music.

The Aztec Sun Calendar teaches us about the power of vibration. Music is sound. Sound is vibration. Vibrational phenomena are experimentally repeatable at any time. They obey definite physical laws like any other force in nature.

The Calendar illustrates how we're always surrounded and influenced by sound and vibration. The modern science of *cymatics* studies the wave patterns of vibration. Cymatic scientists create models and experiments to help us visualize and explore the incredible shapes of sound. They demonstrate how vibrations can induce dynamic patterns of harmony and symmetry into the world around us. (Fig. 80) Hans Jenny, one of the pioneers of modern cymatics, calls this harmonious symmetry the "primal harmonic phenomenon."[7]

The effects of vibration are fascinating to observe. When you study a vibrational field, you can see exactly how each part of the field connects to the impulses and movements of the whole. Cymatic pictures show you interconnected spirals of matter in motion. They give you a graphic demonstration of the principles of the Aztec Sun Calendar.

Fig. 80

Vibrations induce dynamic patterns of harmony and symmetry in the world around us.

The oscillations of sound are very complex. A single note is able to generate an incredible living universe of multiple motions. A simple tone can create a complex series of interweaving relationships that lead from one to another in an endless chain. Sometimes these patterns never repeat.

A vibrational field can exaggerate, suppress and enhance electromagnetic fields.[8] It alters the relationships these fields normally have with one another. All chemical and physical processes change in the presence of vibration.

Since vibration changes the way particles stick

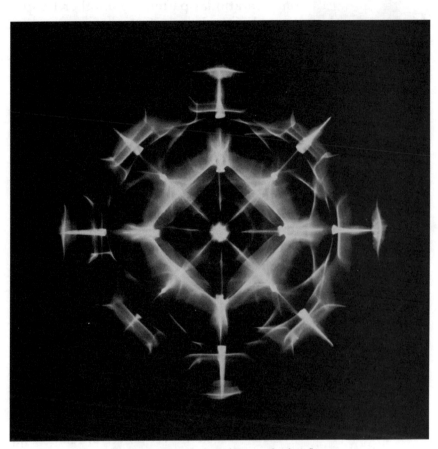

A cymatic picture of a drop of water under the influence
of vibration. From <u>Cymatics Volume II</u> by Hans Jenny.

together, whatever medium it's influencing turns into a dynamic
living liquid. Zones of resonance appear where the effects of vibration intensely magnify. Instead of the smooth, even distribution of
molecules you usually find in a substance, you discover groups of
molecules collecting into patterns.

A single vibration creates many effects at the same time. They
all seem to be happening independently, but they're not. For example, a pile of powder under the influence of vibration can suddenly leap together into a coherent living form. Shift the tone ever
so slightly, and a completely new structure emerges. Transitions from

Sound has a triple aspect. These three inseparable qualities are *pulse, form* and *wave.* Pulse is the essential vibratory rhythm of a sound. Form is the overall shape a sound makes in the medium it's traveling through. Wave is the ever expanding effect of the pulse as it travels out and away from its source. The triple aspect of sound is demonstrated in the Calendar by Tonatiuh's three sectioned earrings.

one vibrational pattern to another happen abruptly. One shape instantly becomes another. There's no in-between stage.

Vibrational forms pulsate. They make vortices. Their phenomena can seem to defy gravity. Keystone Cop scenes appear out of nowhere and annihilate themselves a moment later. The smallest bits of what you thought were inanimate matter seem to make split second decisions before flying off on their unknown missions. Trails and towering bridges erect themselves from one shimmering corpuscle to another. Whole continents rise and fall in perfect topographical detail. Solar systems emerge and explode into oblivion, only to resurface from the depths of stillness. Fractals compound upon fractals.

The Calendar shows us how vibrations often stimulate substances to collect into many spheres that revolve around one another as if they're a universe being formed. A vibrational field can so exactly duplicate the qualities of a dynamic universe, it goes against all common sense to believe these phenomena aren't related in some profound way.

There's a subtle yet powerful relationship between chaos and vibration. Turbulent systems are especially sensitive to vibratory fields. Chaos sets the stage for vibrational events. Sometimes vibration creates what appears to be a chaotic field, but it isn't. The level of complexity in these moments just exceeds our ability to comprehend or perceive pattern.

Most, if not all processes can be modeled as wave phenomena acting on a medium. In complicated vibrational dynamics, we find layer upon layer of simple impulses compounding to produce complex four-dimensional figures. Vibration creates a language of dynamic forms in motion. These living patterns are easily recognized by their simple geometrical configurations. Geometry, it seems, is alive.

Cymatic models such as the Aztec Sun Calendar can help you understand how the space you live in is filled with many forces. They help you learn how to perceive opposites at the same time. You can see opposites unify in a cymatic model when rotating super waves develop and revolve whole patterns as a single unit. These patterns often radiate out past the edges of the vibration, and then reappear from the center of the pattern again. (Fig. 81)

Vibrations tend to create shapes that have definite bilateral symmetry. (Fig. 82) They're very similar to living beings. Vibrational fields can sculpt entire moving, breathing vibrational creatures complete with arms, legs and expressive faces.

Perceiving opposites at the same time.

Fig. 82

The Calendar demonstrates the bilateral symmetry of a vibrational field.

Fig. 81

A vibratory field maintains its integrity and identity even when you physically interfere with it. For example, if you put your finger into a vibrating medium, it becomes a part of the pattern. Sometimes the pattern collects itself around your finger and simply goes on its way. The field and its patterns of motion live independently from the medium they're influencing. A vibratory field can move through and affect different substances, but the substances aren't the field. The medium just gives you evidence the field is there. Buckminster Fuller captured this idea beautifully when he once said: "The wave is not the water. The water merely told us about the wave moving by."

Since sound, oscillations and vibrations are everywhere in nature, it's clear there are many cymatic wave effects at work in every situation. The science of cymatics shows us how a very small shift in vibratory frequency can cause a radical restructuring of form. Could this effect somehow relate to what might happen on August 13, 1999?

Fig. 83

Actively listening can give you important clues to the world around you.

The Earth's geomagnetic frequency is increasing. Greg Braden argues convincingly in his book <u>Awakening to Zero Point</u> that Earth's resonant frequency is on the rise from what was once around 8 Hz to the next stable point in the *Fibonacci* sequence of 13 Hz.* Could this rise in subtle vibration be sufficient to cause a major geophysical transformation? One viewing of a cymatics video could permanently influence your decision.

The Aztec Sun Calendar can teach you how to balance yourself using sound and vibration. It shows you how to orient yourself by actively listening to the world around you. (Fig. 83)

The patterns of nature are vibrating processes.

*If you're into the mysterious qualities of numbers, ponder on this: August 13, 1999 is 8-13-99.

If you can recognize universal rhythmic flows of vibratory cycles, you can enter the flow of nature more consciously. All cycles see-saw. When one side goes up, the other side comes down. Vibration is a unification of opposites. It's the Ollin principle in action. (Fig 84)

It's easy to build your vibrational vocabulary. Sound is the most direct and tangible everyday use of vibration. You can use sound and music to train yourself in the realm of vibration. It's easy, fun, informative, and a powerful healing technique. Vibration is a universal phenomenon. It relates intimately with the behaviors of the energy patterns you meet with every day. It makes good sense to use sound, music and even your voice to familiarize yourself with the qualities of vibration.

Practice active listening. Go for a walk in any modern city. You'll hear a half dozen languages spoken on each block. As you walk, listen through the languages to the universal tones and vibrations inside them. Tone and vibration extend beyond language barriers and cultural differences. Familiarity with them is an essential practice to develop communication skills in our modern world. (Fig. 85)

Learning about sound also introduces you to the ecstatic qualities of vibration. If you develop and skillfully refine your ability to truly listen, many new doors will open for you. You'll come to a real appreciation of the more refined states of human culture. Evolving your sensitivity to sound and vibration leads to expertise in all areas of experience. Best of all, it's your experience, not somebody else's. You don't need to buy someone else's conceptual package.

Sound and vibration are powerful forces in your life. Use them wisely and responsibly. They can help you. Go more deeply into your ability to listen. The Sun speaks.

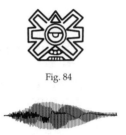

Fig. 84

Ollin is the process of vibratory motion.

Fig. 85

Tone and vibration are universal modes of communication.

Here are some exercises to help you appreciate the power of words and sound:

- Define a period of time not to speak. The amount of time is up to you. Whatever you decide on, stick to it. If you must communicate during this time, do it non-verbally. Simply be mindful of your tendency to speak.

- There's nothing like sound to get you into the present moment. A continuous sound becomes its own kind of silence when you blend with it for awhile. It disappears as though it's not even there. Use any kind of a droning sound to learn how to move from sound to silence to sound. Use the change from sound to silence to keep yourself active and alert.

- Statistically, men are more wired for sight and women are more wired for sound. We all both hear and see, yet there's a ratio of predominance of hearing to seeing that we all embody on a personal level. Examine how you go through your day, balancing seeing, hearing and feeling.

- Listen to Bob Marley and the Wailers, <u>Rastaman Vibration.</u>

Electricity

You're electromagnetic by nature. The Aztec Sun Calendar can teach you how to navigate yourself through our electromagnetic world.

Nobody knows what electricity really is. We only know some of its properties and a few ways to use it. One of these properties is *charge*. Charge is when you divide electricity into two separate parts, one positive, and the other negative. These parts will then do whatever they can to get together again. The power of electricity comes from the strength of the desire of two charges to reunite. This polar force is demonstrated in the Calendar by the relationship of the two Xiucoatl.

The Xiucoatl are the positive and negative aspects of electricity that will do everything in their power to reunite.

Atoms are dynamic electrical systems. The relationships of positive and negative forces in atomic structures determine their qualities. The *nucleus*, or heart, of an atom is made of *protons* and *neutrons*. Protons are electrically positive. (Fig. 86) Neutrons are electrically neutral. This double aspect of the atomic nucleus is demonstrated by Tonatiuh holding one quality in each hand. The outer part of an atom is made of orbiting electrically negative *electrons*, and is demonstrated by the fiery Xiucoatl. Electrons are 1836 times less massive than protons, but they carry most of the electric charge of an atom. An electric *current* is a river of electrons. Any flow of electrons creates both a magnetic and an electrical field at *right angles* to each other. This right-angled relationship of electricity and magnetism is illustrated by the 90° orientations of the Solar Rays. (Fig. 87)

Electricity moves in fractal forms, like lightning bolts, arteries, veins, and the branches of trees.

There's a lot more to the Sun Calendar and electricity. To make that discovery, you'll need to move forward on your journey. For now, there's only one important thing to remember about electricity in your preparations: electromagnetism remains a mystery.

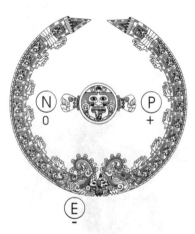

Fig. 86 The Calendar models atomic structure.

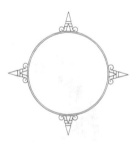

Fig. 87 One of the most fundamental right angles in nature is the relationship of the electric wave to the magnetic wave, demonstrated by the Solar Rays.

Our Spiral Dance

The Aztec Sun Calendar can teach you about cycles and spirals. Nature has a circular/spiral identity. A spiral is a circle that never ends. All circles are single plane glimpses of spirals in motion as they move forward in time. Circles spiral into being. Each spiral is a portion of an even larger circling spiral, and so on into infinity.

Many indigenous legends relate how our universe was born from a spiral contraction. Life affirming cultures of all ages have been deeply fascinated by the spiral and its life giving properties. Wonder at the spiral is an essential human delight.

The spiral was once one of the primary elements of architecture. In ancient Greek design, for example, spiral forms were said to represent Wind and Water. In Gothic architecture, the spiral reflected the winding path of eternal life.

There's an infinite progression of spirals that precisely describe relative proportions of feminine and masculine principles within themselves in a tantric dance between the straight line and the circle. Spirals embody and integrate *both* qualities in their being.

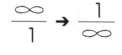

Masculine
Nature

Feminine Nature

Masculine nature runs the danger of becoming too linear, expansive and depleting. Believing the world is going to end is a masculine fantasy.

Feminine nature runs the danger of becoming too circular, repetitive and nurturing. Believing the world isn't going to end is a feminine fantasy.

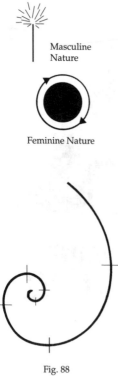

Fig. 88
The spiral of time

Many archaeologists and modern indigenous people discuss the concept of *circular time*. Time also spirals. Your experience of time is subjective. It speeds up as your life moves ahead. This is because each moment is just a fraction of all your experiences. When you're young, this ratio is small. As you move forward in time, each moment gets shorter relative to all the other ones you've gone through. In your first precious moments of life, you're at unity, or infinity. (Fig. 88) This is why your first experiences such as your conception, the time spent in your mother's womb and your birth have such an influential power to form your life patterns. Your sense of time creates a *logarithmic spiral** over the course of your life.

This is one of the reasons you can improve your life by changing your perceptual state. Your state of mind influences the quality and the depth of your sense of time. Depth of experience is another logarithmic spiral that can affect your personal spiral of unfolding time.

As you sit here nearly motionless, reading this book, there are trillions of spiraling motions

$$\frac{\infty}{1} \rightarrow \frac{1}{\infty}$$

The growth of shells and the growth of flowers are very similar. Phi is the common force or quality that unfolds through each of their developments.

* A *logarithmic spiral* is a plane curve produced by a point on a straight line rotating uniformly around a pole or an axis. The point moves at a speed proportional to its distance from the pole. Any curve creating self-similar, or *gnomonic*, arcs is logarithmic. It's the only plane curve where any two arcs are always similar to each other. The only difference between them is their size. The formula to describe a logarithmic spiral can give us a generalization of the patterns of growth and development of a living being.

playing out inside you. You're also sailing through space on multiple spiral pathways as you sit on a point on the surface of the Earth. This point is flying on a spiral path through local space at a velocity of nearly one thousand miles an hour just from the Earth's daily rotation alone. This motion is part of a larger spiral the Earth is making on its spiral path around the Sun, which is also flying along at thousands of miles per hour. The Earth's entire motion around the Sun follows the spiral course of our solar system around our galactic center, which also spirals around the motion of our cluster of galaxies, which is spiral dancing along with other star clusters as we all fly through space at thousands of meters per second towards a mysterious pocket of energy in deep space we call the *Great Attractor*.

Spiral forms predominate in the macro-universe. Spiral motions also abound in the subatomic world. Many aspects of nature take spiral journeys. When you really examine it, it seems like most, if not all, of nature's basic processes spiral either in their forms or through space over time. Energies and forces play themselves out in spirals. Life unfolds and grows along spiral paths.

Logarithmic spirals are the spirals of life. They grow by adding onto themselves, accumulating from within, like the numbers in a *Phi* sequence. Phi is the essential ratio of the *golden proportion*. (Fig. 89) It pops up all over the place in nature. Phi describes a relationship. It's nonlinear and includes the irrational. Phi is interesting because it defines the parameters of growth in living systems. Objects and creatures that embody the divine proportion tend to survive or remain preserved over time.

Iteration is one of nature's basic tools for creating form. The many complexities of dynamic,

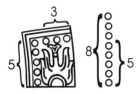

Phi Ratios in sections of the Xiucoatl.

The 8 : 5 phi ratio.

The 13 : 8 phi ratio.

Fig. 89

The golden ratio, or golden proportion, is also called the *divine proportion*. It's formed by dividing any line such that the ratio of the shorter section to the longer section is the same as the ratio of the longer section to the whole line.

A pentagram creates the Phi ratio from its inner relationships.

The pentagram creates Phi. Phi creates the logarithmic spiral.

Each tip of a pentagram is an isosceles triangle.

Each Solar ray has a perfect isosceles triangle at its tip and embodies the golden proportion. The isosceles triangle is mirrored below it in its opposite.

living systems are generated from simple initial conditions. They evolve using a simple game plan. Phi is the most well known and pervasive of nature's iterative equations.

Phi is pyramidal. It builds something new by adding to what's come before. Nature adds the last two terms of a Phi series together to make the next term. Each step in a Phi sequence makes a golden proportion relationship with each of its immediate neighbors. It's golden all the way.

A rectangle with adjacent sides in the ratio of Phi : 1 is called a golden rectangle. This shape has been experimentally proven to be the most pleasing rectangle to the most people.[9] The advertising industry spends billions of dollars to find out what we're most attracted to. Time after time they come up with the same conclusion: the golden ratio, Phi.

The golden section appears repeatedly in the human body. The main one we see is made

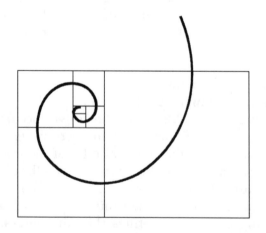

If you take a golden rectangle and cut a square off it, you get a self-similar golden rectangle at right angles to the first. They're the same rectangular shape. They differ only in size. You can also create new golden rectangles by reversing this process and adding squares to the long sides of golden rectangles. Repetition of either process creates a logarithmic spiral.

by the relationship of the total height to the navel in adults. If you have a fairly average skeleton, the relative sizes of your bones have many golden proportion relationships between them. Much of ancient art was based on these relationships, because they evoke an instinctual feeling of beauty.

The proportion of total height to the navel in infants is 2:1, the octave. We grow from octave proportions as a child into golden proportions as an adult. Octave is origin. Phi is adulthood, beauty and life. The journey from Octave to Phi is the path of growth. Phi creates the spirals of nature.

The isosceles triangle also relates with the doubled upside down and reversed pentagram that forms the decagon at the center of the Calendar. An isosceles triangle joins the center of the decagon with any of its sides. The ratio of the radius of a circumcircle of a regular decagon to a side of the decagon is the golden ratio.

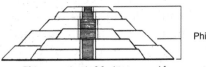

Phi

Phi proportion in Mexican pyramids

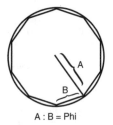

A : B = Phi

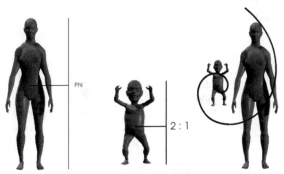

Phi

2 : 1

The journey from octave to phi takes us from infancy to adulthood.

In the realm of music, Phi oscillates between the major and minor sixth. The major 6th is a 3:5 ratio, and the minor 6th is a 5:8 ratio. The musical sixth is shown in the Calendar by the six rattles on the Xiucoatl's tails.

phi

-.618   1.618
-           +

+   -
-1.618   .618

36°
72°

The pentagram relates the five to the six in the circle and the triangle. It does this by uniting the proportions of the phi and the octave by containing the *isosceles triangle*, also known as the *sublime triangle* and the *triangle of the pentalpha* to the ancients. The ratio of the longer side to the shorter base of an isosceles triangle is phi. It has angular degrees of 36 and 72, an octave or doubling relationship as well as a mirroring relationship. The isosceles triangle demonstrates our journey from infancy to maturity, from greenness to ripeness.

Phi has curious relationship with its own negative reciprocal. Phi is the only number that becomes its own negative reciprocal when diminished by one. Phi therefore has a very unique and powerful relationship with the number one.

$$Phi - 1 = 1/Phi$$
$$Phi^2 = Phi + 1$$

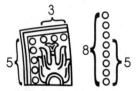

Fig. 90

The Fibonacci sequence moves like a serpent toward Phi. Serpent motions are two dimensional permutations of spirals.

The Fibonacci series is one of the most universally popular examples of Phi. In the Fibonacci series, an even term divided by the preceding odd term gives you a ratio less than Phi, and an odd term divided by the previous even term gives you a ratio greater than Phi. They never touch Phi exactly. They just get closer to it. The farther out you go in the Fibonacci sequence, the closer the relationships get to Phi.

Why is this ratio so important? It's the ideal the vast majority of natural phenomena we've observed in our universe approximate to and head toward. How many phi relationships can you find in the Aztec Sun Calendar?

$$F_n = F_{n-2} + F_{n-1}$$

0,1,1,2,3,5,8,13,21,34,55,
89,144,233,377,610,987,
1597,2584,4181,6765,
10946,17711,28657,
46368,75025,121393,
196418,317811,514229,
832040,1346269,2178309,
3524578,5702887,9227465...

Each section of the Xiucoatl has an L-shaped bar of eight dots. This shape represents both the octave (8) and phi (8:5) the golden mean.

Since *gnomonic*,* or fractal features repeat themselves over and over again in living forms, much of life's geometry is based on logarithmic spirals. Biological systems grow exponentially. They form logarithmic spirals in space over time.

Spirals generate themselves out of a *zero point*. They come from nothing into something along a spiral path. Spirals balance around their zero point. This center is their *axis* of dynamic balance. Logarithmic spirals retain their proportions around their axis as they grow. They're the most user-friendly form of growth. Logarithmic spirals can grow into infinity and still remain balanced and centered. This calm center in the middle of the vortex is the zero at the beginning of the *Fibonacci* sequence. (Fig. 90)

Why would an apparently finite creature make use of the curves of an infinite mathematical spiral? Because the spiral integrates finity with infinity.

The Mexica knew how reciprocating numbers and geometrical forms reveals their magical qualities. They referred to the process of reciprocating as "putting yourself, or the object in question under God."

Here's an example of how this process can tell a story in the Calendar: The twelfth Fibonacci number is **89**. 1 divided by 89 equals .011235813..., the whole Fibonacci sequence. 89 is the 26th prime number, or the mirrored thirteen. The Xiucoatl each have **88** dots on their markings. Their quest for the final dot to complete 89 is the Xiucoatl's quest for Phi.

* A *gnomon* is a portion of a figure that has been added to another figure so that the shape of the whole figure is the same as the smaller figure.

The logarithmic spiral has many expressions in nature. The plant kingdom shows us spiral seeds, shells, and trails of germination. There are spirals in the growth of stems, roots, leaves, flowers and fruits. In animals and man, we find spirals in the formation and swimming motions of sperm. There's a spiral unfoldment of the growing fetus as it's nourished by its left handed spiraling umbilical cord. (Fig. 91) Most mammals have spiral based hearts. The human heart pumps in a spiraling action due to the spiral patterns of the heart muscle itself. Our bones spiral. (Fig. 92) The spiral *cochlea* in your ears distinguish you as a mammal. (Fig. 93)

In plants, spiral growth begins around a stable zero point. Nothing seems to happen at the very center of its vortex. At the periphery of this nothingness, bud shoots appear exactly where two spirals cross over and intersect with each other. New life begins where two spirals cross and relate. (Fig. 94) All major features of a plant's structure appear where two complementary spirals cross. Take a look at any plant to explore and understand how true this is.

Fig. 91
Umbilical Cord

Fig. 92
Bone

Fig. 93
Cochlea

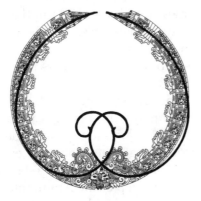

Fig. 94 New life begins where two spirals cross and relate. Events materialize where two spirals meet and relate with each other. The Xiucoatl meet in Phi ratio, expressing the *Double Fibonacci* series.

$Phi^2 = 1+phi$
$Phi^3 = 1+2phi$
$Phi^4 = 2+3phi$
$Phi^5 = 3+5phi$
$Phi^6 = 5+8phi$, etc.

Each bract of a pine cone occurs where the lines of two complementary spirals cross.

Spirals can unfold in two ways.

There are *left handed* spirals and *right handed* spirals. Go for a walk in nature. Notice which way you see the spirals around you moving. This can be wonderfully confusing, and it's a great exercise to train your perceptions. The easiest way to remember the direction of a spiral seems to be a left handed spiral (sometimes called a *sinistral* spiral), starts on the left and moves toward its opposite on the right. It moves in the same direction as the apparent motion of the Sun, like the hands of a clock.*

A right handed spiral (sometimes called a *dextral* spiral), starts on the right and moves toward its opposite on the left.

It's all relative from your point of observation. That is, if two people watch the unfolding of a spiral over time from opposite sides, one of them will observe a right handed spiral and the other will observe a left handed spiral. This phenomenon makes it notoriously difficult to nail down the exact definitions of spirals. The main reason to make the attempt is to discern how spirals can unfold in one of two ways.

There's some academic thought that the direction of the natural spiraling of various life forms comes from their origin in the northern or southern hemispheres. This becomes very interesting to contemplate when you think about how your body often uses opposing spiral structures.

Ammonite

Nautilus

Some spirals in nature failed. We've found fossilized remains of creatures whose spiral forms were inadequate to cope with their changing environmental conditions. An example of this is the *Ammonite*, an ancient relative of our *Nautilus*. The sweep of the Ammonite's curves apparently weren't wide enough to allow it truly to thrive in its shifting watery prehistoric

* Did you know the motion of the hands on a clock represent the movement of the Sun across the sky?

surroundings. Now it's extinct.

We've found some fossils that are identical to animals living today, but they spiral in the opposite direction. The spirals of fossils are often mirror images of their modern counterparts. The implication is that somehow the handedness of their spirals became inappropriate for their times, and only the "lefties" survived. What caused this reversal of spirality, or allowed those with the new spiral to survive while the others were driven to extinction? Was it related to geomagnetic, atmospheric and other environmental shifts enhancing the abilities of a certain form of the spiral? Could this somehow pertain to the "left brainers" and "right brainers" in our society? What about the "whole brainers?" What about the "no brainers?"

Fig. 95

The Sun shines impartially and equally on all.

Curves of growth are spirals. In English, we even name the season of rejuvenation and regeneration after the motivating force of the spiral. The curve of evolution is logarithmic. It defines mathematically uniform growth around a point. Every logarithmic spiral can be defined by a specific geometric progression.

Logarithmic spirals indicate equal distribution of energy. They have a quality of impartiality, like the Sun. (Fig. 95)

Sir Isaac Newton showed us in his <u>Principia</u> that if the laws of attraction obeyed the laws of the inverse cube rather than the laws of the inverse square, the planets of our solar system wouldn't fly around in their elliptical orbits, but would instead spin off into space in logarithmic spirals.

Energy in the form of electromagnetic fields follows the same spiraling lines of equal potential as a spiral vortex in water. Energy flow and biological growth under resistance are consistently observed to be connected with the form of the spiral. Electromagnetic fields always surround and permeate us. Since we grow in relationship to these fields, we grow in relationship to spirals. (Fig. 96) Is there some cubic force at work in the growth patterns of nature?

Fig. 96

The magnetic force generated by an electrical current creates a spiraling vortex motion.

Spirals are always growing past their current boundaries. They seek infinity. We can use their equations to calculate the past, and the probabilities that may come in the future. The message of the spirals in the Aztec Sun Calendar points to a dynamic, progressive and personally empowered philosophy. It reveals some key attitudes to help us create our most positive and holistically integrated destiny as we approach August 13, 1999. They are:

🌀 Stand in and create from the middle ground of your being. Use everything that has come before you to help you achieve your goals.

🌀 Connect yourself with the power of infinity.

🌀 Seek out and promote the unfolding life principle. Sensitize yourself to it, and cultivate it wherever you can.

🌀 Integrate your mature, adult self with your original, indigenous nature. Synthesize the wisdom of your life experience with the purity of your essential origin.

Because of the self-similar nature of nature, all the phenomena you learn about in the Calendar and in the universe are also inside you. You can learn to see spirals and patterns of motion in yourself and your environment.

You're musical. You're electrical. You move in spirals. It's time for your journey.

Here's an exercise to help you appreciate the spiral forms in your body:

Rotate the palms of your hands toward the sky and toward the Earth to see and feel the spiral relationships between the different bones and muscles of your arms. Sense the spirals in your bones. Sense the spirals in your Heart. Sense the spirals in your arteries and veins. How do they direct energy?

Coiled serpent and its base found in Tenochtitlan. Now resides in the Museo Nacional de Antropologia, Mexico City Tenochtitlan.

Your Journey

Creation

Your journey is a story of creation. It's about how you integrate infinity with finity. It spans across all time, touching hearts and minds everywhere. Your journey begins... in the beginning.

Get in to your cosmic canoe. We're going back to the beginning of everything. Take yourself into the primal origins of our universe, and blend with the first moment of creation.

We were born in cosmic fire. (Fig. 97) It was hot. It was dense. The energy there was so high protons and neutrons weren't even able to form or stick together. The primal universe was a *plasma state*. Plasma is the fourth state of matter. The energy of plasma is so high that subatomic particles do not follow atomic structure or order. Our fiery origin was so intense, electrons couldn't find orbital shells to revolve in. There were just an unspeakable number of *quarks*, or *elementary particles*.

The Aztec Sun Calendar describes the genesis of our universe. Tonatiuh is the fiery impulse at the beginning of creation. He is pure cosmic fire. This aspect of the Calendar relates to *Huehueteotl* (Weh-weh-TEH-ohtl), (Fig. 98) the *Old Fire God*.

Fig. 97

Tonatiuh is the primal creation.

Fig. 98

The Mexica described our fiery origins in this poem:

Huehueteotl

Mother of the gods, father of the gods,
The old god, lying in the navel of the Earth, enclosed in a turquoise chamber.
He who is in the waters that are the color of the blue bird,
He who is wrapped in clouds,
The old god, He who lives in the shadow of the land of the dead,
Lord of fire and lord of the year.[1]

Fig. 99

The equality of the three basic forces, or principles, is indicated by the equilateral triangle at the center of Tonatiuh's crown.

Fig. 100

All the matter in our universe was generated from the tiniest quantum fluctuation. Ollin is the primal vibration. It's the original pulse that set our entire universe into motion.

Fig. 101

The masculine solar rays describe the expansion of space.

The early universe was a *singularity*: infinite curvature of the spacetime continuum.[2] Our universe started out infinitesimally small. All places were one place in the original singularity. Everything, including all space and matter, was one. The Calendar represents this infinite curvature and primal oneness by Tonatiuh's circular face. The primal singularity was so dense, even light couldn't get through it. All forces were the same. *Electromagnetism*, the *weak nuclear force* that describes radioactivity, and the *strong nuclear force* that holds parts of atoms together were all equal. (Fig. 99)

The smallest vibrational pulse set our universe into motion. (Fig. 100) It caused a minuscule *quantum fluctuation* that iterated into an extreme and exponential expansion of space. The expansion of space is described in the Calendar by the Masculine Solar Rays. (Fig. 101)

The Big Bang wasn't like a firecracker going off in a gigantic room. Space itself expanded. The Big Bang didn't happen in some incredibly distant galaxy apart from you right now. It occurred everywhere, including right here.

Our universe suddenly inflated at a velocity greater than light. It got very large very quickly, repeatedly doubling its diameter in equal amounts of time. (Fig. 102) Space expanded octave by octave. Physicists call this time the *Inflationary Period*. The expansion of space happened so quickly, the light from many

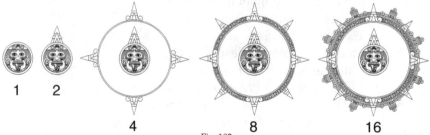

1   2   4   8   16

Fig. 102

The Calendar's doubling progression explains how our universe expanded during the inflationary period.

galaxies still isn't reaching Earth. The universe is much larger than we can detect at this time.

Inflation dispersed the original plasma enough to let light pass through. At that moment, light poured forth. This process is described in the Calendar by Tonatiuh's Tecpatl tongue protruding to speak in light. Physicists call this moment *photon decoupling*. (Fig 103) Light and electromagnetic energies were freed to expand as spherical waves into infinity. (Fig. 104) The tremendous energy of flying photons blasted apart all elementary particles. The Calendar's progression of concentric circles, when coupled with the Masculine Solar Rays, indicates an explosive spherical expansion of energy. (Fig 105)

Inflation created a *phase transition*.* The steady, balanced symmetries of our original singularity uncoupled. The primordial force divided into the four forces we have today. (Fig 106)

The expansion of space stretched out the wavelengths of light and electromagnetic energy until they vibrated down into the *microwave region*. The remnants of these microwaves are the Cosmic Microwave Background Edwin Hubble first discovered in 1965. Expanding space cooled down our universe. Photon blasting diminished, and the strong nuclear force began to grab and hold protons and neutrons together. (Fig 107) Hot energy congealed into cool matter.

Fig. 103

Light poured forth at the moment of photon decoupling.

Fig. 104

The Calendar describes spherical waves that expand into infinity.

Fig. 105

Inflation was a *scalar expansion wave*. A scalar field is a repelling force that is the complementary opposite of gravity.

Fig. 107

The Heart of an atom is composed of two elements, *protons* and *neutrons*, held together by the *strong nuclear force*. The strong nuclear force is illustrated by Tonatiuh grasping the two elements of the heart of an atom, the proton and the neutron.

*A phase transition is a sudden, radical shift in the stable equilibrium of a system.

Fig. 106

The Nahui represent the four forces of gravity, the strong nuclear force, the weak nuclear force, and electromagnetism.

Our universe is mostly space, sprinkled here and there with matter. Matter is made of atoms and parts of atoms. Different types of atoms make our chemical elements.

Atoms are also mostly space. An atom the size of a skyscraper would have a nucleus about the size of a grain of salt. Its electrons would be approximately the size of dust particles, all whirling around the grain of salt at the speed of light.

The nucleus is the densest part of the atom. It's a collection of tiny bits of the insubstantial substance that makes up our physical universe. Each of these bits is just a collection of probabilistic tendencies for vibrations to occur in certain places at certain times. They'll probably be there if you look for them, but they might not be. Atoms collect together into probabilistic patterns to form substances. Matter is whirlpools of vibrations. (Fig. 108)

Fig. 108 The Calendar demonstrates multiple whirlpools of vibrational tendencies collecting around a central vibrating principle.

Fig. 109

There are eight vacancies in an atom's electron shells.

Electrons move around definite paths at specific distances from their atomic nucleus.[3] These paths are called *orbital shells*. They're similar to planetary orbits. Each atom has from one to eight electrons in its outer shell. The Calendar's eight Solar Rays and multiple concentric rings indicate electron shells and the number of possible electron positions in the shells. (Fig. 109) All atoms strive to fill up the eight vacancies in their outer shells. Until they do, they're always seeking for a mate or mates to complete themselves.

Electrons communicate with one another. They pass information back and forth in the form of Tecpatl-*photons*, or light. This communication is illustrated by the Xiucoatl passing Tecpatl-light to one another at the bottom of the Calendar. (Fig. 110) These light messages create changing interval relationships and harmonic variances between the electrons in their shells. They make harmonies resembling the numerical relationships of the musical monochord, or the overtone scale. As we've seen earlier, the eight whole number divisions of the monochord scale are represented by the eight Solar Rays. (Fig. 111)

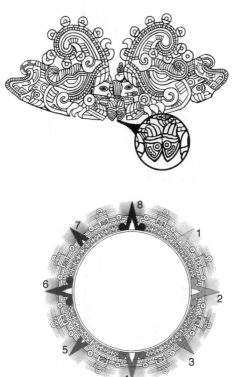

Fig. 110 Electrons communicate with one another by sacrificing portions of their energy in the form of Tecpatl-photons.

Fig. 111 Modern chemistry defines our world as the interplay of two essential electrical properties. They combine and recombine through patterns of emptiness and fullness in pathways of eights.

Electrons get stimulated when they communicate with one another. When they're excited, they jump from shell to shell. They move from one harmonic resonance to another. The saturation of orbital shells with electrons creates modulating harmonic proportions with the nucleus of the atom. The constant proportions of chemistry can all be understood as harmonic relationships. Chemical relationships demonstrate musical intervals and proportions.[4]

The *Pauli exclusion principle* states that no more than two electrons with opposite spins can occupy the same orbital shell. This relationship is indicated in the Calendar by the two opposing spins of the Xiucoatl within a generic orbital ring. (Fig. 112)

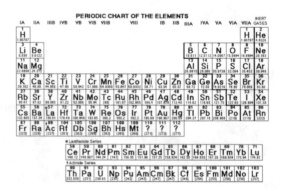

Fig. 110 No more than two electrons with opposite spin can occupy the same orbital shell.

This principle dictates the number of electrons in each orbital shell to give us all the different chemical elements we have today. Orbital shells create unique *structural geometries* as they form relationships with one another. These relationships are where our periodic table of the elements comes from.

The chemical elements repeat themselves in eight different groups of cycles. Elements having the same number of electrons in their outer shells have similar properties and belong to the same groups. The chemical elements spiral. They associate with one another in groups of octaves.[5] The axis of growth for the spiral of elements are the *noble gases*. The electron shells of the noble gases are filled with four pairs of electrons, so they don't long to be fulfilled the way other elements do. They are fully satisfied. Many relationships the elements have with one another can be described as logarithmic spirals.

Some atoms have *isotope* relationships. An isotope has the same number of protons as another atom, but a different number of neutrons. Each element can have up to ten isotopes. There are 20 pure isotopes in the table of chemical elements. There are also 20 *double* isotopes, and the first 20 elements follow an additive sequence of neutrons. (Fig. 113)

Atoms group together into communities called *molecules*. Molecules always strive for maximum structural *symmetry*. This quest leads them to arrange themselves into the perfect three dimensional symmetry of the five *Platonic Solids*.* (Fig. 114)

When an electron is freed from an atom, it goes spiraling away back into infinity. Electrons interconvert with light. A light quantum (the smallest unit of light we know of), with enough energy, can collide with a charged particle, only to disappear and be replaced by a positive and negative *pair* of electrons. This process doesn't seem to change the original particle. Photons have zero mass. Colliding photons create electron pairs that have mass. The higher the energy a light quantum has, the more electron pairs it can produce. This process is illustrated by the colliding pair of Xiucoatl being generated from the emptiness, or the zero point, of 13 Cane. (Fig. 115)

Colliding electrons can also transform into light, which is shown by the Xiucoatl colliding and producing Tecpatl-photons. (Fig. 116)

When electrons pair up, their *wave function*

Fig. 113

Isotope relationships of the chemical elements.

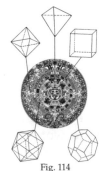

Fig. 114

Platonic Solid relationships within the Calendar.

Fig. 115

Colliding photons of zero mass create electron pairs that have mass.

Fig. 116

Colliding electrons can produce light.

*For an in-depth exploration of the Platonic Solids, please refer to Appendix 1, The Language of the Sorcerers.

predominates.* This means certain wavelike qualities are enhanced in their relationships. Quantum mechanics is also called *wave mechanics,* referring to its waves of probabilities.

Werner Heisenberg discovered in 1927 you can only describe the subatomic realm by mapping its probabilities. This is one of the implications of the famous *Heisenberg Uncertainty Principle.* He taught us how the world of subatomic particles is fuzzy. It's indeterminate. We can only describe how and where particles will probably be. We find probabilities when we explore the world of the extremely small. The deep origins of our universe blend into quantum fuzziness. Quantum stuff almost exists. Probabilities are the only things we can get a semi-firm hold on, because their overall motions average out over time, or in very large numbers, or both.

The quantum principle basically means phenomena jump from state to state, rather than smoothly gliding along from one state to another. Max Planck was the father of modern quantum theory. He got his inspiration from studying the musical overtone scale. Our world works according to quantum principles. Frequency determines the energy of each quantum.** Frequency is like "frequently." It increases when you do something more frequently. In the world of sound and vibration, frequency means how frequently a vibratory wave goes back and forth. Vibrations can be really fast, like ultraviolet light, or really slow, like the creation and annihilation cycles of galaxies and universes. Vibrations can come at any rate.

Quanta are whole number, harmonic relationships. Each subatomic particle has its own *spin.* It vibrates with all other particles in the whole number proportions of the overtone scale. (Fig. 117) Quantum theory is musical by all definitions down to the minutest detail. The spin numbers of electrons, protons and neutrons are all proportional to the whole number overtone relationships of the musical monochord.

---

* A *wave function* is an equation that shows you the behaviors of a quantum system. Wave functions in quantum physics are described as the square roots of probabilities. To learn more about the Mexica view of probabilities, please refer to Appendix 1, Language of the Sorcerers.

** The *Hahn-Einstein equation* illustrates the relationship of frequency and energy very clearly. It's expressed as $hv=mc^2$. It means that Planck's constant times a frequency equals mass times the speed of light squared. The two letters, h and c, are *constants.* They're numbers. They're a ratio. They don't change, because they express a specific relationship. That leaves only two variables in this formula. One of them is mass (m), and the other one is frequency (v). Frequency measures a rate of vibration. When frequency changes, mass changes. You can even express one in terms of the other.

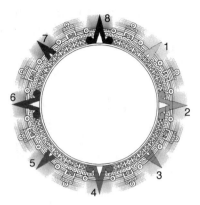

Fig. 117 Subatomic particles vibrate with other particles in the whole number proportions of the overtone scale. The SU³ theory describes how subatomic particles arrange themselves into special unitary spins in symmetrical groups of eights. The rings of the Calendar are quanta.

Out of all possibilities, our universe has settled into mostly harmonious, whole number relationships. Nature changes in quanta. States of matter are quantum flows of probabilities.

Physicists take us on a journey into the infinite when they describe the subatomic world. They tell us things like "Each subatomic particle consists of all subatomic particles.", and "Each particle helps to produce other particles which produce the particle itself."[6]

Our world just keeps getting smaller and less substantial the deeper you go. Nothing can get pinned down. All we've found so far at the most essential level of matter is patterns of motion. Ollin is the essence of motion. The dance of Ollin creates the vibratory patterns of matter. We can't determine exactly what makes up the actual substance of these patterns. All we can know is, for now, the patterns are there. (Fig. 118)

Subatomic particles swim in a sea of *virtual particles*. They alternate between matter and antimatter. Ollin describes the alternation of particles from one realm to another. (Fig. 119) When any system begins feeding back into itself, it

Fig. 118
Matter is patterns of motion.

Fig. 119

Ollin shows us how all matter is vibration. Subatomic particles dance between matter and antimatter.

creates a definite progression of doubling into and out of chaos.[7] Quantum particles follow the path of doubling into and out of our universe from *virtual universes*. (Fig. 120)

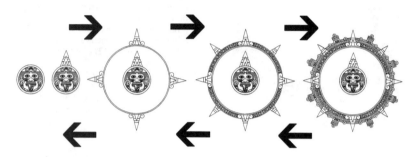

Fig. 120 The Calendar is a matter/anti-matter particle map. It's doubling progression describes the route subatomic particles take as probability waves into and out of our universe.

Subatomic particles are collections of vibrating, looping *strings* of an original ten dimensional geometry that existed in the primal singularity. These ten dimensions are illustrated at the center of the Calendar. They can be visualized as the points of a pentagram and an upside-down pentagram combined. (Fig. 121) These ten dimensions collapsed into our current four dimensions during the phase transition. (Fig. 122) Forces split themselves, and particles multiplied as our universe cooled. Physicists visualize this process as water turning to ice.

Fig. 121

The ten primal dimensions.

Fig. 122

The Nahui represent the four dimensions of our current universe.

Our universe's phase transition left us with one dimension of time and three dimensions of space. The other six dimensions remain in original singularity to this day. (Fig. 123) The center of the Calendar illustrates the four dimensions in current manifestation, and the six dimensions which remain hidden.

*Strings** are curved space.[8] This curvature is again represented in the Calendar by the circular form of Tonatiuh's face. Space itself is the medium of matter. That's how all the stuff in our universe got here. Strings are snakes. They're the essence of subatomic motion. Strings vibrate and coil into different shapes or geometries to create the unique properties of the different subatomic particles. (Fig. 124) The four forces of electromagnetism, the weak force, the strong force and gravity are all qualities of the particle vibrations of strings. Space is dancing with itself. The oscillations of Ollin create matter. (Fig. 125)

The Aztec Sun Calendar teaches us how matter vibrates. Atoms are made from protons, neutrons and electrons. Each of these are made from subatomic particles. Subatomic particles are made from vibrating strings of curved space. Each particle is a resonating chord of strings. Vibration resonates down to the most essential units of matter. Vibration makes something out of nothing. Space itself is filled with an infinity of oscillations and vibrations of every description and beyond. All matter in our universe is attending a perpetual vibrational dance.

Fig. 123

The six dimensions that remain in singularity.

Fig. 124

Strings are snakes.

Fig. 125

Space Dances with itself to create matter.

* Superstring theory says subatomic particles are Black Holes. Particles are made of infinitely curved space. String theory is uniting many branches of mathematics that seemed to be unrelated before. It gives a geometry of form to particle physics.

The Great Mother

Spacetime is the great mother. Einstein's *General Theory of Relativity* implies space is either expanding, or contracting. We know space is expanding from the *Red Shift* observed in light coming to Earth from very far away. The Red Shift shows us the relative speed differences between distant light sources and ourselves as we observe them here on Earth. Since our universe is expanding, the farther away a galaxy is, the greater its Red Shift.[9]

Until Einstein, scientists thought our universe was just spinning around in an infinity of fixed orbits. They thought space was like some kind of giant merry-go-round repeating itself again and again. They didn't think about the inhalation and exhalation of the universe. Until Einstein, only indigenous people were aware of the expanding nature of space. The Aztec Sun Calendar indicates how expansion currently predominates over contraction in our universe, because the Masculine, or expanding, Solar Rays are fully visible. The contractive Feminine Rays are partially hidden from our view. (Fig. 126)

Fig. 126 Expansion and contraction in our universe.

Einstein showed us how space itself has qualities. That's one of the main features of relativity theory. In relative space, matter snakes around the curves and contours of the space surrounding it. There's no force of gravity. Matter flows like water into attractor paths. (Fig. 127) Spacetime geometries create the structures of these paths. The serpent-like watery motion of matter flowing around curved space is demonstrated by the two Xiucoatl flowing around the outside of the Calendar, delicately balancing on the tips of the Solar Rays. (Fig. 128)

Fig. 127

Matter flows like water into attractor paths.

A finite space has one center. The first post-Christian European to appreciate this fact was Giordano Bruno, for which he was torched at the stake in 1600.

Infinite space has an infinite number of centers. The center of infinite space is anywhere. The famous mathematician Wilhelm Gottfried Leibnitz described each center of infinity as containing a reflection of the entire universe.

Infinity can become infinitely large or infinitely small. For example, if you start counting at zero, you can count in both directions, positive or negative, to infinity. Infinity also exists between zero and one. The *reciprocal numbers* start at 1/1, and proceed to 1/2, 1/3, 1/4, 1/5, ever diminishing toward zero. Reciprocal numbers are always one or less than one. They can always be contained in a finite space, even though they approach infinity.

There's a definite relationship between the properties of the square and the properties of space. Let's take light as an example. If you're looking at an object, its brightness decreases by the square of its distance from you. This is an example of the *reciprocal square law*. This law also governs the amount of *attraction* between objects in space. The Feminine Solar Rays describe

Fig. 128

Serpent-motion around curved space.

the square force of attraction. (Fig. 129) Attraction decreases with the square of the radius, or the distance between two bodies. The reciprocal square law governs all non-quantum level interactions in our universe. The square is a natural quality of space itself.

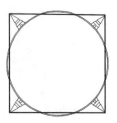

Fig. 129

The four feminine, contractive, attractive directions.

A one dimensional line can contain a point. A two dimensional surface can contain a line, and a three dimensional volume can contain a surface. A *four dimensional* space can contain a three dimensional volume in motion. (Fig. 130)

A one dimensional line can contain an infinity of points. A two dimensional surface can contain an infinity of lines, and a three dimensional volume can contain an infinity of surfaces. A four dimensional space can contain an infinity of (even infinite) volumes in motion. (Fig. 131)

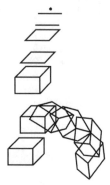

Fig. 130
Four dimensional space.

Space is a four dimensional sphere. It requires a four dimensional map to describe it. General relativity uses four dimensional geometry with time as the fourth dimension. Space-time has no boundary. Our universe is boundless. Space and time are a boundless four dimensional surface.[10] (Fig. 132) This is why the Mexica visualize the Aztec Sun Calendar as a four-dimensional sphere. Each of the four Nahui is a dimension, and its circular shape indicates a sphere, or the qualities of perfect equanimity and equality in all directions.

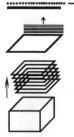

Fig. 132

Space and time are a boundless four dimensional surface.

Fig. 131
Four dimensional space and infinity.

Ours is just one of an infinity of boundless universes.[11] This is demonstrated in the Calendar by the numerous circular Portals and Luminous Pearls that ornament the Ring of Polarity and the Towers. Each of the Portals represents a fractal view of another complete universe within our own. (Fig. 133) Our universe is a Portal within a larger universe, and so on. All universes and multiverses interweave with one another in an incredible multidimensional hierarchy of chaos and order. (Fig. 134)

Fig. 133

Each Portal and Luminous Pearl is an entire universe.

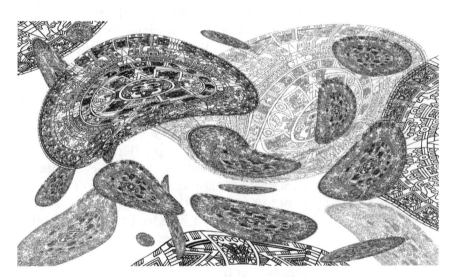

Fig. 134 Ours is just one of an infinity of boundless universes.

All universes connect to mutual sources via interdimensional umbilical cords. These connections come from primal associations within the original singularity. Systems connected at their point of origin remain functionally connected. This remains true regardless of how separated they may appear to be. The Calendar depicts this oneness by containing the whole universe within a circular reflection of the infinitely curved point of creation at its center. Experiments demonstrate this strange quality on a quantum level.

Cause Effect

Cause Effect

Fig. 135

Ollin demonstrates the strange connections of matter through non-local space.

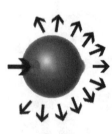

Fig. 136

Since everything in our world is connected, when you create an action in one place, all places respond.

Subatomic particles instantaneously respond to other particles, even though they're separated in space. (Fig. 135) Wolfgang Pauli's Exclusion Principle shows how atoms are able to know instantaneously the state of other atoms, and behave as if they're physically connected. The physicist J.S. Bell deduced in 1964, "no theory of reality compatible with the quantum theory can proceed from the assumption that spatially separate events are independent of each other."[12]

Symmetries are links between subatomic particles coming from a shared common origin. It's a challenge to rationalize it, but the former connection of these particles lives on in some sense. Quantum physics is full of proofs of the undivided nature of our world.

The Aztec Sun Calendar shows us a vast, complex and interconnected universe. If you interfere with one part of a quantum system, it affects all the other parts. (Fig. 136) This happens even if you enlarge the playing area of your experiment to non-quantum levels of size. You could use an area the size of your desk, your living room, or a hundred thousand trillion miles. It's all the same to a quantum system. The parts behave as if they're one no matter how far apart you pull them. Quantum systems react instantaneously. Space and separateness don't seem to exist for them. The quantum world may still live in the original singularity. Matter, at least on the subatomic level, doesn't obey what we believe are the laws of space. Our universe is one, interconnected, living being.

Subatomic particles also have a different sense of time than we do. For example, photons don't have time. Quantum nature still lives in the original singularity with respect to time.[13] The Calendar shows us how all time is one.

Matter and space remember their origins. They retain memory trails of their entire evolution over time. Atoms remember states of being and compounds they've been a part of before. In other words, they learn. They know their history. All energy and matter are convergence patterns of quantum fields. They carry a signature of everywhere they've ever been and everything they've ever done. We're living in a universe of evolving qualities and relationships.

Wormholes are tunnels through spacetime. (Fig. 137) They connect completely different parts of our universe. Wormholes join universes together the same way acupuncture channels relate the different parts of your body with one another. If you look closely at each of the Portals and Luminous Pearls, you'll see that they're cross sectional views of tubes, or tunnels. They indicate pathways of connections on many different levels of magnitude.

We see a diversity of individual things in our universe. Maybe what appears to be separate to us in our four dimensional universe really isn't separate if you look at it from the point of view of the other six dimensions still living in the primal singularity.[14]

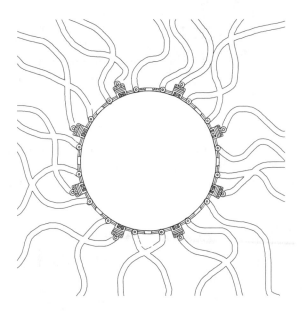

Fig. 137 The Portals and Luminous Pearls are *wormholes* in spacetime.

Let's investigate what we find on our cosmic canoe trip through deep space. You can learn about the history of a thing by examining its structure. Nature's laws reveal the organization and processes of spacetime. Anything you examine can give you clues about where we are and what we came from.

According to current scientific estimates, we can perceive about one percent of the total matter in the cosmos using all our available technology.[15] Cosmologists call the other 99 percent *dark matter*. We know nearly nothing about dark matter because it doesn't emit or absorb light. This makes it difficult to observe directly. So for now, let's focus on the one percent we think we know something about.

Our chemical elements contain their evolutionary history in their basic structure. We believe, for example, the first three lightest and tiniest kinds of atoms, *hydrogen, helium* and *lithium*, were generated in the first stages of life in the universe. These three lightest gases are indicated by the Eagle Feathers on the tops of the Towers.

Big Bang Nucleosynthesis only took a couple of minutes.[16] It converted one quarter of the matter in our universe into helium. This helium is represented in the Calendar by the Luminous Pearls on the tops of the Towers. (Fig. 138) The other three-quarters of atoms remained mostly hydrogen, with traces of lithium. The solar furnaces of stars forged together these lighter elements to compound into the larger, heavier elements we have today, indicated on the Calendar by the Xiucoatl. (Fig. 139) Our elements get cycled and recycled from star

Fig. 138 The Luminous Pearls represent stars. Most stars, like our Sun, are made of Helium.

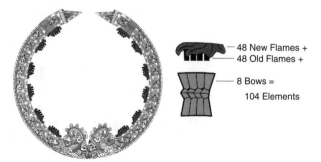

Fig. 139 The Xiucoatl correspond to the 104 elements. Although a regular table of elements will show 106 elements, what they don't tell you is that element number 43, *Technetium*, and element number 61, *Promethium*, only exist for fractions of a second in elaborate laboratory experiments. They have not yet been found in nature.

48 New Flames +
48 Old Flames +
8 Bows =
104 Elements

to star via *stellar winds*. (Fig. 40) This process is shown in the Calendar by our Sun projecting matter outward on the Solar Rays. This matter is picked up by the Ring of Fire, representing the solar winds, and is carried off to distant stars, indicated by the Luminous Pearls.

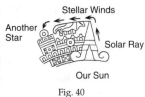

Fig. 40
The chemical elements get recycled from star to star.

Your cosmic canoe trip will take you through *galaxies, clusters* of galaxies, *superclusters, space bubbles* and *voids*. There's cosmic structure as far as we've explored so far. Areas of relative emptiness envelop areas of high density matter. Intergalactic patterns iterate themselves in self-similar fractal geometries. The most recent fractal analysis of the structure of our universe indicates a fractal dimension between one and two. Who'll be surprised if it turns out to be 1.618..., the Phi ratio?

A *light year* is the distance light can travel for one year in a vacuum. You'll discover cosmic structure extending for millions of light years into space. You can sail through great voids of space approximately 300 million light years in diameter. You can ride through infinities of stellar superclusters and across enormous intercluster bridges. You can explore our own *Virgo Supercluster* with its radius of over one hundred million light years.

The galaxies are organized into gigantic space bubbles. Bubble walls meet one another, and can form supercluster complexes millions of light years long. Our universe is a spherical bubble made of other spherical bubbles.

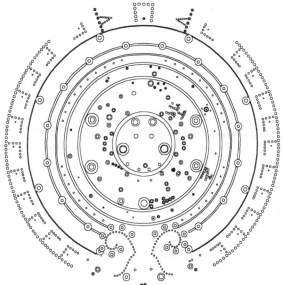

The majority of galaxies are spirals.* Spiral galaxies usually come in complementary pairs. One spins one way, the other spins the opposite way. Both galaxies orbit around a common center of gravity. This relationship is demonstrated by the opposing spiral motions of the Xiucoatl. The many dots on their bellies demonstrate the multitude of stars in a galaxy.

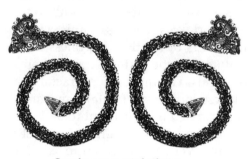

Complementary spiral galaxies.

Most galaxies belong to clusters of galaxies. Each cluster has a motion around its own axis. Clusters surf on expanding spatial waves, and are usually parts of superclusters. Superclusters have their own motions around their own axes, and they also sail along in directions other than those of their general expansion.

Galaxies are born, inhale, expand, evolve, exhale, contract, and die. Our galaxy, the *Milky Way* , is a spiral of constantly expanding space dust. It was formed in a whirling implosion and condensation of gas into matter post-Big Bang. Our Milky Way is the complementary spiral to the larger *Andromeda* Spiral. Both galaxies are microscopic fractions dancing on the edge of the *Local Group,* which is a point of light on the very edge of the Virgo Supercluster.

Our Sun and planets were born from vortexing implosions of gas on a spiral arm at the edge of the Milky Way galaxy. The Sun orbits our galactic center. Our galaxy orbits a gravitational center in the Local Group. The Local Group is part of a community of thousands of galaxies flying toward the constellation *Centaurus,* and so on. It's spirals of relative motion as far as you go.

---

* Edwin Hubble gave us photographic evidence in 1925 that the spiral nebulae really are galaxies. The older parts of the sky contain more spiral galaxies than the younger parts. Nobody knows why.

The Aztec Sun Calendar shows how our Sun balances two forces. (Fig. 141) It generates heat by *nuclear fusion* and expands outward. (Fig. 142) Gravitation also draws the Sun inward and into itself. (Fig. 143) The Sun exhales as it crunches inward and burns hotter. It inhales as it heats and expands, then thins out from the expansion, cools, and begins to collapse inward again.

Fig. 141

Our Sun balances expansion and contraction.

The Sun releases subatomic Tecpatl-photons to produce light. (Fig. 144) Enormous numbers of its atoms liberate photons when their electrons jump from higher to lower orbital shells. The Sun expresses its atomic modulations through light.

The Sun expresses much more than light. Its *electromagnetic field* spins like two giant magnets that cross like an X. The solar field is called the *Solar Quadripole*. Tonatiuh's Ollin configuration at the center of the Calendar depicts the

Fig. 142

The explosive expansion of our Sun.

Fig. 143

The gravitational contraction of our Sun.

Fig. 144

The Sun releases subatomic Tecpatl-photons to produce light.

Fig. 145

Our Sun burns from four proton combinations in helium isotopes of mass 4. It creates a magnetic quadripole.

Fig. 146

The Sun's spinning electromagnetic aura produces the *solar winds*.

Fig. 147

We experience an alternating cycle of seven positive days and seven negative days of solar radiations.

Fig. 148

The twenty eight groups of bars indicating a lunar month, and a solar day.

Sun's electromagnetic properties. (Fig. 145) The Sun sprays out positively charged protons and negatively charged electron particles into space like an enormous pinwheel. (Fig. 146) The Sun's spinning electromagnetic aura produces the solar winds.

The Sun's magnetic field is very strong by our terrestrial standards. The *heliosphere,* or the Sun's electromagnetic radiations, extends well beyond Pluto (Source: *NASA*). Its rotation takes 26 Earth days. As the Solar Quadripole spins around, it creates 13 days of positive radiations and 13 days of negative radiations in one rotation. From a relatively fixed point in space, you would receive half of each radiation at a time, or 6.5 days of positive, alternating with 6.5 days of negative charge. The relative motions of the Sun and the Earth make this cycle appear to last twenty-eight of our days. This is why we experience an alternating cycle of seven positive days and seven negative days of solar radiations. (Fig. 147) This cycle is illustrated by the Portals in the Ring of Polarity. It's an interesting coincidence that from the Earth's perspective, one solar day is the same length as one lunar month. (Figs. 148)

Our Sun rotates on an axis. Because it's made of twisting and exploding plasma, some parts move faster than others. As with liquid being stirred in a bowl, turbulent spots show up here and there. These turbulent areas are *sunspots*. The sunspots rotate in complementary pairs of 11 year shifting magnetic cycles, demonstrated by the dual rotations of the eleven-sectioned Xiucoatl. (Fig. 149)

The planets in our solar system spin in a *vortex*. The closer they are to the Sun, the faster they orbit. The inner planets orbit more rapidly than the outer ones because the gravitational influence on the planets diminishes by the *square*

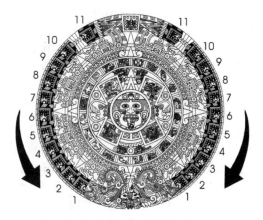

Fig. 149 The 11 year sunspot cycle has definite electromagnetic effects on the Earth and influences our weather patterns.

of their distances from the Sun. (Fig. 150)

Our solar system reveals orders of chaos within orders of order. It weaves complex patterns of probabilities. You may be surprised to learn the orbits of the planets don't follow exact harmonic proportions. Relax. Their orbits are even more interesting than that.

The motions of the planets *exactly* don't follow harmonic proportions. They can't, because their harmonic proportions create enormous resonances in space. The locations in our solar system corresponding to harmonic proportions of the planets are completely empty of matter. These resonance areas send anything entering them flying at high velocity toward one of the planets creating the resonance for that space.[17] Resonant paths are like space tubes. Go to the right resonance point, and you'll be shot straight to the planet of your choice. The gaps in the rings of Saturn occur for the same reasons. Harmonic proportions fill, carve out and define empty spaces. The motions and relationships of our solar system are complex. Planets float into troughs of silence between paths of resonance.

Fig. 150

The closer planets are to our Sun, the faster they orbit in the solar systemic vortex.

Fig. 151
The Earth's electromagnetic field is created by different rates of rotation between its surface and its core.

Guide your cosmic canoe toward Earth, the third planet from the Sun. Earth is the *fourth* planet from the Sun according to the ancient sciences. Modern science hasn't yet discovered the other planet orbiting closer to the Sun than Mercury.

Our watery planet Earth also has an electromagnetic field. This field comes from the Earth's crust whirling at a different rate than its molten iron-nickel interior. (Fig. 151) Here's a switch in the ever-flowing dance of relative meanings of the Aztec Sun Calendar. Its center can also represent the Earth. Planet Earth is the *Iron Heart Mother* in Aztec mythology.

When Earth spins, it creates the rhythmic alternations of day and night. Solar pressure compacts the Earth's electromagnetic field when we face the Sun during the day, and stretches it out on the other side at night. (Fig. 152)

Fig. 52 The solar and lunar days create tangible, measurable fluctuations in the electromagnetic environment of Earth.

The interweaving dance of the different planets and other matter in our solar system add complexity and nuance to the gravitational influences affecting Earth. The rotations of local planets dynamically affect our *geomagnetic field*. For example, the gravitational pull of our Moon increases by a full 6 percent when it comes to *perigee* (the closest point in its orbit) every 27 1/3 days. That's just the gravity of the Moon. There are hundreds of celestial bodies in our local solar system. None of these influences appears too significant when you consider them by themselves. However, if you start adding them all up, you'll soon discover there's an astounding number of twisting, gyrating and spiraling forces acting on our little planet. The Calendar shows these cosmic influences by the Ring of Fire cascading its emanations onto the surface of the Earth.

The Ring of Fire demonstrates the
effects of cosmic rays on the Earth.

Earth orbits inside the Sun's outer atmosphere. Solar activity and magnetic storms create solar winds of radiations and electrically charged space dust. This material gets scooped up and collected in the *Van Allen Radiation Belts* encircling the Earth. (Fig. 153) These highly charged bands of radiation are another important manifestation of the Xiucoatl. They create electrical currents in our upper atmosphere that spirally oscillate between the polar regions. This is what gives birth to the *Aurora Borealis* or *Northern Lights*, which are the fiery outpouring of the Xiucoatl's Ring of Fire.

These radiations in the upper atmosphere come into a rhythmic relationship with the electrical activity of the Earth itself. Their dynamic interplay creates layers of electromagnetic field resonances

Fig. 153
The Xiucoatl are the radiation belts encircling our planet.

The Schumann Bands are an electrostatic field created by the electrical difference between the Earth's surface and our atmosphere. They electrically charge the air around us. Sometimes this charge is powerful enough to create a surprisingly potent shock when you suddenly ground yourself on something like a doorknob or another person.

known as the *Schumann Bands*. (Fig. 154) The Schumann Bands constantly pulsate around our biosphere.

Our geomagnetic field also goes through cycles of its own. This includes complete reversals of polarity over very long periods of time (ten to a hundred thousand years), and smaller variations ranging from one hundred to one thousand year cycles. Our geomagnetic field expresses infinite shades of ever changing nuance. It has a distinct personality at every point on the Earth.

Earth bristles with electricity. Lightning discharges at specific points on its surface to create electromagnetic shockwaves that ping pong between the north and south poles as they echo and fade in intensity. (Fig. 155) The Flames of the Ring of Fire can manifest as lightning. Subterranean electromagnetic undulations course through our planet's interior like gigantic rivers of electrical potentials. They are represented by the five part Ollin-like pattern in each section of the Ring of Fives, which sits below the Earth's crust on the Calendar. (Fig. 156)

Fig. 155
The Flames in the Ring of Fire can create lightning.

The complex interactions of our geomagnetic field and the gravitational fluctuations from the rotations of the Moon and other planets create cycles and spirals. They imbue a definite timing and rhythm to our lives here on Earth. They bestow an ever changing panorama of qualities on our environment as it moves forward in time. Each moment has its own unique character and alchemy.

Currents of interstellar and terrestrial gravitational and electromagnetic waves have passed through our Earth for eon upon eon. They leave tracer pathways through each part of the planet as they go. These rhythms influence the development of all matter and living species over time. They affect the inner structures of minerals and other forms as they shape and reshape chemical geometries. They sensitize, entrain and tune substance and life to specific frequencies and rhythmic patterns. We've coiled cosmic energy cycles into the patterns of our being at every level.

Fig. 156
The Ring of Fives illustrates underground rivers of electrical potential.

Ride an electromagnetic wave into the upper atmosphere of the Earth. A solar eclipse is just beginning. From your vantage point up in the sky, look back out into space. Appreciate for a moment the perfect spatial proportions in the arrangement of the Sun, Moon and Earth. (Fig. 157) As the Moon covers the face of the Sun in the eclipse, their diameters appear to be identical.

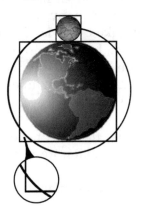

Fig. 157 The *squared circle* demonstrates the relationship between Earth and the Moon in a number of ways. For example, our Moon flies around Earth in 27.32 days. The ratio of the surface of a square to the surface of its inscribed circle is 4:pi=1.2732... Also, the cap in the corner between square and circle is 0.2732. The reciprocal of 2732 is 0.000366. Jolly close to an Earth year. The reciprocal of 366 is 0.002732.

Fig. 158
Quetzalcòatl

Fig. 159
Time and space in motion.

Close to the Sun you find *Venus*. There's an 8:5 Phi ratio of Venusian years to Earth years. With respect to time, Venus and Earth are in golden ratio. Could this be why Venus is beauty in the European tradition?

In the Mexica tradition, Venus is the planet of Quetzalcòatl. (Fig. 158) Quetzalcòatl has many meanings. Often translated as *plumed serpent*, another dimension of his richness means *precious twin*. Quetzalcòatl expresses himself as Phi. He is Life. He is Wind, and the fusion of Earth and Sky. He is sound and the logarithmic spiral. His symbol is the conch shell.

Quetzalcòatl was and still is an honorific term that refers to a person of remarkable development and achievement. Quetzalcòatl is the force that alchemically transforms and can unify opposites. The many expressions of Phi in the Sun Calendar all point to the glory of Quetzalcòatl.

Venus is the brightest natural object in our sky next to the Sun and the Moon. You can see its aura or halo blending with the rays of the Sun as you look past our local planets back out into deep space. The deeper you gaze into outer space, the farther back you're looking in time. Although the night sky appears to exist in normal space and time, it actually stretches out over time. The events you see in the sky at night are taking place over many different billions of years. It can take centuries for light from the stars, nebula and galaxies to reach your eyes. Depending on how far away these objects are, you'll see them at different times. The night sky is a patchwork of celestial events. It has no particular time.

We measure time by movement in space. Time, space and motion are all braided together. (Fig. 159)

Look down to the planet below you. From

this high altitude, you can see structural evidence of magnetic grid lines on the surface of the Earth. One set of them traces a *dodecahedron* with an inscribed *icosahedron*. Rhythmic points of highest and lowest atmospheric pressure occur around the dodecahedral grid. Remnants of the ancient cultural centers are on the icosahedral grid. Many of the Earth's *fault lines* run along both of these grids.[18] (Fig. 160) The Calendar demonstrates the dynamic relationship between these two patterns by the twelve visible sections of the Ring of Sacrifice reflecting the Flames of the Ring of Fire, and the twenty sections in the Ring of Solar Archetypes. The Aztec Sun Calendar represents the forms of the Platonic Solids by their numerical associations, rather than literal drawings. For a detailed exploration of these relationships, please refer to Appendix 1, The Language of the Sorcerers.

The Earth has a nervous system. It has energy meridians running through it, and places on its surface corresponding to acupuncture points on the body. The meridian system of the Earth has Yin and Yang, Tonal and Nagual polarities. Currents of Nagual run along mountains and prominences, indicated by the Portals, or Luminous Pearls on the tops of the Towers. (Fig. 161) Tonal currents create valleys and low places, including the deep subterranean channels to which water flows. (Fig. 162) These are shown by the Portals in the Ring of Polarity, which nest in the center of each section of the Ring of Sacrifice. The drops of blood in the Ring of Sacrifice also represent Water. (Fig. 163)

dodecahedron

icosahedron

Fig. 160
The dynamic relationship between the dodecahedral and icosahedral Earth grids.

Fig. 161 The Luminous Pearls depict currents of Nagual.

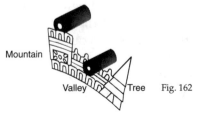

Mountain

Valley   Tree   Fig. 162

Fig. 163 The Portals in the Ring of Sacrifice indicate currents of Tonal.

Fig. 164

The pentagonal structure of water.

Fig. 165

Water clusters into dodecahedral groups.

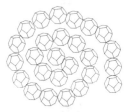

Fig. 166

A helical chain of watery dodecahedra.

Fig. 167

The hexagonal structure of water.

Water follows the Earth's energy meridians and responds to electromagnetic fields. The bonding angles of water guide them into natural *pentagonal* arrangements. (Fig. 164) These pentagons naturally cluster into *dodecahedral groups*. (Fig. 165) These groups then form *helical chains*. (Fig. 166) Electrical currents can circulate through these chains.[19]

Let's ride along with the clouds. It's cold. The suspended drops of water around you slide into *hexagonal* patterns as they begin to freeze. (Fig. 167) Six water molecules come together, uniting in a hexagonal ring to become the heart of a snowflake. Molecular symmetry compounds on itself to create the six directions of growth in the snowflake's ice crystals.

The snowflake projects out soft, exquisitely perceptive tips as it floats in the wind on its long journey through our atmosphere. These crystalline tips feel subtle shifts in temperature, electromagnetic field influences, moisture and particles of matter in the air around them as they grow. All factors influence their tender formation.

Glide along with the snowflake. Freezing tips elongate to provide mother surfaces for new tips, each probing its way through sensitive space. Fresh tips form along the edges of old ones. They diffuse heat and create delicate instabilities. Instability balances with the surface tension of the water to create stability, mating until the snowflake is formed. The snowflake's pattern describes an exact history of its sensitive path.

The Sun returns from behind the Moon, illuminating the sky with brilliant blue fire. Dance with the wind as your snowflake melts back into pure water. Savor the mysterious connection between wind and water that science does not yet understand. Water is instantly responsive to wind in ways physics hasn't been able to explain. (Fig. 168)

Somewhere on the surface of the Earth below you, water is just about to boil. It jumps into a hexagonal state, reflected by tiny bubble *Benard cells* at the bottom of its container. Somewhere else, water is really boiling. Billions of racing molecules suddenly shift into a coherent dance. The chaos of boiling water divides into hexagonal currents of motion. Water takes on a hexagonal quality when you heat it up or cool it down. (Fig. 169 and 170)

Electrical life abounds on this planet. Air ionizes. Electromagnetic resonances resound in the atmosphere. Life processes balance the energies of the Earth and the sky. Our *biosphere* is truly alive. It maintains and increases its organic order over time. The proportions of gases in our air are very different from the chemical equilibrium a chemist might expect to find. The combination of all living creatures on our planet produces the perfect mixture of gases in our atmosphere. We keep the air in a positive state away from equilibrium. Life itself regulates the gaseous envelope of the Earth.[20]

There's thunder. Rain comes down. Streams and rivers swell. Any particular water molecule in a stream follows a spiral thread through the whole stream. It weaves together with trillions of other spiral paths seeking the ultimate attractor. (Fig. 171)

Water remembers. It stores information. The ocean receives all water. It's a living library of all the qualities of history. It holds within itself an infinity of potentials for the future of life.

In the ocean, you find microscopic life forms called *spirillae* and *spirochetes* because of their many spiral forms and motions. These and other tiny protozoa create spiral vortices in the water around them to feed themselves.

Wind   Water

Fig. 168

Science does not yet understand the dynamic relationship of Wind and Water.

Fig. 169

Water takes on a hexagonal quality when you heat it up or cool it down.

Fig. 170

Fig. 171

You find *microplankton* in the sea water. The Aztec Sun Calendar represents them and the drops of water, or the environment they live in, as one coherent system. (Fig. 172) The plankton discharge *sulfur gas* into the atmosphere, indicated by the Eagle Feathers to represent the gaseous state. It's an interesting coincidence that the Towers are the sixteenth division of the Calendar, and Sulfur is element number sixteen. (Fig. 173) The sulfur gas converts into *aerosol particles*, represented by the Luminous Pearls, cushioned up in the sky by the Eagle Feathers. The aerosol particles make attractor points for water to condense around. *Negative ions* form, shown by the five symbol on the Tower. The water collects together into clouds, illustrated by the flames in the Ring of Fire. The clouds protect the living surface of the Earth from too much solar radiation, which is also shown by the Ring of Fire clouds high in our atmosphere.

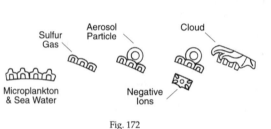

Fig. 172

Temperature regulation in our atmosphere.

Fig. 173

The Ring of Towers is the sixteenth division of the Calendar.

If the clouds get too thick, the temperature drops. Plankton are less active when it gets cold, so their population diminishes. This means fewer clouds, and the Earth warms up again. The cycle continues. Plankton are a part of Earth's temperature regulation system. Even the most microscopic creatures play key roles in keeping us here. The entire web of life creates the environmental conditions it needs to thrive. The microworld and the macroworld interact. They're fractal loops of a single living being.

Water, oil and natural gas create flows of fluid through the Earth. Fluids have a strange coherency to them. They stick together, seek and have intention. Water grows. It develops and even evolves over the course of its cycle. It ripens and matures within the Earth before it gives itself up to nourish and sustain us. Water connects the Earth and the Sky. It descends like a snake into the Earth to regenerate itself. When it's full of energy, it rises like a bird into the sky.

Airborne water seeks out plant life to rain itself onto. The Aztec Sun Calendar shows us how water needs a carpet of vegetation to penetrate deeply into the Earth to complete its full journey. When it rains, water descends into the Earth, where it's warmed.* (Fig. 174) It combines with subterranean gases and minerals in a steamy state (Fig. 175), and brings these substances back up along with it on its path upward. It deposits them in the layers of Earth just below the surface where the roots of the plants and trees are. (Fig. 176) Since the vegetation keeps these upper layers of the soil cool, the steamy water cools down again, and either repercolates down into the Earth or bubbles forth in the form of a cool and refreshing spring. Our ancestors believed *mature water* is the healthiest water to drink. Mature water willingly gives itself from a natural spring. If you ever get a chance to drink this kind of water, you'll notice immediately how good you feel after drinking it.

Water regenerates the upper layers of the Earth's crust at the same time it's regenerating itself. Water can't penetrate the ground as well in places where there's no vegetative covering on the Earth's surface. It just runs off. Its journey remains incomplete and unrequited.

The Calendar teaches us how trees and plants are incredible energy *transducers*. (Fig. 177) They transfer energy from one place to another. When plants drop their leaves, they deposit a blanket of the minerals and metals they've extracted from the deep Earth onto the topsoil. These minerals and metals become the protective skin of the Earth. The mineral skin on the Earth's surface is a *dielectric membrane*, and is demonstrated on the Calendar by the

*The heat deep inside the Earth comes from the decaying radioactive atoms of its original journey from the heart of our galaxy.

Fig. 174
The Solar Rays are water splashing down.

Subterranean Gases
Minerals
Heat
Fig. 175

Fig. 176
The tips of the Solar Rays can be seen as trees growing up out of the soil.

Air { Fire
Water
Earth
The Calendar describes the four Elements of classical alchemy.

Fig. 177
A transducer is anything that translates one form of energy to another form of energy. For example, crystals can convert vibration into electricity, and vice versa.

Fig. 178

The Ring of Polarity is the dielectric mineral membrane of the Earth's skin. The Portals indicate the completion of an electrical circuit.

Ring of Polarity. (Fig. 178) It creates an insulating medium between the negatively charged Earth and the positively charged atmosphere in the sky above. The mineral skin helps to retain the living electrical dynamism between the Earth and Sky. This is one of the origins of the *Metal* element in indigenous medicine. Metal can relate to the skin and other surfaces and membranes in our bodies. When we ingest minerals, we immediately begin to feel them in our skin. Metal is mineral. We mirror the ecosystem in our physiology.

Vegetation, particularly forests, are essential to the continued maintenance of life on Earth. Every plant has its special functions. Planted trees aren't the same as wild forests. When our great forests are squandered, the soil growing our crops becomes depleted. This means our nutrition deteriorates, our quality of life diminishes and our health is endangered.

Soil has very precious magnetic field properties. It supports a delicate system of capillaries and a rich substrate of living organisms. (Fig. 179) They all work together to create fertile soil. The Calendar shows magnetism by the Portals in the Ring of Polarity, which

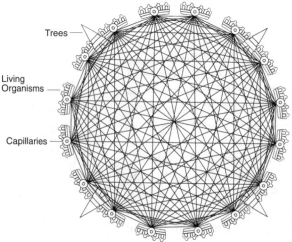

Trees

Living Organisms

Capillaries

Fig. 179

Earth's dynamic living system of capillaries and micro-organisms.

indicate the completion of an electrical circuit. They're also a cross-sectional view of the Earth's capillaries, and the drops of blood are the microorganisms in our soil. We can't simply supplement our soil with vitamins and minerals. Many of its required nutrients and their precise combinations and proportions can be created only by the infinitely precise and elegant alchemies of living plant matter. Vegetation must clothe the Earth to maintain life. This is especially true of the great variety of medicinal herbs, which are our best sources for *biologically active compounds*. Each herb spends its whole life concentrating and condensing a perfect organic proportion of nutrients. When we ingest these herbs at just the right time and in the right combinations, they can help us heal ourselves naturally, effectively and without side effects.

The Calendar shows us how water is the essence of motion. Water needs to follow its natural movements and rhythm to regenerate itself and thrive. Water takes on a natural serpentine flow. It follows graceful spiraling motions and has definite impulses. Water knows how it likes to move. It dynamically responds to the phases of the Moon and the presence of sunlight. Water is the complementary opposite of the Sun and of the element of Fire in the indigenous natural sciences. This polarity is demonstrated when living water moves to protect itself from sunlight. Water retreats from sunlight wherever it can. For example, natural springs protected from the Sun will dry up and even go away when they're exposed to the Sun. When the springs are protected from the Sun again, their water returns.

When the Sun warms up our naked Earth, the deep ground water is unable to rise and nourish the soil. This deprives the plants of their nutrition, and the process of desertification begins. Heating the Earth also releases immature subterranean gases into the air, which contributes to earthquake conditions and poisons our atmosphere. The only safe way to circulate these gases into the surface world is when they're chemically bound with water.

Water can get violent when forests are cut down. Compromising water's cycle of regeneration threatens its strength and vitality. This isn't metaphorical language. It's an observable phenomenon. Water, forest and soil work together. If something interrupts or disturbs the water cycle in any way, it will do whatever it has to do to return the situation to normal. This includes radically shifting weather and flood patterns. The deforestation of our Earth is creating a deluge of water. If we can give up our desire to control water and allow it to do what it wants, we'll all be happier.

Water is a living being. It permeates our entire planet. When it's healthy, everything's healthy. If it becomes unhealthy, everything degrades. Water is the source and the transport mechanism for all of nature's nutrients. It allows you to partake of itself while you're alive. Water is more than just H2O. Water is the Earth's blood. Earth gives up its blood so you can live.

The Shaman's Drum

Fig. 180

The ten intrauterine lunar months.

Fig. 181

The center of the Calendar can represent the uterus, fallopian tubes, fimbria, and ovaries.

The Aztec Sun Calendar describes your journey from conception to birth. Splashdown into your mother's womb at the moment of your conception. The egg waits patiently after spirally twisting herself down from one of your mother's *oviducts*. She waits and prepares for the 10 lunar cycles you'll be spending in utero, poised in her delicate and perfect electrical field. (Fig. 180, 181, 182) Her domain is soft and sensitive to the electromagnetic currents around her. She feels the acid and alkaline changes of your mother's uterus. She knows temperature, *calcium ion* fluctuations, and the point of the entry of the sperm. All factors determine the exact placement and orientation of the egg's electrical axis. The Calendar shows Tonatiuh as the egg, and its axis as the fourth and eighth Solar Rays aligning with the tip of the Solar Dart

Fig. 182 The twenty eight groups of bars indicating a lunar month, and a solar day. The top of the calendar illustrates two partners donating their genetic material.

Seven means *seed* in the language of the sorcerers. Doubling is the process of creation. 7 X 7 = 49.
1 divided by 49 = .020408163264128... creates the doubling process of the Calendar. The Calendar regenerates itself through a process of squaring, reciprocating and doubling.

Fig. 183

Tonatiuh is the egg. He is the essence of potential and creativity.

Fig. 184
The serpent forms of sperm.

Fig. 185
The subtle electrical field of the cell.

Fig. 186
The Xiucoatl are the complementary twin spirals of the DNA double helix.

toward the North along the symmetrical midline of the Calendar itself. (Fig. 183)

Your father's sperm cooperatively migrate on their long journey to the egg. (Fig. 184) They snake their way forward together, using spiral whips of tails, each made from nine groups of cells spirally twisted together.

Sperm meets egg. The new sperm/egg synthesis immediately creates electrical changes in its outer membrane to prevent other sperm from entering. It forms a fresh electrical field with a new axis of orientation. The Calendar indicates the subtle electrical field of the cell by the protruding Solar Rays, and the Ring of Eagle Feathers. Eagle Feathers mean exquisite sensitivity. They demonstrate relationships with the invisible and intangible. Think of the delicacy of a feather. Its very lightness and sensitivity allows a bird to fly. (Fig. 185)

Chromosomes untwist, exposing the precious strands of your DNA to the influences of multiple subtle fields. (Fig. 186) Precisely these moments determine the first transformations of your genetic patterns.[21] Ollin describes the structure of chromosomes. It demonstrates genetic sensitivity to electromagnetic vibratory influences at this very tender stage of life.

The first step of *cell division* is the doubling of the nine part *centriole*. The two new centrioles begin to spin chromosome fibers between them. Cytoplasm divides. An electric current appears along the line where the cell will divide to become two new cells. This electrical axis guides and determines the initial divisions of your cells.

There are eight distinct stages of cell division. The Calendar shows this progression by its eight Solar Rays. Your cells form new octaves of themselves by doubling. They go through each note of the scale on the way.

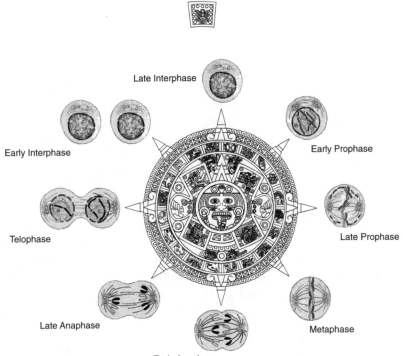

Late Interphase

Early Interphase

Early Prophase

Telophase

Late Prophase

Late Anaphase

Metaphase

Early Anaphase

Your initial division from one to two cells determines your *symmetry*. The symmetry of your body and many of your characteristics are determined by the electrical field at your conception.[22] This symmetry guides the formation of the rest of your body as those first two cells multiply to become your left and right sides. Your first doubling establishes the vertical axis of your spine. (Fig. 187) Your second doubling into four cells establishes the horizontal axis of your hips.[23] (Fig. 188) The Calendar illustrates these first two divisions by its primary vertical axis and secondary horizontal axis

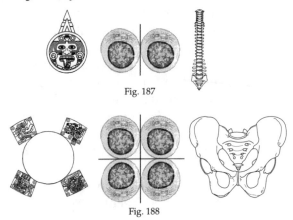

Fig. 187

Fig. 188

Fig. 189

The Xiucoatl form
the gastrula.

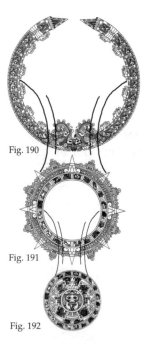

Fig. 190

Fig. 191

Fig. 192

Fig. 190 Ectoderm develops
into the surface of your body.

Fig. 191 Mesoderm

Fig. 192 Endoderm

forming the cardinal directions. These first four cells initiate your three dimensional orientation. Welcome to Earth.

As a fertilized egg, you're a completely unspecialized cell. You divide yourself into groups of other unspecialized cells. In your first part of embryonic development, any of your cells can access any of their genes and any of their chromosomes.

You maintain symmetry on the outside of your body as you develop. On the inside, you differentiate. At three weeks of age, you begin to fold into yourself as a blob of undifferentiated cells to become a little pouch known as a *gastrula*, indicated in the Calendar by the Xiucoatl. (Fig. 189) Then come the first stages of *specialization*. Unspecialized groups of cells migrate to different areas of your electrical field and begin to change into specific types of cells and tissues. They differentiate into three layers of organization that will develop into all the structural features of your body.

First comes your *ectoderm*. (Fig. 190) Ectoderm develops into the surface of your body. It becomes your skin, organs of perception, brain and nervous system, parts of your eyes, the lining of your nose, mouth and anus. Your ectoderm is represented by the Xiucoatl on the periphery of the Calendar.

Your ectoderm creates your *mesoderm*. (Fig. 191) Mesoderm evolves into your muscles, bones and circulatory system, your blood, blood vessels, excretory system, connective tissues, lymph system, heart, cartilage, kidneys, bladder, and linings of your abdominal cavities. Mesoderm is described by the area between the Ring of Sacrifice and the Ring of Solar Archetypes.

Your ectoderm also creates your *endoderm*. (Fig. 192) It becomes your glands, viscera, digestive system, the lining of your respiratory and digestive systems, and parts of your bladder. The endoderm is represented by the center of the Calendar. It also includes the Ring of Solar Archetypes.

Many of your tissues are embryological relatives because they share the same origins. They remain functionally integrated throughout your entire life.

A small pocket forms in the ectoderm along your embryonic electrical axis. It develops close to the area becoming your tail in the lower part of your spine. This area corresponds to your *Ming Men*, or the *Gate of Life* in Asian Medicine. The Calendar describes this area as the point of interaction and communication between the two Xiucoatl. (Fig. 193) This pocket is called the *primitive streak*. Ectodermal cells pour into this pocket to form your mesoderm. Much of the cell differentiation you go through as an embryo arises along the axis of your primitive streak. This axis coincides with that of the Calendar. Its top end becomes your *neurenteric canal*, which is a direct connection between your digestive system and your brain for a time during your development.

Fig. 193

13 Cane rests in the visual center of your brain. Tonatiuh sits at the center of your heart. The two Xiucoatl meet and communicate at your *Ming Men*, or *Gate of Life*.

Electrical currents stream from your primitive streak and connect with your ectoderm at multiple points along your fetal body. The Calendar illustrates this process by the points of the Solar Rays just touching the skin on the Xiucoatl's backs. (Fig. 194) Developing cells follow these

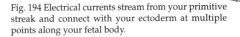

Fig. 194 Electrical currents stream from your primitive streak and connect with your ectoderm at multiple points along your fetal body.

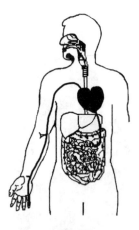

Fig. 195

Structure and paired balance in the meridian system.

Fig. 196

The Aztec Sun Calendar describes many dimensions of the human biofield.

currents to the locations where they will take up residence. Once there, they begin to differentiate and organize themselves into distinct body parts. The electrical field surrounding and saturating you as a developing fetus directs the growth, structural arrangement and positioning of your tissues. Your nerve cells grow parallel to your young electrical field on their way to plugging into the budding organs that will serve you for the rest of your life.[24] Your muscle cells align themselves at right angles to your electrical field.[25]

You develop your upper limbs first, then the lower ones. Limb buds sprout from your mesoderm, covered with a thin layer of ectoderm. Your spinal nerves grow into the buds like roots growing into soil. As they penetrate, the bud cells transform into bone, muscle, sinew and nail.

Almost all your *connective tissues* and most of the areas traversed by your *energy meridians* originate in your mesoderm. Your energy meridians are modes of communication different parts of your body use to communicate with one another. They're the pathways and connections your body parts make on their journey from their origins in the mesoderm to their ultimate forms. Each of your energy meridians permeates and unites with one of your internal organs. Every meridian is also naturally paired with a partner meridian, and wraps around it in spirals. (Fig. 195)

Your meridians and nerves flow outward like great rivers, streams and bubbling springs from your polar axis. They're parts of the subtle electrical gradients forming your electromagnetic *biofield*. (Fig. 196) Many aspects of your biofield are indicated by different parts of the Calendar. For example, the Calendar's concentric ring structure illustrates the physiology of the human *subtle fields*, or *energy bodies*. (Fig. 197) The seven visible Portals on each side of the Ring of Polarity indicate the anterior and posterior aspects of the *chakra* system, and the electromagnetic radiations of the *endocrine* system. (Fig. 198) They also demonstrate the fourteen regular meridians of acupuncture physiology. The Luminous Pearls indicate the eight *extraordinary meridians*.

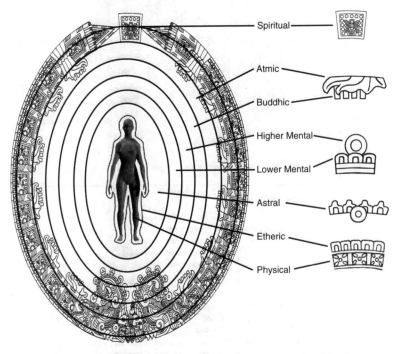

Spiritual

Atmic

Buddhic

Higher Mental

Lower Mental

Astral

Etheric

Physical

Fig. 197 Human energy fields depicted by the Aztec Sun Calendar.

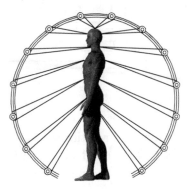

Fig. 198 The relationships of the Portals and the chakra system.

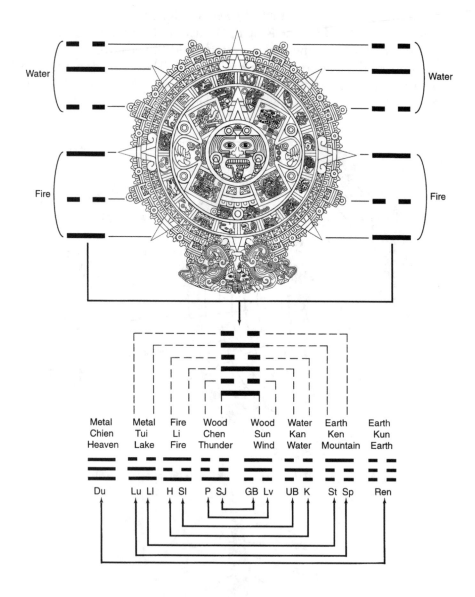

Fig. 199 The alchemical relationship of Water and Fire creates the *Chi Chi Gua* of Acupuncture Meridian Theory, and generates the meridians.[26]

The meridians are also shown through the alchemical relationship of Water and Fire. (Fig. 199)

Your biofield integrates the separate functions of your body into a coherent whole. It's the expression of a unifying principle. Your entire structure, shape, process and pattern is more of who you are than any particular part of you is. Your biofield is a living, organizing impulse in your body. It assists every part of you to communicate with every other part, and helps each fraction of you understand its relationship with the whole you. This living field guides each of your cells through its journey of specialization to maturity. Your biofield can open up and close down the access your cells have to your genetic blueprints. Once your cells mature, your biofield assists them to maintain their optimal health.

Complexity arises in your nervous system. You create a brain. Your eyes snake forward in their journey from your visual center in the area of 13 Cane, leaving a trail of nerve tissue that crosses over itself, left to right, right to left to form the Ollin of your *optic chiasm*. (Fig. 200)

Your *pituitary* appears at the center of this crossing. It sits on the wings of your bird-like *sphenoid* bone. In this aspect of the Calendar, Tonatiuh is the pituitary, and the Nahui are the sphenoid bone. (Fig. 201) Your pituitary is a merging relationship of two unique kinds of tissue. The *anterior* and *posterior* pituitary differentiate and migrate to your brain from separate areas of your body.

The *anterior pituitary* grows out of a pocket that forms in an interaction between the ectoderm and mesoderm of your mouth. It's represented by the lower part of Tonatiuh's face, illustrating his mouth, tongue and digestion.

The optic nerve.

Fig. 200
The Ollin of the optic chiasm.

The pituitary sits on the Nahui, the wings of the sphenoid bone.

Fig. 201
Tonatiuh is the pituitary, and the Nahui are the sphenoid bone.

Fig. 202

The lower portion of Tonatiuh's face is the anterior pituitary.

Fig. 203

Your pituitary uses Tecpatl-hormonal messages to communicate information throughout your entire body.

(Fig. 202) Your mouth and anus are the origin and end points of your *central energy meridian*. Ectoderm and endoderm meet at your mouth and anus. Your *enteric brain* relates to your gut system. It connects with your anterior pituitary, and becomes the master gland of your endocrine system. It sends Tecpatl-hormonal messages to regulate your whole physiology through your network of *hormones*. This is indicated on the Calendar by the Solar Rays of Tecpatl-light streaming forth to communicate with your entire body. (Fig. 203)

How do your hormones work? When you add terms to nonlinear equations, the complexity of their possible outcomes increases exponentially. Small causes magnify themselves through feedback. Your body creates this process through *biochemical catalysts*. Hormones are biochemical catalysts. The presence of catalysts in your body can stimulate order to spring up out of chaos. Your chemical functioning entirely depends on the fractal chemical cascades of your hormonal catalysts. Hormones are how you convert very small bioelectrical signals into large scale biological processes.

Your *posterior pituitary* descends from the *neural ectoderm* of your brain, and is illustrated by the upper portion of Tonatiuh's face. (Fig. 204) It's nerve tissue. Your spinal nerves connect with the posterior pituitary. The Calendar illustrates this connection by the two arcs just in front of 13 Cane. If you imagine you're looking at a cross section of someone's head from the top down, this relationship is easy to see.

Your pituitary is the interface between your nervous system and your endocrine system. It's the center of the electrical feedback, regulation and control of your hormones, and a very important point of synthesis for chemical electrical, electrical chemical you.

You form the four *ventricles* of your brain. (Ventricle means *wind chamber* in Latin.) They fill with cerebral spinal fluid. This is beautifully illustrated in the Calendar by the area in between the Ring of Fire and the Ring of Sacrifice. (Fig. 204) Your cerebral spinal fluid circulates up and down between your spine and skull. It bathes your nervous tissues as it flows over and through your whole body.

Fig. 204 The upper portion of Tonatiuh's face indicates the posterior pituitary. Your brain and nervous system are bathed in cerebral spinal fluid. The highlighted ring on the right is the cerebral spinal fluid. It descends into your spinal column in the area just anterior to 13 Cane.

Nerves branch out from your ectoderm. Impulses begin to travel along your nerves as non-dissipating soliton waves of energy.[27] The Xiucoatl are nerves, and the Ring of Fire shows the off and on firing of the nerve cells. (Fig. 205) You begin to feel as you develop increasing numbers of delicate *sensory nerves*, shown by the Luminous Pearls just under the surface of the skin represented by the Xiucoatl. (Fig. 206) You begin to move as your *motor nerves* multiply and extend

Fig. 205 The off and on firing of nerve cells.

Fig. 206

The Luminous Pearls are sensory nerves.

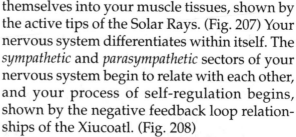

Fig. 207
The Solar Rays are motor nerves.

Fig. 208
The Xiucoatl are the self-regulating sympathetic and parasympathetic nervous systems.

Yes   No

Fig. 210
The decision process.

themselves into your muscle tissues, shown by the active tips of the Solar Rays. (Fig. 207) Your nervous system differentiates within itself. The *sympathetic* and *parasympathetic* sectors of your nervous system begin to relate with each other, and your process of self-regulation begins, shown by the negative feedback loop relationships of the Xiucoatl. (Fig. 208)

You're a relationship of two nearly symmetrical beings. They join together at your midline, and gather around the tree of your spine, cooperating and working together to create the person you're becoming. The relationship of these two creatures creates a front back top bottom polarity that remains with you through life. They form the dual serpents of the arteries and veins generated from your heart, your internal Sun. They're the snakes of your brains, intestines and nervous system. (Fig. 209, next page)

The choices you make as you develop in utero get built right into the structure of your body. They come into being as you advance through each evolutionary stage, shifting from one form to another. You shape-shift many times to get here. Every detail and process of your physiology demonstrates the trail of choices and octave doublings you've made on your journey from a single cell to where you are right now. You're a conglomeration of billions of compiled and coherent decisions. The Calendar shows the act of deciding between options by the razor tip of the Solar Dart, which is its original division from one to two in the process of doubling. (Fig. 210) Each of the decision points in your body preserves the exact conditions of a moment of doubling you went through in your growth. For example, the fluid interiors of your cells retain the environment of the primordial sea in their chemical compositions. Different parts of your brain and nervous system are the

Fig. 209 Coatlique, The Great Mother.

Coatlique (Koh-aht-LEE-kay) is the great mother. She is mother Earth, and the mother of all the Gods. She is the mother of everything. Coatlique is the primal origin.

She is interplay, relationship and the being formed by interactive pairs of complementary opposites. She is the great sound that begets all being. She is the water of vibration. Coatlique is the dark feminine underworld. She reminds us that everything comes from, and returns to, the Earth.

Coatlique is the mother Goddess of the indigenous spiritual practices of the world. She is the Virgin de Guadalupe, Mary and Kuan Yin, whose name means to "actively observe sound." She is the infinite Spiral of Virgins.

The great statue of Coatlique was discovered August 13, 1790. She now resides in the Museo Nacional de Antropologia, Mexico City Tenochtitlan.

Fig. 211

The Ring of Solar Archetypes demonstrates a synthesis of animal, vegetable and mineral natures.

Fig. 212 The Nahui are the four ventricles of your spirally beating heart.

Fig. 213

The Ring of Sacrifice is made from drops of blood. They're similar to tuning forks that oscillate between the two poles of Fire and Water. The drops are also the breasts that nourish you as an infant. The choice between your mother's two breasts is one of the earliest choices you make when you're born into the outside world. Decision accompanies nourishment.

same as those of reptiles and other animals. Your whole being includes and enfolds animal, vegetable and mineral natures. New structures incorporate and include old ones. You're a grand synthesis of life forms. (Fig. 211)

You grow and unfold through myriad spiral forms in utero. These spiral processes become the spirals of your body. Some of your spirals come from long biological organs contracting into the smallest possible spaces. You spiral and internalize structures to economize space, time and energy. Your fingerprints spiral because the electromagnetic patterns and rhythms flowing in and out of your fingers move in spirals. Each fingerprint is totally unique.

The Nahui are the four *ventricles* of your heart spirally pulsating in syncopated rhythm with your mother's heartbeat. (Fig. 212) Since you begin hearing in the womb even before you're born, your first contact with the outer world comes through sound and vibration. The pounding rhythm of your mother's heartbeat provides the steady backdrop for your entire intrauterine journey. This rhythmic sound is your first experience of the shaman's drum. On a deep instinctual level, you continue to compare and reference all rhythm to the beat of your mother's heart.

Your fetal heart begins as a spiral of embryonic tissue. Thousands of spiral patterns wind and unwind through your circulatory system as it grows. The right handed spiral of your pulmonary artery, the right handed spiraling wall dividing your aorta and pulmonary artery, and the spiraling motions of your conical heart muscle itself all occur within the first few centimeters of your circulatory system.

Blood pours in. Your blood moves. The motion of blood is life. (Fig. 213) Fractal trees of arteries and veins transport blood to every part of your body. The way your vessels branch and spread seems chaotic, yet they repeat the same patterns all the way down to the cellular level. Your body uses fractal designs to get blood to each of your cells. It makes dozens of doublings to get your blood into and out of their microscopic world. The ocean of your blood is the vehicle of nutrition for your every cell. (Fig. 214)

Fig. 214

Your blood creates an ocean-like environment for your cells. It's chemically very similar to the waters of the primordial ocean.

The Aztec Sun Calendar teaches us how the alchemical forces of Water and Fire mix in our blood. (Fig. 215) Your blood brings water, nutrition, chemical electrical information,[28] and combustible oxygen to your cells. (Fig. 216) This relationship is described by the Mexica concept of *atlachinolli* (ah-tlach-ee-NOH-lli), or Water and Fire. Often translated simply as *war*, atlachinolli means the dynamic relationship of Water and Fire. It's often represented by two intertwined serpents, one of Water, and the other of Fire.

Fig. 215

The relationship of Fire and Water.

Fig. 216

Oxygen is chemical element number 8. It's the element of the octave. Oxygen modulates itself like chemical music. Its particle spins form a C major scale.[29]

Atlachinolli, the alchemical relationship of Water and Fire.

There's an objective structural relationship between the Sun and your blood. It's the magnetic quadripole. Your red blood cells use *iron* atoms to grab and hold onto the oxygen from your lungs. (Fig. 217) The *hemoglobin* in your red blood cells is iron-hearted. It uses a group of four nitrogen atoms to hold an iron atom at its center, which are the Nahui holding the central

Fig. 217

Tonatiuh is the red blood cell. His hands magnetically grab and hold oxygen from your lungs.

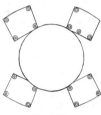

Fig. 218

Hemoglobin has four heme groups of four iron atoms each. Heme molecules create 13 double chemical bonds to make 26 electrons. Iron is the 26th element and is also surrounded by 26 electrons.

Fig. 219

Your hemoglobin forms a magnetic quadripole like the Sun. There are 4 basic blood types, O, A, B and AB. A number of researchers have predicted that a new, fifth type of blood will appear soon that will be immune to most or all the ailments the rest of us suffer from.

circle. (Fig. 218) Iron amplifies and responds to magnetic fields. The electromagnetic field around the iron in hemoglobin creates a magnetic quadripole with its four nitrogen atoms. This Ollin arrangement of alternating north and south poles creates a concentrated magnetic field at the center of the hemoglobin molecule.[30] (Fig. 219)

Your blood is a magnet. Oxygen also has magnetic properties, so it bonds to the magnet of your blood. *PH** changes at the level of your cells alter the geometric structure of your blood just enough to allow your cells to pick up the oxygen. This is just one of the many electromagnetic properties your body uses to maintain life.

Your blood carries much more than simple nutrition. It carries energy from your ancestry to the future. You can invoke tremendous ancestral energies and impulses from the blood flowing through your veins. It holds a graphic history of the behavior of your ancestors, and can tell you where they lived, how they lived, and what they ate. Your blood type is an older and much more integral statement of your ancestry than your race, ethnicity or culture.

Your ancestors blended with their surroundings over time as their environment shaped them genetically. Place is written all over your blood. Ancient farmlands, centuries of migrations, and the excitement of the hunt all have their resonances in your blood. You're building on what came before you. Your ancestors wove a multi-patterned web of interactive cause and effect. They created a massive cultural event, an ongoing story with a cast of thousands you enter into at birth. Everything your

---

* pH is a measurement of hydrogen ion concentrations in a solution. It describes acidity and alkalinity.

ancestors evolved and refined is inside your blood.

Your blood has an intricate array of predispositions and preferences to foods, smells, places, and other people. It contains a set of living guidelines you can use to help yourself attain an optimal state of health and well-being. Dr. Peter J. D'Adamo tells us in his book <u>Eat Right for Your Type</u> how your blood type is an incredible key to your health and longevity. He also says your blood type determines your optimal diet, the kinds of exercise that will most benefit you, and may even be an important component in the kind of personality you have.[31]

You can learn from your blood. All you have to do is remember to listen to it. Your blood resonates with powerful ancestral memories. It has motivating urges and aversions you may not consciously understand. These motivations guide, protect and teach you throughout your life. You surf on waves of ancestral influence. (Fig. 220)

Fig. 220 Waves of ancestral influence are shown emanating from the center of the Calendar in concentric rings.

Your red blood cells are the only cells that sacrifice their own nuclei and DNA to serve your whole being. (Fig 221) They're also the only human cells able to truly *regenerate* themselves.

Fig 221 The sacrificial element of the red blood cell is indicated by Tonatiuh's Tecpatl tongue sticking out.

There are two kinds of red blood cells circulating in your bloodstream. *Mature* red blood cells surrender their nuclei in their process of growth. Because they sacrifice their DNA, they lose their ability to regenerate.

The *Immature* red corpuscles in your blood have the ability to despecialize, respecialize and regenerate into any other kind of cell. Their DNA remains in a dormant state as they float around in a kind of cellular trance. They don't make proteins, and they don't burn glucose for energy like other cells. Immature red blood cells can reverse their stages of development.[32] They can despecialize into prototypal cells, and then respecialize into completely different kinds of cells. They develop according to the information given to them by your biofield in an area that's healing. These cells can completely become whatever they're requested to become. Your red blood cells are the essence of potential. (Fig. 222) They can transform themselves into anything you need them to be.

You manufacture red blood cells at the center of the marrow in your bones. The Calendar can be seen in this light as illustrating a cross section of a bone. (Fig. 223) Immature red blood cells live in the bone marrow of human beings. They rush from your bone marrow into your bloodstream when your body needs to heal.

Your bones spirally twist themselves into shape as you grow and develop in utero. (Fig. 224) After you're born, they constantly rebuild themselves, modifying their spiral curves and adjusting to

Fig. 222

Tonatiuh is the
essence of potential

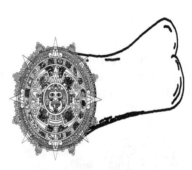

Fig. 223 The Calendar illustrates bone
physiology to demonstrate the essence
of regeneration.

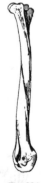

Fig. 224

The spiral
structure of
bone

how you use them. The attractor paths of your daily motion shape your bones. (Fig. 225)

Bone is one of the *semiconductors* of your body. Your bones generate electricity when you put pressure on them. (Fig 226) They also make electricity when you expose them to light, and they generate light when they're creating electricity. Your bones are living LED displays.

Two different materials combine to create your bones. One of them is *collagen*. Collagen is a long protein. It's the main structural component of your body. The other component is *calcium apatite crystals*, demonstrated by the Ring of Fives. (Fig. 227) Collagen and apatite have a highly ordered structure. Your collagen winds itself into a double helix of two complementary spirals. The internal structure of your bones creates itself from thousands of spiral strands winding around one another in complementary directions. (Fig. 228) This structure gives your bones the greatest strength using the least material.

Spirals mean strength. The power in your bones comes from their spirals. Their spiral structure can concentrate or disperse force or energy as they guide their own forces and the forces acting on them into spiral paths.

Fig. 225

Movement shapes your bones.

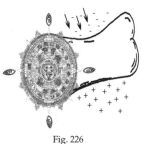

Fig. 226

You create different electrical fields when you put pressures on your bones from various angles. When you bend or stress a bone, the compressed side becomes electrically negative. The stretched side becomes electrically positive.

Fig. 228

The spiraling internal structure of bone.

Fig. 227

The Ring of Fives are the calcium in your bones.

Calcium bonds to the molecules of your bones and nearly all your cells, and is illustrated in the Calendar by the Ring of Fives. (Fig. 229) It's completely interwoven into every function of your body. It's the most abundant metallic element in your physiology, and the fifth most abundant element on the planet. You can find calcium nearly everywhere on Earth. It has a fairly neutral pH compared with other abundant elements your body could use to create life. It's biochemically flexible, dynamic, and electrically efficient.

Fig. 229 The Ring of Fives illustrates the many roles of calcium in your body.

Your tissues conduct electricity by using *ions*. Ions are electrically charged atoms or clusters of molecules. Calcium ionizes. It electrifies. Calcium ions are a vital link in the electrochemical control of your body. Exquisitely subtle variations in calcium ion concentrations trigger almost all your body's activities, including the regeneration and proliferation of your cells.

Many your body's processes don't go directly from one step to another. They go through many subtle stages. Each stage gets passed along and translated from one process to the next through calcium ions. The calcium ion is an electrical physical bridge, and is demonstrated in the Calendar by the "Fives" at the center of the Towers.

The calcium ion levels in your blood can regulate many of your cell functions at the same time. In one of these mechanisms, calcium combines with proteins to create *biological valves* in your cell membranes. These valves regulate the nutritional and electrical properties of your cells, shown by the Towers in the Calendar. (Fig. 230)

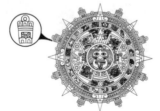

Fig. 230 The central portion of the Calendar is a living cell. The Towers are biological valves and stacked up polar nutrients on the cell membrane.

Your cell membranes have special *calcium ion pores*. Each of these pores contains a *five protein rosette* bound together by calcium. When the electrical potential between the inside and the outside of the membrane increases, the rosette uncoils. This allows more calcium ions into the cell.[33] This dynamic electrical regulation of your cells is illustrated by the relationship of the Towers to the Flames in the Ring of Fire. *Electrical potentials* regulate calcium ion concentrations into and out of your cells. Calcium ions communicate the electrical status on the outside of your cells to the inside of your cells.

Calcium ions also attach themselves to nutrients in your blood. They stack the nutrients up on the surfaces of your cell membranes, also shown by the Towers. (Fig. 231) When these stacks electrically depolarize, calcium ions carry them through the ion pores into your cells. The five protein rosettes usher nutrient stacks into and out of your cells based on electrical field variances.

Calcium ions regulate the electrical potentials of your nerves. They pass messages from one nerve cell to another by translating neurotransmitter substances into electrical activity.

Calcium regulates your body's pH. It combines with the phosphates in your body fluids to create an optimally alkaline environment for your cells. Calcium influences acid and alkaline balances to regulate the progression of your cellular division. Its pH buffering allows your glucose to break down into the 4 *nucleotide* building blocks of your DNA.

Fig. 231

Calcium can stack up to 22 polar compound nutrients at a time with fiery Xiucoatl ionic charges.

Each of your cells contains an entire DNA library of genetic blueprints. These blueprints are instruction manuals that tell your cells how to build things.

Your cell nuclei each hold 23 pairs of *chromosomes*, shown on the Calendar by the 22 sections of the Xiucoatl plus 13 Cane, and then genetically doubled within by the twenty-three visible "Fives" on each side. (Fig. 232) Your chromosomes are made of two very long spiraling strands of proteins. These proteins are your DNA, and are demonstrated in the Calendar by the double complementary spiraling strands of the Xiucoatl. (Fig. 233) Your DNA has different sections. Each section contains protein patterns of biological information. We call these information patterns *genes*. Each of your genes contains instructions on how to create a particular feature of your body, like your hair color or your nasal geometry.

Your cells go through different stages of development and specialization. A young primordial cell can mature into any kind of cell. As it grows up, it loses access to the genetic information it could use to turn itself into another kind of cell. At its final stage of maturity, a cell has access to only one specific set of genes. It uses the blueprints from these genes to maintain its unique position and identity in the environment of your body.

Only one set of genes remains active in each of your mature cells, but all your genes are present in all your cells. Every cell nucleus in your body contains a resonating holographic DNA model of your whole being.

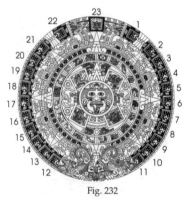

Fig. 232

The Calendar is a map of your chromosomes.

Fig. 233 Ollin illustrates chromosomal structure. The genetic code is based on complementary polarities. The Xiucoatl are the spiraling strands of your DNA double helix. The plus and minus strands of your DNA are primal polarity of Nagual and Tonal.

Your genes are rhythmic patterns of *nucleotide bases*. (Fig 236) Scientists now believe your nucleotide codes reproduce points of decision and change in your growth process. These points of change indicate places your ancestors made choices about how they were going to relate with their environment. Your nucleotide codes recreate the history of your ancestral decisions. This is shown in the Calendar by the four Nahui of your nucleotide bases being guided by the Solar Dart. (Figs. 234)

Fig. 234
The Nahui are the four nucleotide bases.

Nucleotide bases are the elementary components of your genetic library. There are four different kinds of nucleotides. They join together in pairs as they line up along the double helix strands of your DNA to form protein codes. This process is graphically illustrated by the drops of blood in the Ring of Sacrifice aligning in pairs with the Flames on the spiraling Xiucoatl. (Fig. 235) Your genetic library is made up of billions of nucleotide bases.

Fig. 235

Nucleotide bases join together in pairs to form protein codes.

DNA is a four element system that generates a matrix of 64 possibilities through combinations, or relationships, of three out of the four elements at any given time. This is illustrated

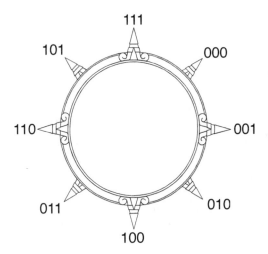

Fig. 236 There are eight possible ways a nucleotide can change its position in a *codon*.

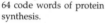

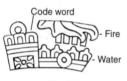

Fig. 237

The Ring of Sacrifice is the 64 code words of protein synthesis.

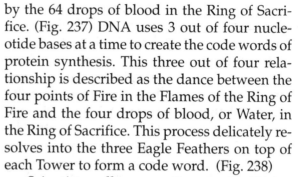

Fig. 238

DNA uses 3 out of four nucleotide bases at a time to create the code words of protein synthesis.

by the 64 drops of blood in the Ring of Sacrifice. (Fig. 237) DNA uses 3 out of four nucleotide bases at a time to create the code words of protein synthesis. This three out of four relationship is described as the dance between the four points of Fire in the Flames of the Ring of Fire and the four drops of blood, or Water, in the Ring of Sacrifice. This process delicately resolves into the three Eagle Feathers on top of each Tower to form a code word. (Fig. 238)

Scientists call your entire genetic library your *genome*. Cells can use parts of your genome for DNA pattern information. Sections of DNA information are called *RNA*. RNA is the tool your cell's DNA uses to create its own distinctive life processes. The active DNA in each of your cells transcribes its information to a special kind of RNA called *transfer* RNA. The transfer RNA takes this information to another kind of RNA called *messenger* RNA. Your messenger RNA then takes this information to the *ribosomes* in your cells. Your ribosomes use this genetic information as a template to create chains of *proteins*. Your cells use these protein chains to carry out their daily tasks. (Fig. 239 and 240)

Fig 239 The Ring of Sacrifice is an incredibly detailed cross section of the zipping and unzipping processes of DNA replication and RNA transcription. The two strands interact with each other by going through the 6 "teeth" of ribosomal translation at the Flames of the Ring of Fire, the points of the Solar Rays and the Luminous Pearls. The lower six teeth are the six coding bases of messenger RNA. The upper six teeth the complementary bases of transfer RNA. They adhere together through *peptide water bonds*.

Fig 240

The Calendar describes the replication, transcription and translation processes from DNA to RNA to proteins. Your ribosomes absorb RNA through their "eyes." Messenger RNA Tecpatl comes in through the mouth. They bond within to form completed proteins.

Proteins are the real work force in your body. They do the jobs your DNA and RNA information are coded for. Your genetic code is a language. It translates sequences of nucleotide bases into *amino acid* proteins, and are represented in the Calendar by the Ring of Twenty Solar Archetypes. (Fig. 241)

Your genetic code is constructed from molecules called *polymers*. Proteins are polymers. They have an amino head and an acid tail. That's why they're called amino acids. Each amino acid has a central carbon atom. The carbon atom links to four other groups of atoms. These groups are the amino group, the acid group, a hydrogen atom and a side chain called an R group.* (Fig. 242 and 243) These amino acids create the proteins that drive your metabolic life.

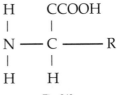

Fig. 242

There are four groups of amino acids, Large polar and Large non-polar, Small polar, Small non-polar. These four groups form a mirrored Ollin-duality.

$$
\begin{array}{ccc}
H & & CCOOH \\
| & & | \\
N & - \ C \ - & R \\
| & & | \\
H & & H
\end{array}
$$

Fig. 243

Nuances in your R groups form a series of 20 different amino acids.

Fig. 241 The 20 Solar Archetypes are your 20 amino acids.

* Your amino acids are made from methane, ethane and ammonium in *tetrahedral* arrangements. In each of them, a carbon or nitrogen atom pulses at the center of a tetrahedron, and hydrogen atoms dance around the four corners. The electrons of the hydrogen atoms repel one another because they have the same electrical charge. The four electrons distance themselves equally around the center. This arrangement naturally forms a tetrahedron, because each corner of a tetrahedron is the same distance from its center. The tetrahedron occurs often in chemistry because it's the simplest three dimensional structure. The Mexica often visualize the center of the Calendar as a tetrahedron, with each Nahui forming one side. Tonatiuh also has a tetrahedral aspect, which is illustrated by the equilateral triangle on his crown. The Mexica were fascinated by the relationship of the tetrahedron and the sphere. For a more detailed discussion, please refer to Appendix 1, The Language of the Sorcerers.

The Center of Perception

Fig. 244

The open legs of the Eagle
illustrate the birth canal and
the birth process. Tonatiuh
is perpetual birth.

Spiral your mammalian path down a river of warm blood. You see light. You're safe. You're being born.

You've gone through a fantastic voyage to get here. You went through an incredible initiation, crawling and clawing yourself all the way from nonexistence through meat, blood and bone just to be born. Respect yourself. (Fig. 244)

Take your first breath and begin your life. You enter this world with the untouched virgin nervous system and self awareness you developed in your mother's womb. You're all *analog*; nuance and quality.

After you're born, you perceive. You connect with everything when you're a baby. Self and other merge in oneness. All energy is alive and real. This is your pure indigenous nature. It wakes up and thrives.

Your perceptions of yourself and your world come, at least in part, from information your nervous system gathers from your environment. Thousands and thousands of bundled nerve fibers compile to form your nervous system. Each of these fibers is a long series of nerve cells. Each of your nerve cells lives in one of two states. It's either completely at rest, building its electrical potential, or it's exploding in fire, releasing its potential and passing it along to another nerve cell. (Fig. 245) The Xiucoatl illustrate these dual aspects of your nerves. Their meeting demonstrates the passing of the fiery Tecpatl-impulse from one to the other. (Fig. 246)

Your nerve cells fire in *binary* patterns. They're either off, or they're on. The tip of the Solar Dart is the essence of this binary yes or no decision. (Fig. 247) You have millions of nerve cells. They create myriad flows of off and on patterns to weave incredible binary symphonies through your being every second of your life. Your nerve cells make cascades of on and off polyrhythms. These rhythms interpret one another to become the vocabulary of your perception. You're a binary creature. Your experiences are electrical interpretations of the multifold interactions of binary mathematics. You have a binary consciousness. Your life is a binary expression of a musical reality. You're living out a binary process from your conception to your perception.

As your experiences accumulate, you begin to perceive your world through a structure. Your nervous system goes *digital*. It organizes incoming information according to *hierarchies* of binary patterns. These digital hierarchies of information become increasingly symbolic as you compile and expand your repertoire of experiences. They evolve into the thought structures that organize your life. The process of building these increasingly complex symbolic structures is

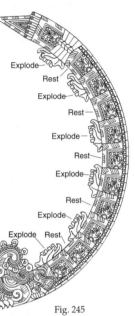

Fig. 245

Neurons are either firing or not firing.

Fig. 246

Passing the Nerve impulse.

off   on

Fig. 247

The binary decision.

shown by the Calendar's fractal doubling progression, which gets more intricately detailed as it evolves. (Fig. 248) Seen in reverse, the Calendar maps the stages of consciousness from the complexity of surface thoughts through successive stages of simplification to the essential core of oneness within.

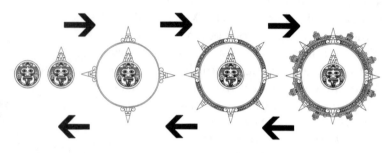

Fig. 248 Your nervous system organizes information into hierarchies of thought patterns.

Your neural firing patterns create and influence your thought structures. Your thought structures also organize your neural firing patterns. It works both ways. Structure influences your perception, and your perception influences your structure. This happens because your habitual thoughts make *standing waves* of rhythmic electrical stimulation. The stimuli of your world set up specific oscillations in the neuron firing patterns of your brain.[34] Your brain converts sensory input into *wave forms*. Your nerves respond to this steady stimulation by grouping together into special patterns. These patterns form interactive or co-active *neural networks*, or *neural communities*. The stimulation of your thoughts changes the structures and arrangements of your nerve cell groups.[35]

Your neural communities order themselves into the organic symbolic elements of your perception.[36] Communities of your nerve cells unite together according to their function. Each group has its own rhythm. Each rhythm associates or connects with the events in your life. Groups of rhythms represent your outer world to your inner world. When information comes into your nervous system, it gets directed to the most similar symbolic area for interpretation, rejection or integration.

Your inner environment as well as your external environment can influence, activate and modify these rhythmic symbols. *EMG*

(Electromyography) and *EEG* (Electroence-phalography) measurements demonstrate how every subtle shift of your thoughts and feelings creates electromagnetic fluctuations in your nervous system.[37] You react the same way electrophysiologically to stimuli from your inner worlds as from the stimuli from the outside world. Your state of mind can alter the electrical potentials all over your body.

Your beliefs and expectations influence your experiences as you stand at the center of an infinity of endlessly self-reinforcing feedback cycles. You're constantly feeding back with the world around you. You perceive your world coactively. You project your innermost processes onto the blanket of spacetime, and your intimate world is a projection of the very structure of the universe. (Fig. 249)

Fig. 249

You stand at the center of an infinity of endlessly self reinforcing feedback cycles.

You access and use your rhythmic thought symbols *holistically*. They cross reference each other. They're fuzzy. They're vague. They acquire relative meanings only in context with other symbols.[38] The information in your consciousness doesn't connect with any particular place in your brain. The ways you store information perpetually shift and change.[39] Your structure modifies with experience as you compile information until it gestalts into new levels of synthesis.

You're creating a hybrid digital-analog nervous system as you move through your life. You use your *analog nervous system* to feel, heal, detect changes in your environment and enjoy quality. You use your *digital nervous system* to handle large amounts of data at high speed.*

You experiment with motion, learn to move in new ways, and build new neural pathways. They open you up to fresh and exciting new perceptions. New discoveries entice you to move in daring new directions. Your feedback cycle of learning expands in a logarithmic spiral.

---

* Increasing amounts of information push your nervous system to go digital. Living in an information age may be the complementary opposite to living in an age where you can enjoy a high quality of life.

Fig. 250

The outer, middle and inner ear, and spiral cochlea.

Fig. 251

Ollin teaches us how vibration translates to electrical impulses that travel down our nerves to communicate our outer world to our inner world. Our perceptions are interpretations of waveforms.

Fig. 252

Your *hippocampus* and *temporal lobes* assist with memory storage and retrieval. The Solar Eagle's claws grasp concepts and retain memories.

Fig. 253

We're designed to perceive and adapt to change.

The Aztec Sun Calendar teaches us how our perception is all about resonance. Take hearing, for example. Your *outer ear* funnels sounds from your environment into your *middle ear*. Your middle ear mechanically translates moving air vibrations into fluid vibrations in your *inner ear*. These vibrations travel as waves up the fluid-filled spirals of your *cochlea*. (Fig. 250) The cochlea's shape mirrors the spiral of ascending and descending tones you hear in the world. The vibrational waves of fluid break just at the point where the geometry of the spiral matches the golden spiraling frequency of the wave vibrations.

Tiny hairs line the inner spirals of your cochlea. They go from coarse to fine up to the tip of the spiral. They vibrate and resonate inside the fluid to stimulate special nerves that translate vibrations into electrical impulses. These impulses flow as binary rhythm patterns to your brain for processing.

Sensory input alters the electrical fields in and around your brain. You experience changes in these fields as changes in your environment. You call the stimulation of the receptors in your ears *sound*, and the stimulation of the receptors in your eyes *light*. It's all translated rhythms of waveforms. Ollin is the center of perception. (Fig. 251)

You travel through time, have experiences and begin to have memories. Your memory traces connect wave patterns through multiple areas of your brain.[40] (Fig. 252) Firing neurons create many levels of patterns that are locally unpredictable, but have overall tendencies.[41]

Our universe is change. Ollin rules. You're hard wired to perceive change. (Fig. 253)

You continue to grow mentally and psychologically in spiral paths. The situations in your life ascend through different keys and octaves. Life events never truly repeat. They're self-similar.

You evolve through each of the four elements over the course of your life. This is reflected in the Calendar through the qualities of its concentric ring structure. You experience sensations, emotions, thoughts and intuitions. (Fig. 254) Then it all comes together in the Big Synthesis.

Air-Thought

Fire-Intuition

Water-Emotion

Earth-Sensation

Fig. 254

You get hungry, select more or less suitable parts of your environment, grind them into mush, and put them inside you. Then you rip them apart chemically to scavenge their electrons for raw materials. Digestion and respiration interplay to produce the energy you use in your daily activities.

Your body's an alchemical boiling pot. It can transmute chemical elements from one into another to sustain its optimal function. You're supremely adaptable.

The biological enzymes in your body can create chemical reactions that in any other circumstances would require enormous amounts of energy to produce. There are chemical spectacles happening in your physiology that, outside a biological system, would take the power of a nuclear fusion reactor or a linear accelerator to generate.

This is where the essence of the new science blends with the ancient science: they both teach us how very specific *combinations* of *subtle* and *indirect* forces can be as powerful, or more powerful, than forceful *direct* ones.

Almost all the biological transmutations your body performs take place within the first twenty elements. The Calendar illustrates these processes by Tonatiuh's intimate relationship with the Ring of Twenty Solar Archetypes. (Fig. 255) You can take the basic building blocks of matter and shape them from one into another. For example, you can convert Sodium into Potassium, Nitrogen into Carbon and Oxygen, Iron to Manganese, and many other chemical transformations.[42]

Fig. 255 Nearly all of your body's biological transmutations take place within the first twenty elements.

Most of your biological alchemy happens by subtly moving around Hydrogen and Oxygen atoms. Oxygen and Hydrogen are the components of water. Your body gets most of its Hydrogen and Oxygen from the water you put into it.

Fig. 256

If you want to appreciate the interactions of Fire and Water in your internal environment, you'll need to develop your *pitzahuacayotl*.

In the practice of classical alchemy, you acquaint yourself with the relationships of Water and Fire within your body. (Fig. 256) If you want to appreciate the dynamic interactions of these forces inside you, you'll need to develop what the Mexica call *pitzahuacayotl* (pee-tzah-hwa-KAI-ohtl). Pitzahuacayotl means *subtlety* and *refinement*. These qualities are demonstrated in the Calendar by the Ring of Eagle Feathers, and especially the three Eagle Feathers on the tops of the Towers. (Fig. 257) They are the elegant, pure and impeccable awareness that can guide you to the highest levels of any situation you encounter, and lead you to the heart of the Sun.

Fig. 257

The Eagle Feathers indicate impeccable awareness, subtlety and sensitivity.

Once you deeply understand and can practically use the relationships of Water and Fire within yourself, you can consciously connect with cosmic Water and Fire.

Here are some exercises to help you build your *pitzahuacayotl* and refine the relationships of Fire and Water in your body:

🦋 Let go of everything. Heighten your awareness of the Water in your body. Move around in your world as Water. Where does Water like to go? What are its impulses?

🦋 Let go of everything. Heighten your awareness of the heat, or Fire, in your body. Where are you aware of it? Does it change? Is it constant? Move around in your world as Fire. Sense how your inner Fire responds to your environment. Where does Fire like to go? What are its impulses?

Fig. 258 Absorbing sunlight is a nutrient that regulates many of your physiological systems.

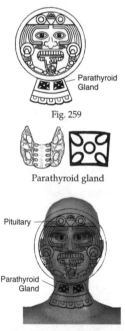

Parathyroid Gland

Fig. 259

Parathyroid gland

Pituitary

Parathyroid Gland

Fig. 260 From this view of the Calendar, the pituitary is shown by the equilateral triangle on Tonatiuh's crown. Its point faces down to demonstrate how it influences everything below it.

Fig. 261 Sunlight is food.

Expose yourself. Feel the light of the Sun. Absorbing moderate amounts of sunlight is a vital part of your good health. Sunshine influences and regulates the calcium ions in your blood. Sunlight and calcium are a unified biological system.

You create *vitamin D* when sunlight touches your electrically active skin. The Calendar illustrates this process by the tips of the Solar Rays touching the Xiucoatl's skin. (Fig. 258)

It's very rare to find vitamin D in foods. The easiest and most natural way to get it is by regularly enjoying sunlight. Vitamin D stimulates calcium binding proteins to pull calcium ions into your blood from your *small intestine*. This is one of the reasons why we call the region of your small intestine your *solar plexus*. Pre-Christian alchemy relates the solar plexus to the element of Fire and the Sun.

The *parathyroid gland* releases a hormone to deposit calcium into your bones. The Calendar illustrates the parathyroid gland as Tonatiuh's necklace. (Fig. 259) Your pituitary gland regulates the activity of your parathyroid gland. (Fig. 260) Sunlight influences and modifies the secretions of your pituitary gland.

Sunlight is food. (Fig. 261) You need it to thrive. Absorbing sensible amounts of sunlight through your eyes and skin is a nutrient that regulates your hormones.

Many different vibrations emanate from the Sun. Visible light is just a small portion of the infinity of vibrations. You interpret some of these vibrations as color, and others as heat. The rest of the Sun's vibrations exist outside a normal person's perceptions, but they still affect you.

Putting it all Together

The Aztec Sun Calendar teaches how life shapes you. What physical forces are at work influencing and contouring your body and your life? We know of only four main physical forces in our universe. They are gravity, the strong and weak nuclear forces, and electromagnetic fields. (Fig. 262)

Fig. 262
The Nahui are the four main physical forces in our universe.

Gravity plays a major role in the macroscopic world of universes, galaxies and planets. Given the relative size of your body, gravity probably isn't a major determining factor in the microscopic moment to moment details of your physiology.

Nuclear forces, as we currently understand them, only influence the world of atoms and the microuniverses they contain. This is the level of magnitude the physicists have been so excited about for the last fifty years. It's one level of the mind/matter connection.

Human beings and other forms of life are able to perceive quantum and gravitational stimulation.[43] Although you can respond to information coming from these very large and very small forces of nature, they probably aren't the primary agents responsible for keeping your system together as an organic being. Is there a

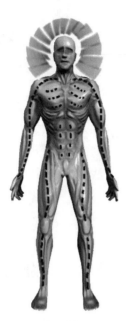

Fig. 263

AC and DC electrical fields in the human body.

physical force that directly relates to our own relative level of size?

Electromagnetic fields are a perfect fit. The areas of magnitude electromagnetic fields influence are the same ones where life as we know it occurs.[44]

The statement "you are electrical" can raise issues with some physicians.* Biochemists went to extended efforts for many years to prove your body is chemical, not electrical.

That didn't turn out to be entirely true. You're both chemical *and* electrical. Modern scientists can detect and catalogue human biofields using *SQUIDS* (Superconducting Quantum Interferometric Devices.) SQUIDS are ultra sensitive magnetic field detectors. These tests show us how you generate *AC* electromagnetic fields around your nerves and muscles, and *DC* electromagnetic fields around your brain.[45] (Fig. 263) If your mother ever wondered if you were AC/DC, she was right.

One of the ways your biofield accesses your physical body is through the process of *semiconduction*. Semiconduction happens in materials with highly ordered molecular structures, like crystals. The regular electron structure of crystals allows electrons to move through them very easily. Electron microscopy has revealed evidence of many crystalline structures in your physiology.

Semiconducting currents are thousands of times more sensitive to electromagnetic interaction than the kind of current that travels down a wire. Semiconductors carry only small currents, but they can carry them over very long distances. Your proteins are semiconductors.

---

* If your doctor tells you electricity has nothing to do with your body, it means she or he has been out of touch with medical research since the late 1950s. Make your decision and act quickly.

You regulate the semiconduction in your connective tissues by *hydration* and *oxygenation*, or by changing your levels of water and oxygen.[46] You influence your semiconduction by tuning the levels of Water and Fire in your body. (Fig. 264)

Fig. 264

The glyph for Atlachinolli, the dynamic relationship of Water and Fire.

Your cellular membranes have *electrical potentials* that hover around ten million volts per meter.[47] The Calendar shows the electrical field of the cell by the Solar Rays protruding beyond its cell membrane. This electrical field is strong enough to align and configure the molecules in your cell membranes into specific structures or patterns. (Fig. 265) These electrical patterns are highly sensitive to, and interactive with, other electromagnetic fields.

There's a positive charge and a negative charge on the surfaces of large biomolecules. These charges separate like the two poles of a compass needle. Molecules of this type are called *electrical dipoles*.[49] Most biomolecules are electrical dipoles. They're like microphones, because they convert acoustic vibrations into electrical signals. (Fig. 266) At the same time, they're also like stereo speakers, because they turn electrical signals into vibrations. (Fig. 267) Electricity and vibration convert into each other at the level of your cells. They create a single electrovibratory field. Researchers call this phenomenon the *Josephson effect*.[50] (Fig. 268)

Fig. 265

The cell's electrical field aligns its molecules into patterns. Vibrational and electromagnetic fields can coalesce and interpenetrate one another.[48] This effect becomes very pronounced in a dynamic living system like your body.

Fig. 266

Fig. 267

Sound   Electricity

Electricity   Sound

Fig. 268

The Josephson Effect

Fig. 269

The biofields around a cell membrane align molecules into patterns.

Fig. 270

Specific frequencies can communicate and convey information to your biological membranes.

Fig. 271

Water can both absorb and transmit frequencies.

The Calendar illustrates how your membrane fields align their dipolar molecules into patterns. (Fig. 269) This produces a situation that's highly sensitive both to vibration and electrical stimulation. Specific frequencies can communicate and convey information to your biological membranes.[51] (Fig. 270) The vital importance of vibrational communication within the body is shown in the Calendar by Tonatiuh's Tecpatl-vibrational influence on the entire sphere of the Calendar. Sound and electromagnetism are equivalent at the cellular level. Your life is electromagnetic and frequency specific.

Dr. Cyril Smith, Simon Best and many others have performed numerous clinical experiments to demonstrate the effects of electrical and vibrational frequencies on human life. In one of these experiments, people who were allergic to a particular substance were exposed to that substance and a frequency at the same time. After a short association period, these people developed an allergic response to the frequency alone. They responded to the frequency and to the initial substance in the same way. These people also developed allergic reactions to *harmonic proportions* of that frequency. On the positive side, they also responded favorably to specific frequencies that neutralize and eliminate allergic reactions.[52] These experiments are a convincing testimony to your body's abilities to discern and discriminate between different rates of vibration.

Smith and Best also learned that water absorbs and transmits frequencies. (Fig. 271) They found they could expose water to a frequency, and the water could then transmit that frequency to a patient at a later time. The water produced the same effects as the original frequency and the original allergen.

Water has a remarkable ability to retain and

record coherent frequencies it comes into contact with. This ability is a basic principle of *Homeopathic medicine*. The homeopathic community has accumulated abundant clinical and experimental proof over the last 150 years of water's ability to absorb and transmit frequencies. This effect probably relates to the reason healers have known about and used holy water since the dawn of humanity.

Using coherent frequencies to heal in the form of sound and vibration is similar, or even equivalent, to the use of Homeopathy. There's an enormous amount of experimental evidence from all over the world supporting these findings.[53] Recently, Dr. Fabien Maman has done extensive research in France demonstrating how musical intervals can even explode live cancer cells in vitro. These same intervals rejuvenate healthy cells.[54] (Fig. 272)

There's no chemistry involved in homeopathy. A healing response can propagate through your body within seconds after taking a homeopathic remedy. This is much faster than any known physiological or chemical mechanisms can explain. Sound and vibration can directly transmit a healing frequency even faster. A sonic vibrational remedy is all around you and within you at the same time. That's the nature of sound. There's nowhere it needs to propagate to. You're inside it. Frequencies influence the normal arrangement of the electromagnetic and vibratory fields around your cells. This conveys information to the aqueous interior of your cells and the micro-organs controlling your cell functions.

The Aztec Sun Calendar teaches us how our cells use electromagnetic and vibrational fields to perceive and communicate with their environment. (Fig 273) Coherent frequencies such as those applied in Homeopathic and Vibrational Medicine speak the language of our cells.

Fig. 272

Using coherent vibrations as a healing tool.

Fig. 273

Your cells use electromagnetic and vibrational fields to perceive and communicate with their environment. Frequencies influence the electromagnetic fields of your cell membranes. Calcium ion exchange conveys nuances of the field to the aqueous interior of your cells. Calcium ion fluctuations affect the replication of DNA and transcription of RNA in your cells.

Might we be able to apply similar methods to healing our entire planet? Could the Calendar hold a key for us to recreate the regenerative technology of the ancients? Could we use this technology to regenerate ourselves and our environment?

On a global scale, maybe. On a personal level, definitely. Perhaps if we can dynamically embody these principles within ourselves, we can create a positive shift in history. If enough of us cast our votes for a regenerative future in our own ways, we can influence our future for the better.

Sounds fluffy and impractical? Consider this: in 1997, the National Institute of Health in the United States finally issued a public statement in which it accepted the use of Acupuncture as a medical, rather than an experimental, procedure. The scientific data they used to come to this decision had been in existence for at least twenty years. There was, however, one critical piece of information that created a permanent quantum shift in the American medical structure. It was one number: 13,000,000,000. This was the number of US dollars spent in 1996 on alternative health care in the United States. In other words, the Americans had already made their decision, acted on it, and put their money where they wanted their future to go. This was sufficient to create a dynamic and completely uncharacteristic shift in the attitudes of the policy makers. Would this shift ever have happened through politics alone? It took about five years of normal, everyday people directing where they wanted their money to go to alter the American medical edifice forever.

When we do what we know is right, things can suddenly, miraculously change.

The Aztec Sun Calendar teaches us about regeneration. It demonstrates how a special electrical field appears if you get harmed or injured in any way. Scientists call this special field the *current of injury*. This current continues until you grow new nerve root tips in the place you injured. Your new nerves split up and snake into the area of the injury. They form little bulbs at their tips that contact the epidermal cells in the deep levels of your skin. This relationship is shown very clearly in the Calendar by the edges of the Luminous Pearls contacting the skin of the Xiucoatl. (Fig. 274)

Your nerve tips complete an electrical circuit. The connections they make form the exact electrical signal your immature red blood cells need to trigger their despecialization and begin the process of regeneration.* [55] This process is shown by the active relationship between the Ring of Fire and the drops of blood in the Ring of Sacrifice. (Fig. 275)

The current of injury reverses polarity. (Fig. 276) It gets stronger, and the damaged area heals.[56] The electrical field involved in regeneration isn't the typical nerve impulse you read about in physiology books. It involves extremely minute levels of electricity occurring at very specific voltages and frequencies. This field is a direct current (DC) that flows *around* your nerves. It comes from an entirely different function of your nervous system than anything the biomedical scientists thought existed before. It appears to originate in the *reticular activating system* of your brainstem. Your reticular activating system influences your sleep cycles and focus of attention.[57] It's located deep within your brain in the area of 13 Cane. (Fig. 277)

Your nervous system coordinates the individual activities of your body into a single, coherent whole. Biochemical science has focused mostly on the *neuronal* parts of your nervous system. The impulse and neurotransmitter process explored and advocated by the biochemical scientists is the *digital* aspect of your nervous system. It's made from long chains of coherent oscillations in groups of nerve cells working together in unison. Scientists call these oscillations *action potentials*.

There are special groups of cells surrounding each of your nerve cells. Some of them are the spiraling *Schwann cells*, which are one manifestation of the Xiucoatl. Schwann cells create

Fig. 274

Your nerve tips complete an electrical circuit.

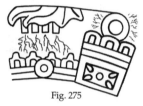

Fig. 275

Electrical signals trigger your immature red blood cells to begin the process of regeneration.

Fig. 276

The current of injury reverses polarity, and the damaged area heals.

Fig. 277

13 Cane is in the area of the reticular activating system.

---

* Regeneration begins when nerves can contact the epidermis. An injured area can regenerate if there's damage to its motor nerves, but not if there's damage to its sensory nerves. A damaged area requires a nerve supply in its first few days of healing. After that time, you can cut the nerve and the area will still regenerate.

Fig. 278

The perineural cells are the Xiucoatl. The neuron itself is the section of the Calendar ranging from the tips of the Towers and points of the Solar Rays to the Ring of Solar Archetypes. The nerve impulse is Tonatiuh, Ollin and Tecpatl.

Fig. 279

The three main centers of electrical activity in the body.

Fig. 280

Your heart's rhythm connects your entire being.

an insulating sheath around all your nerves. There are a number of coverings around your nerve cells. They are your *perineural cells.* (Fig. 278) Perineural cells constitute much more of the mass of your nervous system than your neurons do. Your perineural nervous system creates an electrical environment that integrates your whole body. It's important in healing and the maintenance of your health. Regeneration, healing and energy function are the *analog* aspects of your nervous system. They're perineural.

The main centers of electrical activity in your nervous system come from your brain, heart and lumbar areas. (Fig. 279)

Your heart creates your strongest electromagnetic fields. It generates a pervasive rhythm. Any point in your body can detect the electromagnetic wave of your heart known as the EKG pulse.

Your heart generates a persuasive rhythm. It influences every one of your cells. Many other rhythms accompany your heart in a polyrhythmic rain that emanates from you at all times. The Calendar illustrates your heart's rhythm by Tonatiuh, your heart, expressing Tecpatl, and emanating Tecpatl-vibratory rays throughout your being. (Fig. 280) Electrical pulses from one part of your body can conduct to any other part. Each of them communicates specific information reflecting the qualities of their origins.

The next strongest fields of your body come from your brain and eyes. One of the energy circulations described in the ancient medical classics issues from your eyes, flows all over your body, and returns to your eyes again. (Fig. 281)

Your *sacral nerve plexus*, related to what the Chinese call the *Lower Dan Tian* and the Japanese call the *Hara*, is the third strongest electrical field in your body. (Fig. 282) Your center of gravity is the center of your biofield and of your polar axis. Your natural center of gravity rests in your Lower Dan Tian or Hara.

There's simply no way you can experience or understand your indigenous nature without understanding and experiencing your Lower Dan Tian. It's the origin of your physical body, where your original primordial cell divided from one into two.[58] Your Lower Dan Tian lives in a state of primal singularity. It exists in a world before the division of Tonal and Nagual. In classical alchemy, your Lower Dan Tian is the source of your Fire and Water. It's a place where you can develop power. It's the home of what the Europeans call *gravitas*. It's a place of transformation and birth, and the source of your creative energy as it steps from the realm of potential into everyday reality.

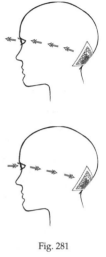

Fig. 281

Fig. 282

Here are some exercises to help you understand and appreciate the functions of these three centers in your body:

🪷 Animals can regenerate more effectively than most humans. Animals regenerate so well because they have a higher proportion of nerves in their body tissues than humans do. Human beings have concentrated much of their nerve supply into their heads to create big brains. Many of your nerve cells are in your brain.

The "empty" aspect of 13 Cane relates to the process of regeneration. It means to clear your mind, and end mental and psychological duality. This creates a field for you to get your attention down into your heart and Lower Dan Tian to regenerate yourself spiritually and physically.

If you focus your intention into your Lower Dan Tian for extended periods of time, you can optimize your ability to regenerate yourself. This is a very practical application of the Ollin principle.

 Experiment with placing your attention and awareness at each of the three major electrical centers in your body. How does this influence your perceptions of yourself and the world? It can become pathological to over or underdevelop your knowledge, heart or power without balance. Your physical, emotional, mental and spiritual health come from the dynamic and harmonious relationships of these three elements. They dance in living communion with one another when you're in your natural state.

If you spend much of your time working or running around in empty activity, invest more time in meditation to develop your potency.

If you spend much your time and energy giving to others, develop your power. Replenish yourself. Maybe you can find a way to give more effectively that fosters and empowers the independence of those you're giving to.

If you spend much of your time meditating and doing esoteric practices, sensitize yourself to perceive right timing, the right location and the right people with whom you can do something to actively improve the world around you.

Contemplate what the most appropriate ratio of these three elements is for you. Develop them all, and develop flexibility.

Your biofield orients and arranges your atomic parts, and your atomic parts taken as a whole create a physical foundation for your biofield. Your biofield creates electromagnetic patterns, and structure follows. Different aspects of your body can and do drop away as your cells come and go, yet your biofield remains as your body incorporates new cells. Your biofield lends you continuity through the processes of change. It directs the growth, development, orientation and regeneration of all your tissues.[59]

Fig. 283

The Aztec Sun Calendar teaches us about movement. Your body's motions generate specific types of electrical fields. (Fig. 283) Every movement you make changes the qualities of tension and relaxation in your tissues. When your tissues change, the qualities of your biofield change. These alterations convey electromagnetic information to your cells, which modifies their calcium ion currents. The currents stretch, crunch and otherwise tweak the *microfilaments*, *microtubules* and *microtrabeculae* connecting all your cells with one another. Your cell structures, shapes and functions adapt themselves to these changes. Your life processes are both chemical and electrical. Chemistry and electricity interact with each other in living feedback cycles.

You emit a rhythmically oscillating, undulating biological field. It interacts with the hormonal and cellular chemistry of your body. Electromagnetic and vibratory phenomena are very important influences at the biomolecular and cellular levels of your life. Even the slightest change in a cell's environment will alter the electrical potentials across its cell membrane. This in turn alters and regulates the cell's functions.

Each of your tissues responds to specific frequencies and amplitudes. The vibrational preferences of each part of your body change cyclically over time. All your subcellular structures, cells, and collections of cells have vibrational and electrical "sweet spots" or resonances that affect them more strongly than other frequencies do. Specific frequencies can act as *catalysts* in chemical reactions. A catalyst is a substance that can greatly magnify chemical reactions. Your hormones are examples of biological catalysts.

Some catalysts can create reactions between substances that wouldn't happen at all without the catalysts being there. Catalysts are relationship enhancers. *Enzymes* are biological catalysts. All enzymes are proteins. Proteins are recombinant chains of your 20 types of amino acids. (Fig. 284)

Fig. 284 Proteins are recombinant chains of your 20 types of amino acids.

Fig. 285

The relationship of the Ring of Fire and the Ring of Sacrifice demonstrates *resonance*.

Fig. 286

Resonance may explain the lock and key mechanisms of enzymes.

Nothing in the chemical structure of enzymes can account for their tremendous power. Scientists believe enzymes are so powerful because they create *resonance phenomena*. Resonance happens between an enzyme and its *substrate*. Researchers such as Herbert Frolich and others suggest these resonance phenomena are the mechanisms of the lock and key properties of your enzymes.[60] (Fig. 285) The Calendar demonstrates resonance through the relationship of the Ring of Fire and the Ring of Sacrifice harmonizing, reflecting and interlocking with each other in a dynamic relationship of Water and Fire. (Fig. 286)

There are about 3000 different types of

enzymes in each of your cells. If you calculate how many different kinds of chemical reactions can occur between these enzymes and their potential effects on your cellular chemical processes, you can begin to appreciate the intricate web of subtle complexity each of your cells sponsors. How can all your billions of cells work together, and also interact with your surrounding environment? You're truly a miracle of organization.

The Aztec Sun Calendar teaches us about symmetry. Your body remembers its original cellular symmetry to create the dynamic Ollin of your body. (Fig. 287) Your sense of symmetry is exact. An excellent practical example is in the ancient art of acupuncture, which uses your body's sense of symmetry to diagnose and cure many illnesses with astonishingly mathematical precision.

Your body connects with itself in an upside down and backwards reflection. Your two sides mirror each other and form a quadripole. Your left foot connects with your right hand. Your right hand connects with your left foot. Your lower left abdomen connects with your upper right abdomen, and so on. Your nervous system perceives and generates symmetry

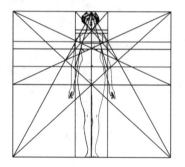

Fig. 287 The symmetry of your nervous system divides your body into 4 quadrants, just like the Sun.

Your body remembers its origins. It retains memory trails of your entire evolution over time. These trails are your energy meridians. Your skin is highly electrically active. Meridians are pathways of lowered electrical resistance through your skin. This means the areas of the meridians conduct electricity better than the places that don't have meridians passing through them. Many people can feel the sensations of their meridians opening up when they receive acupuncture.

Your energy meridians connect the vast panorama of your physiology. Your inner world reflects to the surface of your body through your meridians, appearing as zones of electrical abundance and depletion on your skin. Your meridians oscillate together to form an overall picture of your internal environment. Your biofield transmits a broadcast of your inner world to your outer world. (Fig. 288)

Your meridians conduct biological current. A wave rhythm conducts through your meridian system in a 15 minute cycle. It circulates 96 times in 24 hours. This daily rhythm is shown in the Calendar by the sum of the Flames in the Ring of Fire and the drops in the Ring of Sacrifice. (Fig. 289)

Fig. 288

Your inner world reflects to the surface of your body through your meridians.

Fig. 289 The Calendar demonstrates the daily cycle of electromagnetic energy through the body.

Fig. 290

Tonatiuh is your core potential. He is the essence of creation and creativity.

Your meridians are rivulets of energy. They branch off from and circulate your core energy all over your body. They're not your main energy core. Neither are your chakras. Neither is anything else you can rigidly define. Your core energy is an ocean of potential. (Fig. 290) At the center, or heart of your being, you are pure potential. On the outside, you have tendencies and probable behaviors. You're fuzzy and somewhat predictable. All systems work together. There's only one system.

The Aztec Sun Calendar teaches us about the integration of chaos and order. It shows how the patterns of neurons firing in your brain are mostly irregular. Biological current passes from area the of 13 Cane to the front of your head while you're awake. It reverses when you go into deep trance or deep sleep.[61] Chaotic activity in your waking brain is slight. When you go into ritual states of trance or sleep, chaotic firing patterns increase. Chaos heals. Chaos regenerates.

The natural rhythmic electrical impulses of your healthy heart are mostly regular. Your heart also includes subtle flowing variations in its timing. If the interplay of your heartbeat and your breathing becomes too regular and simple, it can lead to health problems. If the rhythm of your heart becomes too chaotic, it can also cause problems. Your heart is nourished and thrives on the integration of chaos and regularity. (Fig. 291)

A healthy body incorporates chaos and order creatively, the same way nature does. You're a part of nature. You can regenerate yourself if you observe nature and apply what you learn personally.

Your body is a great work of art. Great art of any kind isn't about conformity. It explores the exciting relationship between chaos and order. It's about doing nature your own way.

Fig. 291
Your heart is nourished and thrives on the integration of chaos and regularity.

Rending the Veil

The Aztec Sun Calendar teaches us about electromagnetic and vibrational life. You're alive. Anything that's alive uses electromagnetic and vibrational fields to get information about its environment. Just look into the world of nature to observe the sublime vibrational sensitivities of small animals. Examine the exquisite responsiveness of insects and the delicate motions of their antennae. Have you ever watched the pure subtle field navigation of single celled protozoa? Creatures such as the *amoeba* make extensive use of vibrational and electrical fields to sense and maneuver in their surroundings. Many fish are famous for their ability to detect extremely minuscule electrical fields. Some fish can generate and even discharge enormous amounts of electricity to protect themselves.

You have all these capabilities within you, too. All you have to do is develop them. You can receive and interpret electromagnetic fields. You can become a highly trained electro-vibratory athlete.

You use electromagnetic fields to communicate information from one part of your body to other parts of your body. Your cells use frequencies that extend even into the range of light to communicate with one another and maintain homeostasis. (Fig. 292)

You emit coherent radiations all the way up to the ultraviolet part of the spectrum.[62] (Fig. 293) Dr. Fritz Popp and others have demonstrated how cells use frequencies of coherent lightwave channels as one of their communication links.[63] Human cells have been observed to emit *biophotons* in both visible and ultraviolet frequencies.[64]

You also use electromagnetic fields to communicate with the people and other animals around you. In 1987, Russian scientists shocked the world with their research into biophotons, your body's ability to emit light. Some of their most interesting findings revealed how you actively sense and respond to *infrared emissions* from the people in your environment. They also detected that your body emits both audible and ultrasonic sound.[65]

Human beings have demonstrated field sensitivities at the fringes of what the most advanced equipment of theoretical physics has to offer. Your ability to pick up on subtle fields is so accurate you can even detect single quanta of electromagnetic radiations.[66]

Your body is like a radio telescope. All your cells work together to detect minute electromagnetic fields. The Calendar shows this cooperation by its many converging patterns. (Fig. 294) You constantly scan your environment for electromagnetic fluctuations and resonances. There are many ways you can detect these gossamer changes in your surroundings.

How do you make these quantum level stimuli sensible to the rest of you? Your hormones

Fig. 292

Tonatiuh is the cell in Tecpatl communication.

Fig. 293

Your body emits both light and sound.

Fig. 294

Your whole body works together to detect fluctuations in your electromagnetic environment.

and enzymes are chemical amplifiers. *Biological amplification* is similar to the chemical cascades that occur in your body when it responds to hormones. Your hormones trigger enzyme reactions. These reactions create very large chemical mobilizations which affect larger and larger structural and perceptual levels in your body. Their progression is demonstrated by the doubling sequence in the Calendar. (Fig. 295)

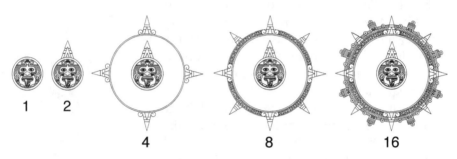

Fig. 295 Your body uses hormones and enzymes as *chemical amplifiers*.

Your sensitivity to electromagnetic fields is equal to the level of electromagnetic radiation you emit. This is shown in the Calendar by the Solar Rays, or your energy emissions, extending to the same line as the Luminous Pearls, or the limits of your perceptions. (Fig. 296) The levels of energy you transmit can get to be very intense in certain situations. For example, if you're having an allergic reaction, or you're very highly stressed, you can discharge enough electricity to seriously interfere with the electronic equipment you come into contact with.[67]

Fig. 296 Your sensitivity to electromagnetic fields is equal to the level of electromagnetic radiation you emit.

All life uses electromagnetic fields, resonance and coherency in its essential biological functions. Coherency relates to precision of frequency. Living systems use highly coherent electromagnetic energy to communicate internally and with one another. These frequencies range from the ultraviolet portion of the energy spectrum all the way down to Extra Low Frequencies (ELFs).

We're living in a time of exceptional changes. August 13, 1999 may be a turning point for our planet in many ways. Successful life forms can adapt to very subtle changes in their environment. The most perceptive ones are most likely to survive and thrive.

You live on the Earth. Earth has a magnetic field. Anything you do automatically references to the warp and weft of this field.

The Earth's ambient electromagnetic field surrounds you right now. It's formed by the complex and shifting relationships between the geomagnetic field and the charged ions in our atmosphere. Lunar rotations, our journey around the Sun, the motions of other planets and even measurable transgalactic forces influence the Earth's geomagnetic field from space. Your local geological formations, the distribution of the ground water in your area, and many other natural and man made factors all affect the behavior of geomagnetic waves as they swirl and flow around you.

The Earth's magnetic field orients itself toward the north and south poles. It also spins around its axis, giving it another definite polar orientation.* (Fig. 297) The Earth's field radiates in different directions. Depending on where you are and when you're there, its orientations and subtle fluctuations can influence your biofield in a number of ways. Even though the variations of the electromagnetic field of the

Fig. 297

The North/South polar axis. The Calendar shows us how motion revolves around a central axis. This motion creates cyclic rhythms here on Earth. We experience these rhythms as the rotations of the Geomagnetic field. Many phenomena build themselves around these supremely delicate subtle forces.

* Your biofield also has a vertical orientation, just like when you were developing in your mother's womb.

Fig. 298

Orientation in the geomagnetic field.

Earth are just barely perceptible using ultra-modern measuring techniques, they still affect you. Their ability to influence you relates to their frequency, or quality, more than their strength.

Each of your cells is sensitive to these fields. This is true even down to the genetic level. The genes on your chromosomes can move and re-orient themselves to respond to changes in your environment.[68] Your DNA can respond and adapt to the surroundings it finds itself in.[69] It can change within certain parameters to do what it needs to do to thrive. The DNA helix even oscillates in resonance with the micro-waves you're exposed to.[70] Weak magnetic fields can also influence your DNA activity.[71]

Your orientation in the geomagnetic field gives your entire body incredibly precise data. (Fig. 298) It gives you clues to the qualities of energy surrounding you. It helps you determine your exact location on the planet, and what physiological adjustments you need to make to optimize your functions there.

Homing pigeons can navigate for hundreds of miles blindfolded. They use magnetic refer-ences.[72] Pigeons and a number of other animals have small magnetic crystals in their skulls. They use them as biological compasses to ori-ent themselves through the shifting waves of the geomagnetic field. Human beings have similar magnetic crystals in their *ethmoid si-nuses*.[73] The Calendar demonstrates this feature of our anatomy in the place where the Xiucoatl meet. If the Calendar is placed over the top view of a skull with 13 Cane aligned with its correct position at the back, the Xiucoatl meet at the ethmoid sinuses. Their opposing spin directions indicate how we use this area for orientation and navigation. (Fig. 299)

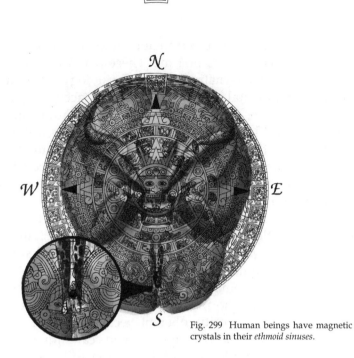

N

W   *E*

S

Fig. 299 Human beings have magnetic crystals in their *ethmoid sinuses*.

Your biofield can change its intensity, reverse directions, and modulate into different frequencies. We've already learned how every electrical field creates a complementary magnetic field at right angles to itself. Changes in your electrical field also cause changes in your magnetic field, and changes in your magnetic field cause changes in your electrical field. Magnetic information doubles the set of variables your body uses to guide and differentiate each of your cells through the constantly shifting electromagnetic fields of your environment. (Fig. 300)

The Aztec Sun Calendar teaches us about personal integration with the cosmos. Environmental fields affect your personal biofields by modulating your body chemistry. Your body is designed to blend with and respond to the subtlest of natural fields.

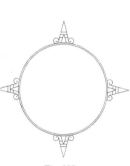

Fig. 300

The right angle relationship of electricity and magnetism is demonstrated by both Masculine and Feminine Solar Rays.

Some environmental electromagnetic patterns are big enough to affect all of us at the same time. These patterns show up in the daily and seasonal alternations of our physiology. We each respond to these environmental shifts in our own way according to our constitutions and level of personal development. Your biofield goes through seasonal fluctuations.[74] It changes according to environmental electromagnetic fields, weather changes, and a number of other factors. For example, your *circadian rhythms* are affected by Schumann wave fluctuations and other Extra Low Frequency patterns in your surroundings.* [75]

Environmental fields are biologically significant even though they're very subtle and their fluctuations are slight. Living creatures usually show a *logarithmic response* to environmental stimuli. This means a small stimulation can get a big reaction.

Man-made electromagnetic fields are much more powerful and coherent than the ones normally occurring in nature. Since your body uses extremely low intensity coherent electromagnetic fields to regulate itself, man made electromagnetic fields can influence you very powerfully. For example, rates of depression and suicide are statistically higher in areas near high voltage lines.[76] This phenomenon has nothing to do with psychological or placebo effects. The statistics are the same whether the lines are above ground and visible, or below the ground and people don't know they're there.

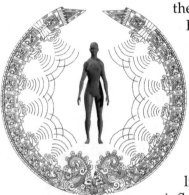

External fields directly influence all your cells. They don't affect you because of the sheer amount of power they're emitting. They're significant at very low, almost undetectable levels. They're potent because their frequencies occur at or close to your own biological frequencies. Since environmental fields are a lot like the fields of your body, they can influence, inhibit or enhance your biology. It's not their strength that makes them strong. It's their similarity to your own natural living waveforms.

---

* *Circadian rhythms* are biological cycles of activity and non-activity.

Here's a simple test you can perform to become aware of the electromagnetic fields that constantly surround you.

🦋 Check your environment for electromagnetic fields with a small transistor radio jammed in between stations on the AM setting. Walk around with the radio and listen to what happens when you walk by objects like rheostat switches and television sets, even when they're turned off. Your body is constantly aware of these frequencies and fields.

Many of your biological functions are electrical. For example, bioelectrical fields regulate the opening and closing of the ion channels in your cell membranes. All your nervous signals are electrochemical. Fields constantly influence your cells to accept, reject and process ions and other substances from their surrounding medium. Electromagnetic fields can also directly influence your biochemical reactions.[77] These fields alter the pH of the chemicals in your body and even rearrange their geometrical structures.

The geomagnetic field influences the membrane permeability of all your cells at the same time. The qualities of your entire physiology are affected by this natural field.[78]

The gentle fluctuations of our geomagnetic field cause a tidal action on your body chemistry. You surf on electromagnetic waves. There's abundant evidence that fluctuations of the natural electromagnetic fields surrounding us have profound statistical influences on human behavior and well being. These fluctuations especially include those caused by *solar flares*.

Your environmental and biological fields are very subtle. Your physiology is sensitive to specific frequencies and amplitudes of energy. This sensitivity is illustrated by the Ring of Eagle Feathers in the Calendar. (Fig. 301) Your biological catalysts translate and

Fig. 301

Your physiology is sensitive to specific frequencies and amplitudes of energy.

amplify these waveforms to influence and regulate all your normal physiological functions.

It works just like a cell phone. Cell phone towers are everywhere. They spew out thousands of frequencies into your environment all the time. Fortunately, your phone doesn't ring every time anyone makes a phone call. Your phone picks up only the frequency with your number attached to it.

Many of your body's most essential biochemical reactions occur at extremely low levels of electrical potential, but they're very frequency specific. Weak electromagnetic fields can affect you even more powerfully than strong ones if they come at you with a frequency that can influence one of your physiological systems. This happens because the frequency creates resonances with certain parts of your biology.

Resonance creates *entrainment*. Entrainment occurs when any two objects vibrate at close to the same frequency. The vibrations of the two objects will tend to equalize and move into synchronization with each other.

It's like tuning a radio or television. You tune its frequency until it resonates with the frequency of the TV or radio station's transmitter. When the two frequencies synchronize, you get a TV picture or radio information.

This isn't just a dandy new age philosophy. Resonance is the scientific foundation of all our wireless communications such as telephone, radio and television. Resonance is also the operating principle for many of our modern high-tech weapons systems. (See page 280.)

Here's a more positive example. We know an oscillating vibrational field will induce a resonance at a specific frequency and strength for any chemical element. All chemical bonds have their own *vibrational signatures*. They have distinct and unique patterns of vibrational and rotational frequencies. These are the phenomena measured by spectroscopy to determine the chemical structures of various materials. You can even take special pictures of this process. This is the principle behind *Nuclear Magnetic Resonance Imagery*. If you know someone who has had an MRI done at a hospital, they've tasted the fruit of the science of resonance.

The Mexica used the science of resonance to promote the life principle in themselves and the world around them. For example, they used specific frequencies in their agricultural practices both to promote the healthy growth of their crops and reduce harmful pests. Sometimes these frequencies were applied directly, but most often they were applied to the water used to irrigate their crops. The water carried the vibrational frequencies where they needed to go.

Another example. Your brain is highly sensitive to electrical and magnetic fields resonating at or around its own operating frequency and amplitude.[79] Your brain and your nervous system oscillate. They're susceptible to resonance with the rhythms around you, especially the Schumann resonance.

EEG monitoring shows us your brain creates oscillating electrical waves in frequency ranges from around .5 to 30 Hz.* Your brainwaves work in the same frequency range as the Schumann waves rhythmically pulsating around the Earth's ionosphere. Electromagnetic waves emanating from the Sun influence the Schumann resonance. Fluctuations in the Schumann Bands create gigantic magnetic field waves. These "magnetic storms" sweep around the Earth in the same frequency range in which your brain operates. Our Sun influences your brain via the Schumann resonance.

Environmental resonances affect your electromagnetic field sensitivities. They form resonances with your brain, influence you, and entrain you with the rhythms of nature.

*Hz, or hertz, defines frequency as the number of wave peaks or cycles that occur in one second.

Does this stuff sound kind of wacky to you? Do your common sense, good scientific thinking and healthy skepticism keep you far away and safe from such New Age philosophies? Well, these impractical sciences don't scare off the military. The armed forces of every developed country in the world have been using these technologies since the 1950s. There was a very famous incident of the microwave bombardment of the US embassy in Moscow in 1953. Project Pandora, Project Big Boy, Project Sanguine, the Woodpecker Signal, and many other military operations are a screaming testimony to the reality and power of this technology. If you want some truly hair raising accounts of the kind of things that go on in the world of ELFs and EMFs, pick up a copy of <u>Microwave News</u>.

The military has developed and refined an entire technology of *consciousness weaponry*. These are devices that control and manipulate our abilities to perceive. They are weapons that can put you into a vegetative sleep. Some of them can induce sounds and even spoken commands inside your head. The Walter Reed Army Institute of Research dramatically demonstrated this ability in 1973, when pulsed wave audiograms delivered spoken auditory commands directly into Dr. Joseph C. Sharp's brain.[80]

Right now, the US Navy is testing Low Frequency Active Sonar systems in the ocean off Hawaii's Big Island. This testing is maiming and destroying whale and dolphin life for thousands of miles. This is not science fiction. This is real. It's happening as you read this book. Is there some essentially valid reason why we consider it appropriate to use this technology for the purposes of destruction, but scoff at the idea of using the same science for constructively building a better world?

The dream of a new kind of technology isn't a far-flung, pie-in-the-sky ideal. We have it already in many forms, but how are we using it? Our current use of technology is glamorous, explosive and generally destructive. It provides instant gratification. Regenerative technology requires a different, more long-term attitude toward life. It takes a mature, integrated mind and attention span to appreciate it. To properly use the technology of the ancients, we need to have respect for the rhythmic cycles and timing of nature's qualities and nuances. It's more like a successful intimate friendship than a frenzy of subjugation. If we focus on the proper use of this technology, maybe we can regenerate ourselves and our environment.

The Aztec Sun Calendar teaches us about rhythm. You need to be in rhythm with the pulse of your environment if you want to thrive. You need to synchronize with your world. There are a number of ways you can do it. For example, a 10 Hz frequency can get you into natural rhythm and restore your biorhythmic cycles. It's a kind of home base frequency.

Earth generated enormous electromagnetic pulses at approximately 10 Hz a long time ago in the Precambrian era.[81] Prototypal life forms entrained with these waves of rhythms. They became the first spiral form creatures. The physiology of all life on Earth replicates and reflects self-similar patterns of our geophysical history and origins.

10 Hz is the dominant brainwave rhythm in all animals. It entrains us with the electromagnetic vibration of the Earth. A 10 Hz frequency will renormalize the circadian rhythms in people who have been isolated from the geomagnetic field. Astronauts use this frequency while they're in space to keep their biology from going haywire.

We're healthy when all our cells are working together with mutually beneficial rates of vibration or oscillation. We get sick when something upsets the natural rhythms of these vibrations. Some pathogens even use harmful radiations, or vibrations, to take over our internal environments.[82]

One of the purposes of the traditional indigenous sciences is to enhance our entrainment with the healing rhythms of natural fields. The modern world interprets the indigenous sciences in an overly simplistic way. We've described them as some kind of rudimentary awareness of yearly agricultural cycles. The reality is something much more profound and intimate. Indigenous people can have very personal and ecstatic connections with the unique qualities of time and space in each moment. A person with an intact indigenous nature directly experiences the wonders of cosmic and terrestrial waves of influence.

Many of us have been culturally conditioned to reject the possibility that astrological events could affect us in any practical way here on the surface of the Earth. It's a new/old prejudice that continues to hang on even though there's compelling, well established evidence to the contrary.

People in the communications industry know planetary phases interfere with radio and television transmissions. Planetary influences definitely affect our weather. We've known since the 1800s how our geomagnetic field fluctuates in waves as our Moon revolves around the Earth. Our geomagnetic field becomes most intense with the full moon. Anyone who works at a police station, hospital, psychiatric institution, or other profession dealing with large numbers of people can tell you how the Moon affects masses of people. An adept physician can explain to you how a full moon affects bleeding.

Other events in space like solar winds and even more distant occurrences all have influences on your body and your environment.* (Fig. 302) There's an entire field of research devoted to this study called *cosmobiology*. Many cosmobiologists believe events in space cause fluctuations in our electromagnetic surroundings to create these effects.

Fig. 302 The claws of the Sun, each grabbing a heart, indicate that the magnetic fluctuations of the Sun influence you. They affect your physiological functions and the ways you think, feel and behave. This image is also one more indicator of the great process of decision and choosing the middle path that exists between extremes. It teaches you how to be creative. It teaches you how to speak with light.

For example, researcher Giorgio Piccardi discovered how periods of solar eruptions can enhance certain chemical reactions by as much as 350 percent. He also found magnetic storms and the 11 year sunspot cycle can affect chemical processes.[83] In another study, Professor Frank Brown, Jr. found metabolic activity in various plants and animals follows the phases of the Moon.[84] Other researchers have found that rainfall patterns are related to lunar cycles.[85] So are the electrical potentials of trees,[86] the electrical potentials around your head and chest areas,[87] and many of the fluctuations and cycles within your blood.[88]

*Quantum effects are non-linear and frequency specific. The *Photoelectric Effect* demonstrates how even a single quantum of light traveling from a distant star, if its frequency is correct, can bump an electron off an atom here on Earth.

These researchers and hundreds of others have learned how interplanetary influences can deviate test subjects from statistical behavioral and physiological averages. This is remarkably similar to the precepts of indigenous medicines, where much of diagnosis measures deviations from a time based mean.

The most generally accepted version of how these influences affect us goes like this:

Planetary positions affect chemical reactions.[89] This probably happens through the mechanisms of *resonant amplification* within the Solar magnetic canals.[90] (Fig. 303) These resonances can affect the Earth's geomagnetic field. (Fig. 304) Your *pineal gland* is very sensitive to weak magnetic field changes.[91] (Fig. 305) The fluctuations of our geomagnetic field affect us chemically and systemically through our pineal glands. (Fig. 306)

The path of the pineal gland is only one of many ways electromagnetic fields can influence you. You have layers and layers of

Fig. 303

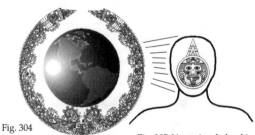

Fig. 304

Fig. 305 Your pineal gland is highly sensitive to changes in your electromagnetic environment. These changes may be an important component in the regulation your body's internal cycles.

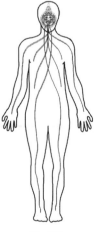

Fig. 306

mechanisms in your body that are sensitive and responsive to electromagnetic fields. You receive signals from the minutest subatomic particles, to your atoms and molecules, to your cells, tissues, nervous and hormonal systems.

The new sciences try to take into account the multiple pathways of interactive forces at work on you at all times. The influences of nature are a convergence of subtle forces. When these subtle environmental factors combine together coherently, they create very powerful effects.

Remember the reciprocal square law? It states the influence one object has on another decreases by the square of the distance between them. It shows you that no matter how far away from you something is, it's still affecting you on some level. It may seem that this influence is very, very tiny. It would appear to be unimportant. Insignificant. But what happens when as many subtle and oblique factors as there are in the entire universe compile? What happens when the infinity of these microscopic effects add up over vast amounts of time?

Nobody can say for sure. The answer must be really fuzzy. The only thing we can say is the system includes everything. There are no unrelated events, because there aren't any isolated systems. Everything is significant.

No moment is reproducible. This time we're sharing here and now is unique. Just think of all the complex interactions of gravity, electromagnetic fields and spirals of motion in the universe, all tugging and nudging within and around you right now. Our universe is in motion. It's not repeating itself.

The Aztec Sun Calendar teaches us about balance and harmony. There's a balance somewhere between your inner and outer environments. Connective tissues permeate every part of your body. They communicate information from your external fields to your internal fields.[92] They're the physiological bridges between your inner biological world and the outer world in which you live and move and have your being.

Some of these bridges have no known direct relationship with the old physiological models. For example, your acupuncture points are locations of intense interactions between your inner and outer electromagnetic environments. Some of your meridians act as reservoirs to collect and refine energy from your surroundings. Your meridian system integrates parts of your body that wouldn't otherwise appear to be connected. It's highly sensitive to specific informational, vibrational, and electromagnetic input.

The fields of your body respond to the fields of your environment. Small fluctuations in your ambient environmental field can amplify into very large effects internally by influencing your chemical and hormonal catalysts. It's a perfect regulatory system.

You're connected by a thread to the sky and the vast system of meridians connecting the entire universe. The cycles of the sky are the cycles of your meridians. The interactions of Water and Fire in your body are self-similar fractals of the interplay of cosmic Water and Fire.

COUNTDOWN

AUGUST 1999						
S	M	T	W	T	F	S
1	2	3	4	5	6	7
8	9	10	11	12	**13**	14
15	16	17	18	19	20	21
22	23	24	25	26	27	28
29	30	31				

There's only one Friday the 13th in 1999. Guess when it is? For years, many sensitives have had dreams about August 13, 1999, and others have dreamed about strange and unusual things happening during the entire week of August 13, 1999.

Until a few years ago, the tour guides at the anthropological museum in Mexico City Tenochtitlan stated with absolute conviction that August 13, 1999 is going to be the end of the world as we know it. More recently, their orations have become more timid. Now they tell us 13 Cane simply indicates "a time of great change."

August 13, 1999

What can we expect for August 13, 1999? According to our current level of scientific knowledge and understanding, it's impossible to predict. There's no way to prepare specifically. We don't know what's coming.

On a more human level, we have the world situation briefly described at the beginning of this book. The modern world presents us with a vastly complex social and political picture. Prediction of the future based on current events at this level can easily lead to nonproductive hysteria. Is there any other way to obtain information that might help us round out our understanding of August 13, 1999 ahead of time?

One of the primary techniques of investigation an indigenous scientist uses is to look at a single issue from multiple perspectives. This was the method used in asking a number of different astrologers from completely different astrological backgrounds their studied opinions regarding August 13, 1999. Each of them gave their predictions for the time period in and around August 13, 1999, for the location of Mexico City Tenochtitlan. None of them knew about the Aztec forecast. They weren't prompted or prepared in any way.

The astrologers came up with a very interesting and challenging insight: from an astrological point of view, the day we're talking about might not happen exactly on August 13, 1999. Each of them independently produced the date of *August 11, 1999* as being a day of exceptional astrological importance. They also individually concluded this difference might be because of discrepancies between our own calendar and the Aztec Sun Calendar.

A number of western astrologers and a Chinese astrologer gave their analyses. Here's what they found:

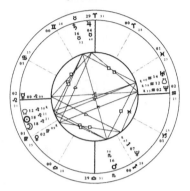

The picture the western astrologers paint for us of August 11, 1999 is surprisingly similar to our original definitions of 13 Cane.

1) The last solar eclipse of the twentieth century happens on August 11, 1999. The New Moon Solar Eclipse will occur in Mexico City Tenochtitlan at 5:08:32 AM.

2) There's a grand cross of planets in the fixed signs of Aquarius, Scorpio, Leo and Taurus. These are the four beasts of the Apocalypse referred to in the Biblical Book of Revelation. A Sun and Moon conjunction in Leo opposes Uranus in Aquarius. Mars in Scorpio opposes Saturn in Taurus. All planets square each other.

3) Mercury in Leo opposes Neptune in Aquarius. They both square Jupiter in Taurus. This is a fixed T-Square.

4) A total of 8 out of 10 planets are in fixed signs.

5) Venus is retrograde and at its helical setting, where it disappears into the rays of the Sun. With this movement, Venus will no longer be visible as the Evening Star. It will reappear again several weeks later as the Morning Star.

What does it all mean? This is an archetypal chart of massive and fundamental change. Some astrologers call it an earthquake chart. It indicates a major cataclysmic event that will transform values. Sources of stability break and fall apart. There's an overthrow of old political structure, and a rebirth of a new order. A possibility of global financial meltdown accompanies a massive redistribution of wealth and a new financial system.

Whatever is going to happen, the chart indicates it will attract international recognition. There's a quality of families being ripped apart by internal tensions, and a sudden fall of the father figure.

There's a possible outbreak of war over territorial disputes, accompanied by an unpredictable chain of catastrophic events.

The movement of Venus on this day indicates a time of major social crisis. It's classically a time to dread with the utmost respect. Since this motion happens at the very moment of the solar eclipse, it sends the impact of this action off the charts.

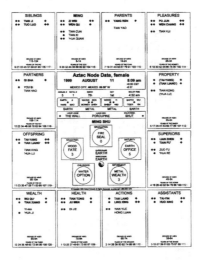

The Chinese astrology for August 11, 1999 reveals some fascinating perspectives. The solar eclipse relates to a time where astrological focus is on the *Emperor*. Heaven shows displeasure on an eclipse date. There are indications the Emperor isn't doing his job correctly. The affairs of state are out of alignment, and the ruler needs to take appropriate actions to mend them.

The Emperor is a bridge between Heaven and Earth. Fate completely backs up the Emperor on this day. The *Fate, Superiors* and *Offspring* palaces are very bright and positive. There's a good foundation of support for what will occur. *Zi Wei*, the Star of Fate, is in the Fate palace. The atmospheric energy of this time backs up responsible actions. This is the best possible moment for such an auspicious and powerful situation.

Yang Ren, the star of Sacrifice, is in the palace of *Parents. Tan Lang*, the Hungry Wolf star, and *Ling Xing*, the Alarm Bell star, are in the Actions palace. There's a calling out of misconduct. *Tian Yue*, the Heavenly Halberd, indicates strong support from seen and unseen partners. Even in the heat of accusations, this support assists the Emperor to do the right thing.

August 11, 1999 is the first day of the Water Monkey month. It's a bright, warm and auspicious day. It has the intuitive ability to present people with what they need just before they need it.

The energy of this eclipse rules the period until the next eclipse. If for some reason the Emperor doesn't succeed on this day, the ministers will have to clean up for him on the very auspicious day of August 13, 1999.

The western astrologers didn't find anything of major importance on August 13, 1999 compared to August 11, 1999. Robert Fenwick, Chinese astrologer for the Academy of Celestial and Mundane Arts in Santa Cruz, California,[1] did. Let's take a look at the Chinese chart for August 13, 1999.

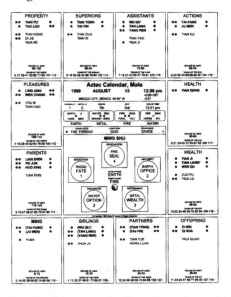

This fire Fowl day is the most challenging day of 1999. Its image is one of a person who could easily become a hoodlum or a rogue unless their grandparents care for and guide him or her. In this case the person will succeed and can become great. *Wen Chang*, the star of Literary Brilliance, indicates the grandparents are the ones holding a special knowledge, and they will be the ones to pass it on.

There's no inherent center for this time. It's a picture where the Emperor dies and no one claims the throne. The empire breaks up. It is a dangerous time of civil war. This is a situation where the parents never showed up for the children. Now the children are taking over the parents' role.

On this day, the Fate palace has no stars of its own. It borrows all its stars from other palaces. This indicates profound influences coming from other people. The Fate palace borrows *Ju Men*, the Great Gate star. It invites a hero to come in and do great things.

The largest element for this day is *Seal*. People have something to express. They want to come forward and speak. The hero can help people express themselves in a positive, constructive way.

The *Wealth* palace is bright. There's a sense the changes are good if the proper influences are in place. As the energy shifts, the situation responds appropriately. Even if there's a disaster, money and energy come along with it. Brightness in the Health palace indicates it will be easy to get help if it's needed.

August 13, 1999 is a day of inner *Fire* and outer *Earth*. There's plenty of internal energy to match the external situation. It's a time that shows a martial arts spirit, and is cautious walking on the edge.

To give us yet another perspective of this time, Vernon Mahabal, director of the Planetary Palmistry Institute in Oakland, California,[2] gives us his appraisal. Vernon has studied thousands of people's palms from all over the world for many years, and he's found some very interesting correlations. Although an exact day is not evident, mid August 1999 appears to be the beginning of major changes in people's lives. He sees a time of great family turmoil and upheaval, geographical changes and mass migrations. There's a move toward decentralization of society and the creation of small, self-sufficient, ecologically based communities. Values get redefined on all levels. People will begin to seek spiritual solutions to material challenges. They will learn to penetrate into the hidden underlying causes behind events. There's a quality of respiritualization and the return of a personal experience of God. This includes an essential, direct relationship with a God who is a sentient being rather than a distant abstraction.

When this many self-similar patterns show up from such a variety of completely unrelated disciplines, a good indigenous scientist will tell you something's going on.

NASA tells us 1999 is going to be a time of the most intense solar storms we've ever seen. The Sun may speak with us on August 13, 1999.

An enormous magnetic storm emanating from the Sun might not seem like such a bad thing to you. Consider this: our last period of concentrated sunspot activity was eleven years ago in 1988. It caused magnetic waves large enough to disrupt communications systems all over the world, blow out power stations in Canada, and produce the *Aurora Borealis*, or the Northern Lights, as far south as Jamaica.

Think about it: electromagnetic devices store and process nearly one hundred percent of the vital information of our information age. Electromagnetism in one form or another is the basis of every bit of our technology. Take a look around at how much of your life depends on the stable, predictable responses of our electromagnetic world. Your car, appliances, all communications, the storage of food, your money in the bank, and many other things all depend on it.

That's the good news. There's something much more important to consider. Your biofield is extremely sensitive to even minor fluctuations in our electromagnetic environment. Your body could translate a massive fluctuation of solar magnetism into almost any biological signals.

The solar flare cycle already is growing in intensity. Many sensitive people are experiencing a strange combination of tiredness, heightened awareness of energy fields, loss of long-term memory with an accompanying ability to stay present in the current moment, easy confusion, disorientation and an intensified ability to discern patterns. Some people are even beginning to feel a tingling or a sensation of pressure in the area of 13 Cane.

In some ways, it's a comical scene: all the New Agers bumbling around in an Alzheimer's like syndrome. But this is real. It's happening right now. We don't know how many people it's going to affect, or how it's going to affect them, or for how long.

Then again, maybe the effects won't be so dramatic. Will we be able to understand, or even perceive, the events that take place on August 13, 1999? Will it turn out to be some kind of subtle event that only the indigenous world will perceive in the moment, and the rest of us will catch the fallout in the years to come? Will we all just be sitting around on August 13, 1999 asking ourselves if we feel anything yet?

On a more worldly note, if something on the level of a popular uprising does take place, what are the chances of finding out about it? Let's be real. We live in a time when they even lie about the weather on TV to make money. It's no secret. Popular media are power tools. Television and other forms of mass communication have progressively replaced reality for much of the modern world. Many of us have been conditioned since early childhood to adopt a conceptual reality, rather than the reality we directly experience. Concepts are easy to manipulate.

How can we take proactive, creative and personally responsible positions to prepare for August 13, 1999?

It's not advisable to stay glued to your television on August 13, 1999. Be a part of what's happening instead. Any project performs much better when it's under a deadline. We've been acting like there's an infinite amount of time to get ourselves together here on planet Earth. There's not. Let's use August 13, 1999 as a deadline to create the world we want to live in right now. It may seem like an impossible, or at least highly improbable task. But, sometimes, it's very important to take on a highly improbable task. This is one of those times. Let's do it.

Look at the Aztec Sun Calendar. 13 Cane is at the polar opposite of the Xiucoatl facing each other in creation, communication and creativity. They hurl themselves at their goal, completely risking all. If we use the Ollin principle of balancing complementary opposites, we can rise to the occasion to which 13 Cane calls us.

We hang in the balance. How can we best prepare for August 13, 1999? By learning to listen. Nature always wins. It's also always speaking with us. If we can learn to listen, we can survive August 13, 1999, and a lot more. We can unlock and unfold our highest destiny.

Listen to nature. Since your body uses highly sensitive electrical currents and fields to regulate itself, the electromagnetic fields you come into contact with can influence you. Fluctuations of the geomagnetic field especially affect you. Your biofield is in constant contact with the electromagnetic pulse of the Earth. It biologically entrains you with its fluctuations. Your biology works in rhythmic synchronization with the pulse of the Earth. Go with it.

Your brainwaves oscillate in the same frequencies as the Schumann resonance. Natural events in the sky profoundly influence all biofields on Earth. Environmental fields affect the fields of your body and your cells, where vibration and electricity are equivalent. Coherent waveforms stimulate your cell membranes to send specific chemical messages into and out of the interiors of your cells. You're intimately connected with a universal and interactive chain of cause and effect.

A river of electrons is flowing through and around your body every moment of your life. It connects you with ever larger and smaller dynamic rivers of electrons in an infinite electrical cascade. You are at one with this infinity.

Before the electromagnetic noise and pollution of the modern world, the delicate whispers of nature's electromagnetic fields were all there were for your analog nervous system to perceive. There were only beneficial electromagnetic radiations. You could be aware, and it was wonderful. No luxury can compare with the soft, warm flow of our geomagnetic field.

However, if your environment becomes polluted with toxic electromagnetic fields, or you're overloaded with too much information, you'll have a natural tendency to retreat into your digital nervous system. It's too painful to allow your analog system to continue operating at its normal level when your surroundings are not well. Many people who have highly developed analog nervous systems are having a very difficult time these days.

Even though it's challenging at times, it's still beneficial to operate in analog. It shows you where it's OK to be and where it's not. It helps you experience quality in your life, with all its highs, lows, subtleties and passions. One of the prime features of creative people is their ability to perceive and appreciate nuance. They enjoy using their analog nervous systems. As more and more people go digital and abandon their analog nervous systems, the analog users are gaining a qualitative informational edge.

Your analog nervous system is wired for health and longevity. So is your digital nervous system. If you learn to pay attention to your perceptions, your life will improve. Begin to listen to and follow your indigenous nature. It always knows the most creative solutions to every challenge.

One way, perhaps the most constructive way, to meet squarely and positively influence what we will face on August 13, 1999, is to cultivate and integrate with your indigenous nature. As we each blend with our greater field of being, we can help to direct the course of our destiny in the fullest, most creatively empowered direction possible. We create our future step by step and day by day. We build it in many small ways that subtly and persistently multiply themselves into being. Each person you meet connects with our future somehow, and does his or her part to guide you on your path.

You can learn to listen by developing your associations with the natural fields around you. You can strengthen these connections just as surely as you can make your body strong through exercise. Your biofield is a small part of a vast and interconnected flow of energy. It connects you with the objects and other living beings around you. It blends you with your local environment, the Earth, our solar system, and interstellar currents and oceans.

You're a dynamic and connected system in motion. Your indigenous nature is completely at one with the fields of nature. It's intimately reflective of your environment. The energy meridians of the Earth are your energy meridians. The phases of the Moon, the tides and the seasons are all you. Cultivate your awareness of the beautiful oneness of nature. It will help you understand and benefit from your integration with the whole of creation.

It's going to take a synthesis of instinct, intellect, information and intuition to face the challenges of August 13, 1999. Cultivate a relationship with your indigenous nature. Begin to develop and use your intuition and instinct every day. Set aside August 13, 1999 to do exactly what your instinct tells you to do. Whatever it is, no matter how crazy it seems, as long as you're respectful of yourself and others, just do it.

Life is your journey. It's a dynamic outpouring of energy you can sculpt, shape and direct over time. Gently guide the flow of your attention toward a more noble, dignified and authentic expression of who you're becoming. The more completely you go into this process, the more consciously you'll be able to navigate yourself in the flux of our changing world. Use the tools of listening, feedback and balance. Respond to small things before they turn into big things. Everything is on your spiral path of progress, transformation, strengthening and refinement.

Unify opposites. Look for patterns. Trust your indigenous nature. Go for synthesis. Follow the central principle. Return to the pulsing heartbeat of nature. Get Sun, fresh air, eat well and connect with the Earth's geomagnetic field. Trust who you're becoming. You'll know what to do when the time comes.

Many people aren't aware of the subtle energies of nature on a conscious level. If you want to sense and constructively use these energies, you'll first need to build and refine your own energy. You'll need to cultivate coherency in your biofield to operate your nervous system at this level of awareness. You'll need to develop your *pitzahuacayotl*.

You can store and apply your energy to increase your levels of sensitivity, focus and improve the coherency of your electromagnetic field. This process is similar to tuning a radio. A radio exactly focuses in on a very small, thin waveform. Then it makes the waveform louder so you can hear it. Learn to listen for and move toward your most positive future. Amplify it. Embody it. Allow yourself to connect naturally with the millions of others who are responding to the Call.

Do your exercises. You can enjoy some very interesting and health-giving benefits if you invest your time and energy this way. The world of your indigenous nature will open up to you in a vast and exciting panorama. As you unite with your own nature, you'll be able to appreciate and unite with the nature in your environment.

You can make intelligent use of the information in the electromagnetic fields of nature. It's a scientifically established reality. All life, including human beings, has been creatively using this information forever. We've only recently, briefly, forgotten how to do it consciously. Nowadays, the most natural things in the world are being reintroduced to us as the latest scientific breakthroughs, systems for personal development and the ultimate in spiritual growth. It's a good thing. We can really use it at this point in history.

But here's the real deal: all these wonders exist inside you. They're just waiting to come out and improve your life and the lives of everyone and everything around you. All you have to do is simply give yourself the time and space to allow them to develop naturally, and they will.

You can create coherency in your life and in your world. You can blend with nature and discover its intimate secrets. You have choice. You can know the events of August 13, 1999, and be a part of them as they occur. Something in the air is just waiting to happen. Listen for it. It's the Call. Go with it. Your innermost calling is what will guide us all into the best possible future. Whatever your calling is, it's time for you to go do it, with *oquichehualiztli*.

You can influence what will happen on August 13, 1999. The things you do make a difference. You're always adding your thread to the web of life, perpetually empowering yourself and the rest of us at the same time. You matter. Every little thing you do affects us all. Actively involve yourself with August 13, 1999. Look for right timing. Make your moves. Respond to the Call. Your actions are building our future.

Revolution

Have you heard? There's a revolution in Mexico. Part of the Mexican revolution is composed of the long time oppressed indigenous people of Mexico, who are doing their best to create decent lives for themselves. Yet underneath this revolutionary fabric, there's something deeper going on. It's something more profound and persuasive. It's inclusive, creative and bursting with compassion. It kindles an ancient ancestral fire in your blood. You can see it in the eyes of people everywhere.

There's a revolution taking place inside you and all of us right now. It's a revolution that strives upward for possibilities.

We're at a rare and precious moment in history. It's a critical time for people everywhere to look to the wisdom within themselves. It's a time to seek out those who have unique and important insights. It's time to find the handful of remaining Elders, the grandparents, the people of wisdom, and ask them humbly and respectfully if they will hold our hands as they teach us to remember all we've forgotten.

The great indigenous traditions of the world are like a giant tree. The Mexica called this tree *Ahuehuetl* (ah-weh-WEH-tl), the ancient wise one. Its roots connect the entire globe. The cultural ancestry you came from intertwines with these roots. You're a leaf on this tree. Its sap flows from deep in the Earth right through your veins. You're nourished by the Sun. You help keep this tree alive moment by moment with each breath you take.

Five hundred years ago, who would have dared to predict the grandchildren of the conquered would dance the sacred dances of their ancestors again? And who, in the most heightened states of awareness, could have foretold that in our generation, the generation of 13 Cane, the grandchildren of the conquerors would also dance the sacred dances and learn the indigenous sciences?

They're the ones who, in their wisdom, chose to build a bridge between their time and ours. They're the ones who built great monuments of stone. They're the ones who knew we would dance the sacred dances again.

They're the ones who knew we would dance them together.

Appendices

The Language of the Sorcerers

A Hierarchy of Symbols

You begin forming connections between your outer world and your inner world when you're developing in utero. By your fifth month of prenatal development, you've established the foundations of your neural system. The initial neural networks you formed in the uterine environment give you a sensory base line, or your original perception of self and other.

This state of original perception may be what the ancient sorcerers called the "Prebirth state," "Preheaven Chi," and the "Original Face before you were born." Your Original Face is your indigenous self. You can empower it. You can disentangle it from your acquired and imposed belief systems and assist it to effortlessly and objectively become what it wants to be.

You can speak with your Original Face. It speaks the language of your inner symbolic patterns. Geometry, nature and the way you process information all involve the same types of relationships. It's self-similar all the way up and all the way down.

Your nervous system gathers information from your environment and internalizes it into a hierarchy of symbols. The deeper you go into your consciousness, the more abstract and mathematical these symbols become. These symbols are the language of the sorcerers.

Geometry

We're witnessing a great rebirth in the appreciation of geometry in the modern world. This language of natural mathematical and geometrical relationships speaks with all people and spans all cultures. Geometry is transcendent. It's universal.

The discovery and appreciation of geometry are important parts of the development of any culture. It's a language that gets rediscovered time and again whenever a group of individuals attains a ripened stage of development. Any culture that has endured the test of time has based itself in some way on the structure of nature and its geometries.

The language of geometry isn't something you need to learn. It evokes an understanding from deep inside you. Geometry is your mind's link with higher orders of energy through the panorama of nature.

Geometry trains you how to experience your world as energy patterns. Learning about these patterns can help you cooperate more effectively with nature's movements. This helps you to be more successful in every situation, because nature always wins.

There's a natural magic in the structure of number and geometry. When you become aware of this magic, nature can come to life and influence you in a variety of beneficial ways. The patterns of nature are the patterns of your awareness. They're hardwired into your nervous system as pathways of information processes. Once you begin to perceive your world as patterns of nature, life becomes increasingly beautiful, fascinating, fun and engaging. The rebirth of our appreciation of geometry is the rebirth of our indigenous perception.

Everything in nature is in dynamic flow, yet the patterns stay the same. Which is more real? The pattern, or the part of the pattern you can see and touch right now? Everything you can observe is somewhere in a process of unfolding through stages over time. We tend not to see a whole pattern at once. It's revealed only as time goes on. The whole story and the story of the whole are contained in the geometry of every event. When you learn how to read nature's order, you can begin to let go of the fearful projections you cast upon it.

Geometry is the poetic language of nature. Why do modern schools make every attempt to separate geometry and math from nature? Many of us go into a kind of catatonic state if we think we're going to have to deal with math. It's as if math was an abuse we suffered in childhood. If we learned language the way we learn math in school, we'd be living on a silent planet.

One of the current trends in science is the attempt to explain and map the forces of nature using the hyper-dimensional effects of geometry. The idea is that all the forces in nature come from abstract geometries relating with one another. Every part of nature we've discovered so far has shown us geometrical and mathematical roots.

Fractal geometry is another modern scientific trend. Fractals map the complexities of nature very accurately.

Classical, or *Euclidean* geometry maps the general divisions, boundaries, and domains of nature very accurately.

Geometry is very important in the world of atoms and chemistry. Varying geometrical relationships between the same atoms can create different substances. For instance, the switch from a random to a *tetrahedral* structure creates the difference between plain glass and quartz crystal. The difference between coal and diamond is also the difference of a tetrahedral structure.

The beauty of the natural constants of science is that they express the relationships between things in terms of the specific qualities of numbers. There's a lovely harmony that's part and parcel of the qualities of numbers themselves and their simple relationships.

Geometry and number are a kind of in-between world, between existence and nonexistence. You can find geometric forms on the way into and out of creation. They're the forms living energy fields create as they interact with one another over time.

Nature's designs evolve out of processes. Nature designs to address a specific purpose or a multitasking set of purposes. This level of structure is precisely where the ancient and the new worlds meet in timeless observations that reconfirm themselves age after age.

The ancients had a wonderful and profound appreciation for the world of numbers. It was a world they wove into every aspect of their lives, from science to art to religion to philosophy. For example, the Pythagoreans of ancient Greece knew the realm of pure number was one of highly abstracted archetypes, or *eidoi*. In this world of abstraction, each of the numbers had its own name and personality characteristics. Number relationships were studied as personal relationships.

The Mexica sorcerers had a very unique and integrated understanding of the structures and qualities of numbers and the roles they play in the creation of our world. They knew how the realm of numbers has physical laws similar to the ones we have in our world. Their science used the knowledge that numbers have very distinct individual personalities and demonstrate clear patterns of relationships when they interact with one another.

Life is about relationships. Relationships express themselves as ratios and proportions. Ratios and proportions create geometry and number. Life follows abstract geometrical pathways. Numbers are qualities. They're the essence of relationships. It's odd we've divided the sciences into the quantitative and the qualitative. Quantitative is completely qualitative. Nothing could be more qualitative than numbers.

The Pyramid of Nature

The individual events in our lives seem to occur at random. However, if you examine your life and the world around you from a slightly larger perspective, you'll find an order permeates this randomness. If you take samples of many different situations, you'll begin to notice there's order, pattern and rhythm in the random events. The larger your samples are, the more order you'll find.

Pascal's triangle is the fractal form *Pyramid of Nature*. It has everything to do with the real world, because it exactly describes the probabilistic behavior of all phenomena, groups of phenomena, groups of groups of phenomena, etc. They all follow the Pyramid of Nature from chaos to order.

The Pyramid of Nature gives you a perfect illustration of *stereoscopic mathematics*. People who work with statistics use it to calculate probabilities. For example, if you randomly throw three coins into the air and let them fall, what are all the possible head and tail patterns that will result? You'll find there are eight possibilities.

They look like this:

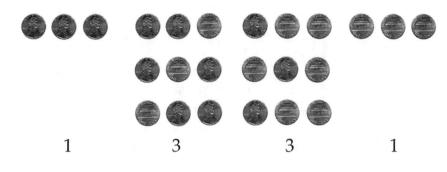

| 1 | 3 | 3 | 1 |

1 3 3 1 is line 3 of the Pyramid of Nature. (See next page.) You can find the answers to tossing any number of coins by referencing the line with that number.

Cascades of binary yes or no decisions create the events in your life. The forces around you affect you. The more in touch and in tune you are with yourself and the world around you, the more clearly you'll be able to discern between the actions you really want to take and when you're just being swept away by the tide of events.

You'll find choice at the center of the Aztec Sun Calendar. (Fig. 307) Choice is the ability you have to go one way or the other in a decision process. The Calendar profoundly empowers and reminds you of your freedom of choice. At the same time, it also acknowledges and deeply respects your destiny. You are at choice with what will happen to you on August 13, 1999. With your freedom comes personal responsibility and accountability for your actions. This naturally fosters your sense of self-worth and self-respect. You are in the driver's seat of your life.

Where on the curve of events do you want to put yourself?

Fig. 307

The Solar Dart is the essence of choice.

The eighth Solar Ray emphasized by the tip of the Solar Dart indicates the Pyramid of Nature very elegantly. It brings you back to the philosophy of choice.

The Pyramid of Nature

$$2 = 2^1 \rightarrow \quad 1 \ 1 \qquad \rightarrow \quad 11 = 11^1$$
$$4 = 2^2 \rightarrow \quad 1 \ 2 \ 1 \qquad \rightarrow \quad 121 = 11^2$$
$$8 = 2^3 \rightarrow \quad 1 \ 3 \ 3 \ 1 \qquad \rightarrow \quad 1331 = 11^3$$
$$16 = 2^4 \rightarrow \quad 1 \ 4 \ 6 \ 4 \ 1 \qquad \rightarrow \quad 14641 = 11^4$$
$$32 = 2^5 \rightarrow \quad 1 \ 5 \ 10 \ \ 10 \ 5 \ 1$$
$$64 = 2^6 \rightarrow \quad 1 \ 6 \ 15 \ 20 \ 15 \ 6 \ 1$$
$$128 = 2^7 \rightarrow \quad 1 \ 7 \ 21 \ 35 \ 35 \ 21 \ 7 \ 1$$
$$256 = 2^8 \rightarrow \quad 1 \ 8 \ 28 \ 56 \ 70 \ 56 \ 28 \ 8 \ 1$$

1 9 36 84 126 126 84 36 9 1

1 10 45 120 210 252 210 120 45 10 1

The Pyramid reveals how nature expresses itself in powers of eleven.

The number two is a fundamental constant in nature.

The Pyramid of Nature generates itself from cascades of yes or no decisions. It's a mirror image you can read either way from the middle.

The Pyramid of Nature generates powers of eleven. When you get to the fifth line in the Pyramid of Nature, the powers of eleven appear to break down. However, when you take decimal places into account, the lines perfectly transform into progressive powers of elevens.

This is much simpler than it sounds. It works just like when you're adding numbers. For example, the fifth line, 1 5 10 10 5 1 becomes 1 **6 1 0** 5 1. 161051 is 11 to the fifth power, etc. This is an absolute proof the Mexica had and used the decimal system.

Each Xiucoatl has 11 visible sections. These sections illustrate how the Pyramid of Nature works in powers of 11.

▲ Every number in the Pyramid of Nature is the sum of the two numbers above it.

▲ The sum of the numbers in any row is two times the number of the row.

▲ The sum of all the numbers in the row above any row is two times the sum of the numbers in the row minus one.

▲ The sum of any series of numbers going diagonally equals the number to the right and just below the last number in the series.

▲ Pick any number in the pyramid. There are exactly that many ways to get to that number at that location from the top of the pyramid.

▲ These are just a few of the many fascinating properties and applications of the Pyramid of Nature.

The *Sierpinski triangle* takes the Pyramid of Nature and makes the odd numbers one color, and the even numbers another color. It helps you distinguish patterns of Nagual and Tonal.

Look what happens:

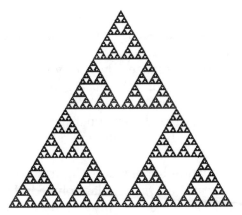

Sierpinski triangle

The Pyramid of Nature contains repeating self-similar patterns of Nagual and Tonal.

Let's take a closer look at one of these inner pyramids:

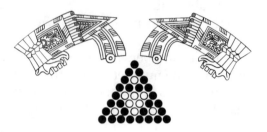

Each Xiucoatl has a number six on its tail. When the 2 Xiucoatl interact, they create 6x6= 36. Each Xiucoatl also has a series of nine groups of four bars coming from its tail. 9x4=36. 36 units in the Pyramid of Nature takes you to the eighth level, or octave of the pyramid, where it reaches the next layer of self-similarity. The rattles on the Xiucoatl's tails indicate how sound, rhythm and vibration create our world.

The Pyramid of Nature demonstrates an eight stage fractal structure of propagation. At every octave of lines, the pattern doubles. Nature creates in octaves. Nature doubles.

Reciprocal Space

The Aztec Sun Calendar teaches you how the natural world uses geometry in its processes of creation.

The forces of nature equalize. They're symmetrical. They radiate into infinity in all directions. A *regular* geometrical figure is any shape with perfect symmetry.

A *sphere* has perfect three dimensional symmetry. Any structure relating to space has to dynamically embody the qualities of the sphere.

You can create any number of regular figures in two dimensions. However, you can create only *five* regular polyhedral forms in a three dimensional space. These are the only five regular convex shapes you can get to fit exactly inside a sphere. These figures are the *Platonic Solids*. They're called Platonic because they have *nonsexual relationships* with one another.

Just kidding. We call them the Platonic solids because Plato was one of the last Europeans to publicly catalog and convey fragments of the ancient indigenous sciences.

The Platonic Solids are:

The tetrahedron.

The octahedron.

The cube.

The icosahedron.

The dodecahedron.

Since *triangles, squares* and *pentagons* are the only regular shapes that can enclose a volume of space without leaving any gaps, nature uses these forms to create spatial geometry. The Platonic Solids are made of the simplest possible geometrical elements. They're built from equilateral triangles, squares and pentagons arranged in the simplest possible three dimensional relationships. They form regular shapes.

The five solids demonstrate *equality* and *equanimity* because they divide a sphere equally in all directions. The surfaces of a Platonic Solid are *congruent regular polygons*. This means each of its faces is the same.

The Platonic Solids create themselves from iterated shapes, lengths and angles. They naturally construct and complete themselves through iteration in three dimensional space.

The *volumes* of the Platonic solids are the spatialized forms of musical harmonic intervals. They're the structural elements of the architecture of space.

A central concept to the Platonic solids is *reciprocity*. Reciprocity means that if you find the exact center of each surface of one of the solids, and then connect each of these centers with lines, you'll make another figure inscribed inside your original figure. These two shapes have a *reciprocal* relationship with each other. If you then find the centers of the surfaces of your new inscribed figure, and join those points, you'll have a tiny replica of your initial figure inscribed inside the two others. This process continues into infinity. In nature, the Platonic Solids pulse back and forth between reciprocals.

The octahedron and the cube are reciprocal with one another. (Fig. 308) So are the icosahedron and the dodecahedron. (Fig. 309) The tetrahedron is reciprocal with itself. (Fig. 310)

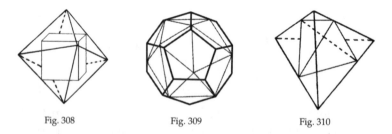

Fig. 308   Fig. 309   Fig. 310

The ancients considered the dodecahedron to be a model of the universe. The dodecahedron is a three dimensional projection of the pentagon. It's a geometric representation of the harmony of all elements within the whole. The dodecahedron was said to guide the harmony of the cosmos. Each of the other solids relates to the essential qualities of the four *Elements*.

The Platonic Solids embody the four Elements and the four states of matter. There's also a fifth state of synthesis.

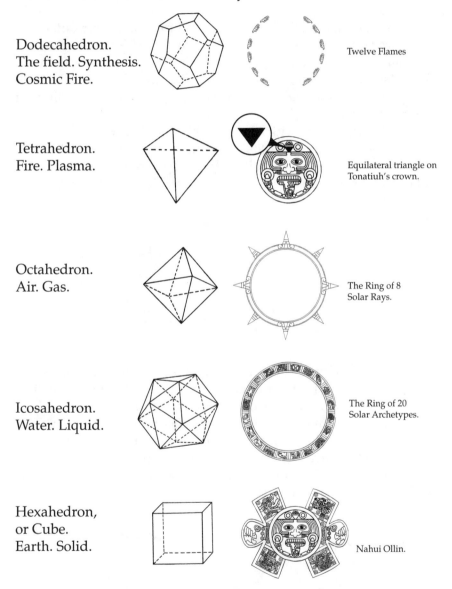

Dodecahedron.
The field. Synthesis.
Cosmic Fire.

Twelve Flames

Tetrahedron.
Fire. Plasma.

Equilateral triangle on Tonatiuh's crown.

Octahedron.
Air. Gas.

The Ring of 8 Solar Rays.

Icosahedron.
Water. Liquid.

The Ring of 20 Solar Archetypes.

Hexahedron,
or Cube.
Earth. Solid.

Nahui Ollin.

The Mexica used the numbers and shapes associated with the Platonic Solids to represent them on the two-dimensional surface of the Calendar. The equilateral triangle on Tonatiuh's crown symbolizes a tetrahedron.

The indigenous sciences consider *sincerity* and *congruity* between the inner self and the outer self to be the foundation of good health and integrity.

The Calendar teaches you about the fusion of your outer and inner worlds. The inner cube of the Sun, your Heart, reciprocates with an octahedral outer form that touches and communicates with the outer Fire of space, the outer Sun. The outer Octahedral Air reciprocates with the inner cube of Earth. Tecpatl is the medium of communication going both ways.

Earth reciprocates with Air. Remember how the Earth exchanges gas with our atmosphere? Most indigenous cultures refer to the body energy as breath, or Air, and the physical, solid body as Earth. The solid self (Earth) reciprocates with the outer self through energy (Air).

The inner cube reciprocates with the outer octahedron in the form of your inner self reciprocating with your outer self, and your outer self reciprocating with your inner self.

Cosmic Fire reciprocates with Water. Electromagnetic waves are waves of Cosmic Fire. Cosmic energies are the 12 flames in the Ring of Fire. They communicate to and through your 12 meridians. You have 6 Yang meridians and 6 Yin meridians, represented by the Luminous Pearls and points of the Solar Rays that mediate between the Ring of Sacrifice and the Ring of Fire. Your 13th central meridian connects with 13 Cane, the silent attractor. The universe is you and you are the universe. (Fig. 311)

The dodecahedron of Cosmic Fire reciprocates with the icosahedron of your inner world of Water. There's a reciprocal oscillation between your inner and outer worlds.

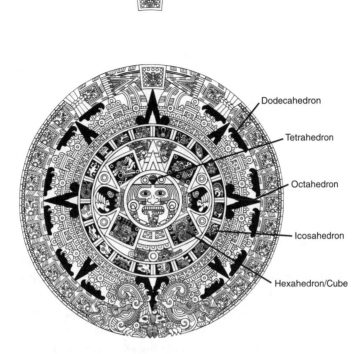

Dodecahedron

Tetrahedron

Octahedron

Icosahedron

Hexahedron/Cube

The Aztec Sun Calendar depicts a tetrahedron, within a cube, within an octahedron, within an icosahedron, within a dodecahedron.

The Meridians, and their connection to 13 Cane.

Fig. 311

Fire reciprocates with *Fire*.

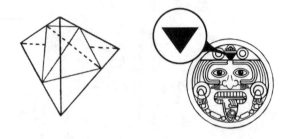

The Mexica were masters of tetrahedral geometry. The ratio of a tetrahedron to its inscribed sphere is two to one. The relationship of the sphere and the tetrahedron creates an octave. The ratio of the volume to the area of a tetrahedron is also 2:1. The tetrahedron creates an octave relationship with itself. A tetrahedron inscribed within a sphere touches the surface of the sphere at the its apex and at 19.47 degrees of latitude. This location plays a very prominent role in the geography of every planet in our solar system.

It's an interesting coincidence that 1947 is exactly one Mexican century of 52 years before 1999. Did anything significant happen in that year? The only seemingly important global events in 1947 were the breaking of the sound barrier, the discovery of the element *Promethium*, the discovery of the Dead Sea Scrolls... and the division of India and Pakistan.

Spiral of the Virgins

Prime number: Having no integral factors except itself and unity. Having no common measure other than unity. A prime number can be divided only by itself and one.

In the earthy and esoteric language of the sorcerers, prime numbers are called *Virgin numbers*. Prime numbers are Virgins because they only let themselves and God get inside them.

There's an amazing thing about prime numbers. Each one is completely unique. Since they can be expressed only by one and themselves, they're the atoms of the number world. They're the elements of numbers, because you can't reduce them. Prime numbers are primal numbers. They're essential qualities.

If you examine the primes as a whole, you'll discover an interesting pattern. This pattern is called the *Spiral of the Virgins*.

Here's how you find it: if you begin counting the list of all whole numbers from zero to infinity, the number of prime numbers you'll find decreases as the numbers you're counting increase in size. The distribution of prime numbers follows the spiral of the natural logarithm. The natural logarithm is *Euler's number*, e.*

Since all physical phenomena conform to laws involving the natural logarithm, the frequency and distribution pattern of the prime numbers have measurable relationships with all physical phenomena.** The virginal quality of the prime numbers winds through the sequence of all numbers in a logarithmic spiral.

If you take a deeper look into the Spiral of the Virgins, something incredible, something miraculous happens. Except for the numbers 1, 2 and 3, prime numbers always occur in pairs around a multiple of six. Any number showing up next to a six that isn't a prime

---

*e=2.718...The number of prime numbers is x/e times x. The prime numbers have a definite relationship with e, the natural logarithm.

**Nature seems to use prime numbers and prime number sequences in the creation of life. Johnson Yan gives an excellent explanation of how the prime number sequence relates with the nucleotide sequences of DNA in his <u>DNA and the I Ching</u>.[1] Dr. Peter Plitcha discusses his version of the Spiral of the Virgins in his book, <u>God's Secret Formula</u>.[2] He calls it the *Prime Number Cross*, and relates it to many chemical and physical phenomena.

number is either a square number, or the product of two earlier prime numbers. The entire sequence of numbers is a logarithmic spiral around prime number twins. This spiral weaves like two serpents alternating between the qualities of the square, and the qualities of a spiraling logarithmic sequence. The Spiral of the Virgins embodies the synthesis of the square law and the cube law.

Because of the relationship of the square numbers and the prime numbers, the Spiral of the Virgins appears to blossom from the basic nature of space itself. The prime numbers are even more elemental than atomic structures. They're attractors. The sequence of all numbers expresses the living qualities of the spiral. Are numbers the backbone of life? Are numbers alive?

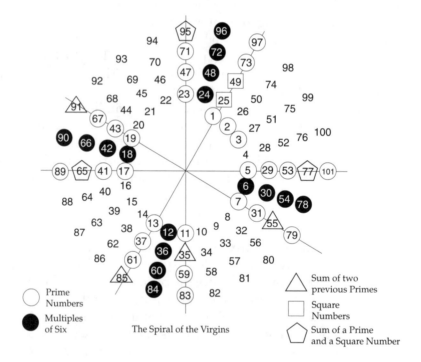

The Spiral of the Virgins

Prime Numbers

Multiples of Six

Sum of two previous Primes

Square Numbers

Sum of a Prime and a Square Number

Prime numbers are born as twin pairs around multiples of six. Any number next to a multiple of six that isn't prime is either a square number, the sum of two earlier primes or the sum of a prime and a square number. The primes naturally divide the circle into four sections with sixes marking the quarters. The Spiral of the Virgins arranges itself in rings of eight primes, or four pairs of twins.

The Mexica sought for and were aware of patterns in numbers and relationships between them.

The structure of the number six in the sequence of numbers gives us a beautiful logarithmic spiral. Six rules the 1 dimensional line by the golden section created by the 6x6=36 degree angle of the pentagram. (Fig. 312) Six also rules the 2 dimensional surface through the optimum efficiency of the hexagon in dividing spaces. (Fig. 313) Six rules 3 dimensional volume via its doubled octave form of twelve in spherical packing arrangements. (Fig. 314) The number six rules 4 dimensional spacetime through the logarithmic spiral of prime numbers. (Fig. 315)

Fig. 312   Fig. 313   Fig. 314   Fig. 315

The Xiucoatl enter reality with sixes on their tails. They are a mirror reflection on either side of multiples of six. The Xiucoatl are the prime numbers.

The Exercises

Doing the Exercises

Whoever you believe you are, you have an indigenous side to you. Let it live.

Your ancestors did special practices to keep in touch and in tune with themselves and their world. Living oral traditions preserved and passed on some of these practices for generation after generation, and we can still benefit from them today.

Your life can become more magical and interesting through the simple practice of these exercises. They can open up an incredible universe for you if you allow them to. They can help you understand and embody for yourself the origin and substance of both scripture and science. They can help you experience how refinement is more powerful than brutish power. They can help you learn how to combine your sensitivity with right timing to take appropriate action in the world, and manifest your creativity in the best possible ways.

These exercises may seem very simple to you at first. Even though they appear to be easy on the surface, it takes a lifetime to master them. The work involved is mostly internal. You can use these practices to help you refine conflicts and contradictions out of yourself. This process will help you to embody your essential self more coherently. The more clearly you can live from this coherency, the more effective, potent and long lived you and your actions will be.

Doing these practices will help you enhance your awareness of natural energy fields. Increasing your sensitivity this way may lead you to a heightened ability to regenerate and heal yourself, and an increased capacity to heal and nurture others.

If you choose to go deeply into the study and practice of these exercises, you will, over time, unlock a potential for genius within you. You may even attain the rapture of the saints and a deep mystical understanding of the oneness of all things. If you can integrate and develop any of the qualities of this philosophy, you'll have the basis for a very fulfilling lifelong practice of personal evolution.

Doing these exercises is extremely practical. It won't earn you academic accolades, but, in the real world, you'll have the right stuff. You don't need to depend on any special teachers or masters to do these practices. There's no need to go through any more initiations than you've gone through already. You can benefit from these teachings in an everyday way. There's no need to go to unusual extremes.

You may experience embarrassment, shame, pain, frustration or boredom when you practice. This is similar to the special kind of embarrassment some people feel when they try to sing in front of others. Singing reveals a certain nakedness of the inner self. These kinds of sensations are directly proportional to the degree your indigenous nature has been repressed. Therefore, the more you feel any of these inhibitions, the more you stand to gain from doing the exercises.

Your mind doesn't have to "get" the practices. They're definitely not about that. Experiment with them. Make them your own.

Getting in touch with your indigenous self doesn't mean jumping up and down and becoming a human didgeridoo. The rapid depolarization of control you may experience when you do your practice isn't the indigenous part. All that stuff is just on the way to your becoming more indigenous as you shake off all your old baggage. The state of being indigenous defines refinement and perfection. It can express itself through you in any form. Whatever shape it takes will be full, perfect and evolving.

Religious training may have taught you to believe your indigenous nature is evil. Please be patient with yourself as you practice. Most of us have a deep fear of freedom when we get really close to it. Relax. Your indigenous self is naturally virtuous. These practices are safe and self-regulating. They'll teach you how to be flexible in your mind and body. They create a structured and safe environment to help you let go of rigid control. Rigidity in any form constitutes a loss of the essential principle you're developing. If you go into any single exercise too narrowly, your benefits will begin to diminish until you shift the emphasis of your practice. This is a self-correcting and self-balancing system. Practice different exercises at different times.

You don't need to wade through libraries of written material to master this art. All you need to do is practice. You may believe you don't have the time to do these exercises. Of course you don't have time to do the exercises! The entire modern world is predicated on the fact that you don't have time to do the exercises. Do the exercises. When you make your practice a priority, you'll suddenly, magically, have the time. Here's a secret: the exercises give you more time when you practice them. They help you become more connected, coherent, and efficient. They're an investment of energy. Hold an attitude of investing your time and energy. Do you invest more time than you spend? Or do you spend more time than you invest?

There's no right or wrong way to do the exercises. None of them is more important or advanced than any others. They all build on and connect with one another. Familiarize yourself with all of them. Practice whichever one is right for you in the moment.

Beware of the "can't" syndrome. This means rather than practicing and investing your energy in a creative direction, you become discouraged and just give up. Remember what you're doing and persevere. Be creative. Have fun with the process.

If you're chronically depleted, do whatever you need to do to get out of your state of exhaustion. Build your energy back up. Become healthy and aware. Follow your spirit. Create your dreams.

If you're tired, rest or sleep. If you're hungry, eat. If you're thirsty, drink. If you want to retrieve your indigenous self, it's helpful to learn how to listen to, understand and follow your natural impulses. Most of us closed off our perceptions of these impulses when we were young. It takes time and patience to reactivate them.

This practice doesn't negate or override your mind. You're always in control of what's happening. Your mind allows the many aspects of yourself to come together and integrate in a constructive and responsible place.

Practice isn't about forcing yourself to do anything. It's a dialogue between you and your energy that develops an intimate relationship over time. Practice is there for you to discover, cultivate and refine your relationship with yourself and your environment. Refining your sense of self is your best guide and protection in every life situation.

Doing your practice realigns you with your indigenous nature. It helps you ritually return to nature's simplicity. As you return, all things will naturally converge into great good fortune for you.

Psychotherapists and musicologists from all around the world have noticed an interesting coincidence: there's a point in deep healing where people begin speaking what sounds like an indigenous language. Don't be concerned if this happens to you when you're practicing. Just let it do its thing and run its natural course.

Centuries of repressed expression can come out of the closet and live when you do these exercises. Go slowly. You have plenty of time. We've repressed our indigenous selves, our connections with God and with nature for a very long time. The great collective neurosis of the modern mind wasn't built in a day. Let it dissolve organically.

Modern definitions of psychological and mental health and disease come to us from Euro- and Judeocentric value systems. They have little or no validity in other cultural contexts. Let them go when you're practicing. True mental and emotional health can accept, enjoy and integrate a wild nature and the bliss of the irrational. Keep your dialogue open between the rational and the irrational. If you get locked statically into one or the other, it can lead to challenges.

Your practice is never over. You're not going to get a colorful belt or a certificate for practicing. All you'll receive is a constant process of growth. Each step you take is a magnificent accomplishment.

The Exercises

Your life will improve when you do these exercises. You'll become happier, more intelligent, better looking, and more connected with a world you feel good about. Your ancestors developed and refined these tools since the dawn of humanity. These tools are your inheritance. It's an honor to practice them. Please respect them.

First, a couple of tips:

- 🦋 Take off your shoes whenever and wherever you can. Maintain your electrical contact with the Earth.
- 🦋 Don't overly define what your indigenous nature is. If your surface mind gets an exact definition, it will probably demonstrate a tendency to copy what it thinks you should be doing instead of just allowing you to be yourself.

🦋 1. Finding your spot.

Wherever you go in life, it's important to find your spot. Animals always gravitate to a *power spot* when they're recuperating, regenerating or just getting comfortable. It's easy to observe domestic cats and dogs doing it in their daily routines. They'll enter a space, and walk around inspecting it until they find just the right place to be. Once an animal finds its spot, it will stay there. The spot nourishes it and makes it strong.

Wherever you are right now, find your spot. Simply stroll around with a loose and unfocused mind. You'll notice as you do this the quality of the space you're in will come alive. It will begin to communicate with you. Nature returns when you appreciate it.

As you inspect your surroundings this way, you'll discover special places where you suddenly feel better or stronger than you did before. Another sensation you might have is similar to being stuck, glued or suctioned to the ground or the air around you. This is your spot.

You don't need to habituate one power spot. They can, and do, change and move around. Each time you practice, find your spot. Go to the place that's most comfortable for you whenever you practice. Go there, be there, and for the moment, unite with it.

🦋 2. Simple standing

Find your spot. Once you're there, close your eyes. Let go of everything. Blend with the space around you. Loosen your knees slightly and breathe naturally. Simply notice the sensations and impulses you have as you stand there. For now, just observe your impulses as they come and go. Don't act on them. Keep letting go of anything that comes up. You'll sense a natural rise and fall of whims, thoughts and feelings. Let them go.

Blend with the space until you sense it's time to stop. Then slowly open your eyes. Rub your palms together until they feel warm. Gently massage your face. Lightly stroke your entire body using downward motions. Begin at the top of your head. Work your way down to your feet. You are complete.

🦋 3. Allowing movement.

Find your spot. Once you're there, close your eyes. Let go of everything. Blend with the space around you. Loosen your knees slightly and breathe naturally. Simply notice the sensations and impulses you have as you stand there.

Let yourself become sensitive. Allow yourself to move naturally. Your body will refine its position and orient itself exactly the way it wants to. Any movement, from the most subtle to the most dramatic, is appropriate. There's no need to force anything. If your body wants to move, let it move. If it wants to be still, let it be still. Any position is fine.

Follow the rise and fall of your natural impulses until you sense it's time to stop. Then slowly open your eyes. Rub your palms together until they feel warm. Gently massage your face. Lightly stroke your entire body using downward motions. Begin at the top of your head. Work your way down to your feet. You are complete.

🪬 4. *Finding Your Indigenous Rhythm*

Find your spot. Once you're there, close your eyes. Let go of everything. Blend with the space around you. Loosen your knees slightly and breathe naturally. Simply notice the sensations and impulses you have as you stand there.

Let yourself become sensitive. Allow your hands to move naturally. Permit your deep indigenous self to use your hands to tap out its natural rhythm on your body. Any rhythm, from the most subtle to the most dramatic, is appropriate. There's no need to force anything. You don't have to hang on to any particular rhythm. Simply observe where it wants to go, and go there with it. If it wants to be loud, let it be loud. If it wants to be soft, let it be soft. Any rhythm is fine.

Follow the rise and fall of your natural impulses until you sense it's time to stop. Then slowly open your eyes. Rub your palms together until they feel warm. Gently massage your face. Lightly stroke your entire body using downward motions. Begin at the top of your head. Work your way down to your feet. You are complete.

✸ 5. *Finding Your Indigenous Voice*

Find your spot. Once you're there, close your eyes. Let go of everything. Blend with the space around you. Loosen your knees slightly and breathe naturally. Simply notice the sensations and impulses you have as you stand there.

Let yourself become sensitive. Allow your natural rhythm to come into your breath. Any rhythm of breathing, from the most subtle to the most dramatic, is appropriate. There's no need to force anything. You don't have to hang on to any particular rhythm. Simply observe where it wants to go, and go there with it.

If your voice wants to make sound, let it. Let your voice do what it wants to do. If it wants to be loud, let it be loud. If it wants to be soft, let it be soft. Any sound is fine. There's no need to force anything. If you want to sing, sing. If you want to scream, scream. If you want to be silent, be silent.

Follow the rise and fall of your natural impulses until you sense it's time to stop. Then slowly open your eyes. Rub your palms together until they feel warm. Gently massage your face. Lightly stroke your entire body using downward motions. Begin at the top of your head. Work your way down to your feet. You are complete.

✸ 6. *Four Directions*

Using a compass or the Pole Star, determine which way is North.

Find your spot. Once you're there, close your eyes. Let go of everything. Blend with the space around you. Loosen your knees slightly and breathe naturally. Simply notice the sensations and impulses you have as you stand there. Appreciate your spot for a while by doing exercise number one, two, three or four.

When you feel ready, slowly turn your whole body to the right until you face East. Let go of everything. Blend with the space around you. Blend with the energy of the East. If your body wants to move naturally, let it move. If it wants to stay still, let it. Remain in the East until you sense it's time to stop.

When you feel ready, slowly turn your whole body to the right until you face South. Let go of everything. Blend with the space around you. Blend with the energy of the South. If your body wants to move naturally, let it move. If it wants to stay still, let it. Remain in the South until you sense it's time to stop.

When you feel ready, slowly turn your whole body to the right until you face West. Let go of everything. Blend with the space around you. Blend with the energy of the West. If your body wants to move naturally, let it move. If it wants to stay still, let it. Remain in the West until you sense it's time to stop.

When you feel ready, slowly turn your whole body to the right until you face North. Let go of everything. Blend with the space around you. Blend with the energy of the North. If your body wants to move naturally, let it move. If it wants to stay still, let it. Remain in the North until you sense it's time to stop.

When you've completed each of the four

directions, slowly and sensitively turn your whole body to the right until you come into an exact natural resonance with your spot. Appreciate your spot for a while by doing exercise number one, two, three or four.

Follow the rise and fall of your natural impulses until you sense it's time to stop. Then slowly open your eyes. Rub your palms together until they feel warm. Gently massage your face. Lightly stroke your entire body using downward motions. Begin at the top of your head. Work your way down to your feet. You are complete.

7. *Thirteen Directions*

Using a compass or the Pole Star, determine which way is North.

Find your spot. Imagine your spot is at the exact center of a circle. The optimal radius of this circle is the distance of your outstretched arms.

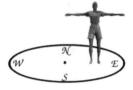

Standing at the center of this circle, close your eyes. Let go of everything. Blend with the space around you. Loosen your knees slightly and breathe naturally. Simply notice the sensations and impulses you have as you stand there. Appreciate your spot for a while by doing exercise number one, two, three or four.

When you feel ready, slowly turn your whole body to the right until you face East. Carefully and sensitively walk to the East edge of your circle, keeping the field of your awareness intact as you go. Let go of everything. Blend with the space around you. Blend with the energy of the East. If your body wants to move naturally, let it move. If it wants to stay still, let it. Remain in the East until you sense it's time to stop.

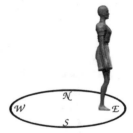

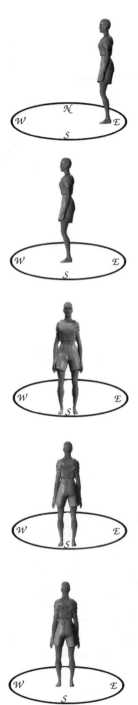

When you feel ready, slowly turn your whole body to the right 180 degrees until your back faces East, and you're facing your spot at the center of the circle. Let go of everything. Blend with the space around you. Blend with the energy of the East. If your body wants to move naturally, let it move. If it wants to stay still, let it. Remain in the East until you sense it's time to stop.

When you feel ready, carefully and sensitively walk back to the center of your circle, keeping the field of your awareness intact as you go. Appreciate your spot for a while by doing exercise number one, two, three or four.

When you feel ready, slowly turn your whole body to the left until you face South. Carefully and sensitively walk to the South edge of your circle, keeping the field of your awareness intact as you go. Let go of everything. Blend with the space around you. Blend with the energy of the South. If your body wants to move naturally, let it move. If it wants to stay still, let it. Remain in the South until you sense it's time to stop.

When you feel ready, slowly turn your whole body to the right 180 degrees until your back faces South, and you're facing your spot at the center of the circle. Let go of everything. Blend with the space around you. Blend with the energy of the South. If your body wants to move naturally, let it move. If it wants to stay still, let it. Remain in the South until you sense it's time to stop.

When you feel ready, carefully and sensitively walk back to the center of your circle, keeping the field of your awareness intact as you go. Appreciate your spot for a while by doing exercise number one, two, three or four.

When you feel ready, slowly turn your whole body to the left until you face West. Carefully and sensitively walk to the West edge of your circle, keeping the field of your awareness intact as you go. Let go of everything. Blend with the space around you. Blend with the energy of the West. If your body wants to move naturally, let it move. If it wants to stay still, let it. Remain in the West until you sense it's time to stop.

When you feel ready, slowly turn your whole body to the right 180 degrees until your back faces West, and you're facing your spot at the center of the circle. Let go of everything. Blend with the space around you. Blend with the energy of the West. If your body wants to move naturally, let it move. If it wants to stay still, let it. Remain in the West until you sense it's time to stop.

When you feel ready, carefully and sensitively walk back to the center of your circle, keeping the field of your awareness intact as you go. Appreciate your spot for a while by doing exercise number one, two, three or four.

When you feel ready, slowly turn your whole body to the left until you face North. Carefully and sensitively walk to the North edge of your circle, keeping the field of your awareness intact as you go. Let go of everything. Blend with the space around you. Blend with the energy of the North. If your body wants to move naturally, let it move. If it wants to stay still, let it. Remain in the North until you sense it's time to stop.

When you feel ready, slowly turn your whole body to the right 180 degrees until your back faces North, and you're facing your spot at the center of the circle. Let go of everything. Blend with the space around you. Blend with the energy of the North. If your body wants to

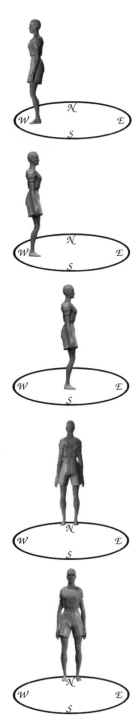

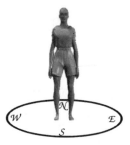

move naturally, let it move. If it wants to stay still, let it. Remain in the North until you sense it's time to stop.

When you feel ready, carefully and sensitively walk back to the center of your circle, keeping the field of your awareness intact as you go. Appreciate your spot for a while by doing exercise number one, two, three or four.

Follow the rise and fall of your natural impulses until you sense it's time to stop. Then slowly open your eyes. Rub your palms together until they feel warm. Gently massage your face. Lightly stroke your entire body using downward motions. Begin at the top of your head. Work your way down to your feet. You are complete.

Someone who stands in the center of his or her being is always the model of the adept, the sage, the person of wisdom and power.

Cult Busters

As our public awareness of energy fields and alternate realities grows, there are increasing numbers of energy masters- and complete charlatans- coming out into the public to teach.

Our modern culture trains us to be sitting ducks for all kinds of quackery and fakery. The gaping holes in our modern psychology are screaming to be filled. Charlatans all around the world are well aware of our situation, and they're emigrating in droves to turn our innocence to their advantage.

We're all very new to the world of energy. Getting taken by a charlatan is easier than you may think. Beware of the bogus. Fortunately, it's easy to identify a charlatan, false guru or cult. Run any situation you find yourself in through the following questions to see where you stand. You may be surprised at what you discover. Make your evaluations, and take appropriate action.

- Do the people you're involved with demand secrecy of you in any way?

- Do they ask you for endless amounts of money, especially under the guise of taking you to "new spiritual levels?"

- Do they want to marry you so they can change their citizenship?

- Do they spend more than ten percent of their time talking about themselves?

○ Do they coerce, scare or intimidate you in any way?

○ Do they use your sense of guilt to their advantage?

○ Do they manipulate you in any way?

○ Do they speak pseudo-spiritual drivel to manipulate you?

○ Do they purposefully make you feel less than in any way?

○ Do they claim a right to anything based on their heritage, "lineage," ancestry, racial or cultural background?

○ Do they tell you their way is the only way?

○ Do they tell you their way is the best way?

○ Do they tell you you'll be part of a "special group" if you do what they say?

○ Do they lack humor in their interactions?

○ Are they critical of people who don't follow their teaching?

○ Are they habitually angry, or rigidly fixed in any other emotion?

○ Are they on some kind of superiority or inferiority trip?

○ Do their words contradict their actions?

If they demonstrate any of the above to you, be thankful. They've shown you they have no true development. Get out of there as fast and as completely as you can. If they threaten you, call the police and make a report. If the police are involved with the cult, do whatever you have to do to save yourself. Get as far out of town as you can, immediately. Tell everyone you know exactly what happened. Break the silence. Remember, they have no power. They can't harm you in any way.

Many of these groups want you to join forces with them. Their financial livelihood depends on it. The truth can never be reached in these organizations, because everyone is literally invested in their own point of view. This is particularly true of the American New Age movement, which has somehow utterly confounded the concepts of spirituality and marketing. The people involved often depend on the financial success of the group in order to survive. They are completely attached to the outcome of their process in every way.

Does the group encourage you to let go of your personal desires? Do they want you to give everything to them? Do they emphasize devotion to the group rather than cultivating your own devotion and personal relationship with God and your own spiritual essence? More manipulation happens in the name of impersonality and spiritual progress than all other reasons combined. You're the only one who can know what your sacrifice is. Nobody else can tell you what to do.

Do they try to force you into a mold of who they want you to be? Or do they help you become all you *can* be?

Many of these groups train people to conform to a typical cancer profile. The *cancer personality* is characterized by self-pity, self-deprecation, passivity, a compulsion to please, and the inability to rise from depression after a traumatic event.[3] Cancer cells differentiate into a more primal state than normal cells. Cancer is often a frustrated expression of a repressed indigenous nature that isn't allowed to express itself in any other way. People who compromise themselves get cancer. The more compromised a person is, the more likely it is he or she is developing cancer. The modern world is riddled with it. The more modern the life style, the more cancerous its people have become.

There are some basic differences between a cult and a group of friends. A cult coerces or forces its members into having the same beliefs. If you don't believe, they force you to believe, or they force you out of the cult. This process can be extremely oblique and persuasive. They can mask it in a variety of ways so you don't even know it's happening. Most people involved with a cult don't realize it until after they escape.

A group of friends is totally different. You can believe anything you want in a group of friends. The group acknowledges, accepts and appreciates the diversity of its members. Nothing needs to control the group in any way to keep it together. It is together.

True authority is distinguished by two things: humility and humor. Humor is the context of wisdom. Lack of humor is diagnostic of ignorance and repressive control.

You can spot a cult by two things: arrogance, and a group of people who want to attach themselves to an authority figure in order to gain a sense of protection and power for themselves. Most cults know to look for people who are desperate for an authority figure to tell them what to do. These systems thrive on and reinforce deep passivity. The cult leaders use these feelings to hierarchize their perceived relationships with others. They do whatever they can to control their environment. This situation leads to a paradoxical reversing of energy. The true power of the cult leader desiccates over time. Anyone's best parts would wither in such a controlled and rigid environment.

These groups encourage you to pass both blame and praise onto the authority figure, rather than taking it yourself. They tend not to develop your own sense of accountability and self respect. When the right time comes, you'll know and live your truth from within. Humility is a natural dimension of power. Sincere humility doesn't have a rigid structure. It can't be enforced. Learn to respect natural wisdom again. You're ultimately responsible for yourself. If you don't choose to exercise your right of responsibility, other people will be happy to make your decisions for you. For a price.

Are you putting up with abuse in any form? Why? Train yourself to have unconditional self-respect.

Do you do what you know is right, or do you just do what you're told? Teach yourself to rely on what you personally sense is the truth rather than going on hearsay. Educate yourself.

Find your own natural level of associations. Don't allow yourself to be lured into relationships of convenience. Do your friends help you create a positive future? Do they encourage you to improve your life, or do they just commiserate with you and lament your so-called fate? Do the people around you support you, or do they bring you down?

Ferret out victimized psychology at its roots. End bottomless passivity in all forms. Check yourself for negation or sarcasm that goes beyond healthy and good humored discernment. If it's present, you're upset about something. Find out what it is and deal with it.

Are you stuck in rigid, endlessly repeating patterns, or are you creative, successful and having fun? Return yourself to common sense and leave behind convention. Check every situation you encounter for competency and accountability.

How does your daily life reflect cosmic order? Seek out those of wisdom, and seek your wisdom within. There are no more chosen ones. We're all in this together.

Chief Seattle's Reply

1854 - United States President Franklin Pierce makes an offer to purchase a large portion of Indian land. This is Chief Seattle's reply.

How can you buy or sell the sky, the warmth of the land? The idea is strange to us. If we do not own the freshness of the air and the sparkle of the water, how can you buy them?

Every part of this Earth is sacred to my people. Every shining pine needle, every sandy shore, every mist in the dark woods, every clearing and humming insect is holy in the memory and experience of my people. The sap which courses through the trees carries the memories of the red man.

The white man's dead forget the country of their birth when they go to walk among the stars. Our dead never forget this beautiful Earth, for it is the mother of the red man. We are part of the Earth and it is a part of us. The perfumed flowers are our sisters; the deer, the horse, the great eagle, these are our brothers. The rocky crests, the juices in the meadows, the body heat of the pony, and man-all belong to the same family.

So when the Great Chief in Washington sends word that he wishes to buy our land, he asks much of us. The Great Chief sends word he will reserve us a place so that we can live comfortably to ourselves. He will be our father and we will be his children. So we will consider your offer to buy our land. But it will not be easy. For this land is sacred to us.

This shining water that moves in the streams and the rivers is not just water but the blood of our ancestors. If we sell you land you must remember that it is sacred, and you must teach your children that it is sacred and that each ghostly reflection in the clear water of the lakes tells of events and memories in the life of my people. The water's murmur is the voice of my father's father.

The rivers are our brothers, they quench our thirst. The rivers carry our canoes, and feed our children. If we sell you our land, you must remember, and teach your children, that the rivers are our brothers, and yours, and you must henceforth give the rivers the kindness you would give any brother.

We know that the white man does not understand our ways. One portion of land is the same to him as the next, for he is a stranger who comes in the night and takes from the land whatever he needs. The Earth is not his brother but his enemy, and when he has conquered it, he moves on. He leaves his father's graves and his children's birthright is forgotten. He treats his mother, the Earth, and his brother, the Sky, as things to be bought, plundered, sold like sheep or bright beads. His appetite will devour the Earth and leave behind only a desert.

I do not know. Our ways are different from your ways. The sight of your cities pains the eyes of the red man. But perhaps it is because the red man is a savage and does not understand.

There is no quiet place in the white man's cities. No place to hear the unfurling of leaves in spring, or the rustle of an insect's wings. But perhaps it is because the red man is a savage and does not understand. The clatter only seems to insult the ears. And what is there to life if a man can not hear the lonely cry of the whippoorwill or the arguments of the frogs around a pond at night? I am a red man and do not understand. The Indian prefers the soft sound of the wind darting over the face of a pond, and the smell of the wind itself, cleansed by the rain or scented with the pine cone.

The air is precious to the red man, for all things share the same breath: the beast, the tree, the man, they all share the same breath. The white men, they all share the same breath. The white man does not seem to notice the air he breathes. Like a man dying for many days, he is numb to the stench. But if we sell you our land, you must remember that the air is precious to us, that the air shares its spirit with all the life it supports. The wind that gave our grandfather his first breath also received his last sigh. And if we sell you our land, you must keep it apart and sacred, as a place where even the white man can go and taste the wind that is sweetened by the meadow's flowers.

So we will consider your offer to buy our land. If we decide to accept I will make one condition. The white man must treat the beasts of this land as his brothers.

I am a savage and I do not understand any other way. I have seen a thousand rotting buffaloes on the prairie, left by the white man who shot them from a passing train. I am a savage and I do not understand how the smoking iron horse can be more important than the buffalo that we kill only to stay alive.

What is man without the beasts? If all the beasts were gone, man would die from a great loneliness of spirit. For whatever happens to the beasts, soon happens to man. All things are connected.

You must teach your children that the ground beneath their feet is the ashes of our grandfathers. So that they will respect the land, tell your children that the Earth is rich with the lives of our kin. Teach your children what we have taught our children, that the Earth is our mother. Whatever befalls the Earth befalls the sons of the Earth. Man did not weave the web of life, he is merely a strand in it. Whatever he does to the web, he does to himself.

Even the white man, whose God walks and talks with him as friend to friend, cannot be exempt from the common destiny. We may be brothers after all. We shall see. One thing we know, which the white man may one day discover-our God is the same God. You may think now that you own him as you wish to own our land; but you cannot. He is the God of man and his compassion is equal for the red man and the white. This Earth is precious to him, and to harm the Earth is to heap contempt upon its Creator. The whites, too, shall pass; perhaps sooner than all other tribes. Contaminate your bed, and you will one night suffocate in your own waste.

But in your perishing, you will shine brightly, fired by the strength of the God who brought you to this land and for some special purpose gave you dominion over this land and over the red man. That destiny is a mystery to us, for we do not understand when all the buffalo are slaughtered, the wild horses are tamed, the secret corners of the forest heavy with the scent of many men, and the view of the ripe hills blotted out by talking wires. Where is the thicket? Gone. Where is the eagle? Gone.

References

The Call, Inquisition, Come Together and The Birth of Science

1. Tompkins, Peter, *Mysteries of the Mexican Pyramids*, p. 25.
2. *Ibid.*, p. 16.
3. Meyer, Michael and William Sherman, *The Course of Mexican History*, p. 87.
4. Bray, Warwick, *Everyday Life of the Aztecs*, p. 111.
5. Meyer, *op. cit.*, p. 79.
6. Gomora, Xokonochtletl Antonio, *Juicio a Espana*, Mexico,Tlamatini, 1988.
7. Bray, *op. cit.*, pp. 75-80, 92, 147-151.
8. Oxford English Dictionary
9. Tompkins, *op. cit.*, p. 5.
10. Searle, S., "*The Church points the Way*," *The New Scientist 3*, January, 1974
11. Michell, *op. cit.*
12. Moctezuma, Eduardo Matos, *Treasures of the Great Temple*, p.149-151.
13. Tompkins, *op. cit.*, p. 217.
14. *Ibid.*, p. 253-5.
15. *Ibid.*, p.p. 279-80.
16. *Ibid.*, p. 264-75.
17. *Ibid.*, p. 241-52.
18. Harleston, Hugh Jr., "*A Mathematical Analysis of Teotihuacan,*" Mexico City, XLI International Congress of Americanists, October 3, 1974.
19. Brennan, Martin, *The Hidden Maya.*
20. Johnson, Charles William, *Science and Ancient Artwork* http//www.earthmatrix.com
21. Oxford English Dictionary
22. Einstein, Albert, *The World as I See It.* New York, Philosophical Library, 1934.
23. Oxford English Dictionary
24. Cook, Theodore Andrea, *The Curves of Life,* New York, Dover Publications, 1979.
25. Oxford English Dictionary
26. Tompkins, *op. cit.*, p. 11.

Preparations for Your Journey

1. Tompkins, *op. cit.*, p. 34.
2. Feigenbaum, Mitchell J., "Quantitative Universality for a Class of Nonlinear Transformations," *Journal of Statistical Physics*, 1978.
3. Henri Poincare, late 1800s.
4. Hodgkin, Huxley and Eccles, in Briggs and Peat, *Turbulent Mirror,* p. 129.
5. Berendt, Joachim-Ernst, *The World is Sound - Nada Brahma.*
6. *Ibid.*
7. Jenny, Hans, *Cymatics, Volume 2*, p. 112.
8. *Ibid.*, p. 41 ff.
9. This research began with Gustav Fetchner in 1876, and has been reconfirmed hundreds of times ever since.

Your Journey

1. Translated by Eduardo Matos Moctezuma, from *Treasures of the Great Temple*, p. 95.
2. Hawking, Stephen, *A Brief History of Time*, New York, Bantam, 1988.
3. Niels Bohr, 1913. from Plichta, Peter, *God's Secret Formula*, p.160.
4. Berendt, Joachim-Ernst, *The World is Sound - Nada Brahma*, p. 67 ff.
5. John Newlands, 1864.
6. These have become generic phrases in common use among physicists.
7. Briggs and Peat, *op. cit.*, pp. 62-65.
8. Andrew Strominger, 1995, in Ferris, *op. cit.*,p. 227.
9. Edwin Hubble, 1929, *Ibid.*, p. 45.
10. James Hartle and Stephen Hawking, 1982. *Ibid, p. 251.*
11. Andrei Linde , 1990, *Ibid.* p,244.
12. Berendt, *op. cit.*, p. 106.
13. David Bohm, *Wholeness and the Implicate Order,* 1980.
14. John Wheeler and Richard Feynman, 1965, in Ferris, *op. cit.,* p. 287.
15. *Ibid.*, p. 121.
16. Steven Weinberg, *The First Three Minutes,* New York, Basic Books, 1977.
17. KAM, 1954, in Briggs and Peat, *op. cit.*, pp. 123-5.
18. Goncharov, Moroz, and Mokarov in Tompkins, *op. cit.*, p. 326.
19. Smith, Cyril W. and Best, Simon, *Electromagnetic Man, Health and Hazard in the Electrical Environment,* London, p. 271.
20. Lovelock, J.E. *Gaia: A New Look at Life on Earth.* Oxford, Oxford University Press, 1979.
21. Gerhart, J.C., et.al, 1981, *A Reinvestigation of the Role of the Gray Crescent in Axis Formation in Xenopus Laevis,* Nature, 292:511-516.
22. Dubrov, A.P. *The Geomagnetic Field and Life: Geomagnetobiology,* N.Y, Plenum Press, 1978.
23. Matsumoto, Kiiko and Birch, Stephen, *Hara Diagnosis: Reflections on the Sea,* p. 181 ff.
24. S. Ingvar, 1920, in Becker and Selden, *op. cit.*, p. 86.
25. Smith and Best, *op. cit.*, p. 62.
26. Developed by Dr. Chao Chen, China and Dr. Richard Teh Fu Tan, San Diego, California.
27. Briggs and Peat, *op. cit.*, pp. 128-9.
28. Nordenstrom, Bjorn" Biologically closed Electrical Circuits: Clinical, Experimental and Theoretical Evidence for an Additional Circulatory System" also G. Taubes, "An Electrifying Possibility," *Discover,* April 1986, 22-37.
29. Berendt, *op. cit.*, p. 68.
30. Plichta, *op. cit.*, p. 97.
31. D'Adamo, *op. cit.*
32. Becker, Robert and Selden, Gary, *The Body Electric*, p. 140.
33. Linas, 1982.
34. Hebb, D. O., *The Organization of Behavior: A Neuropsychological Theory,* New York, John Wiley, 1949.
35. Freeman, Walter and Skarda, Christine, "Spatial EEG Patterns, Nonlinear Dynamics and Perception: The Neo-Sherrington View," *Brain Research Review, 10* (1985)
36. Changeux, J-P., *Neuronal man: The biology of the mind.* L. Garey (Trans.), New York, Pantheon, 1985.
37. Becker and Selden, *op. cit.*, p. 240.
38. Malsburg, C. von der (1986). *Am I Thinking Assemblies?* In G Palm & A Aersen (Eds.), *Brain Theory* (pp.161-176). Berlin: Springer-Verlag.
39. Edelman, Gerald, "Group Selection as the Basis for Higher Brain Function," in *The Organization of the Cerebral Cortex,* F. O. Schmitt et al, eds., Cambridge, MIT Press, 1983.
40. Freeman and Skarda, *op. cit.*, p. 147.
41. Garfinkle, Alan, "A Mathematics for Physiology," *AmericanPhysiological Society,* 1983.

42. Louis Kervran in his *Biological Transformations*, (Brooklyn: Swan House Publishing Company, 1972) and Peter Tompkins and Christopher Bird in *The Secret Life of Plants* (England: Penguin Books, 1973) have shown that true alchemical transformation of elements can occur within biological systems.
43. Smith and Best, *op. cit.*, p. 63.
44. Becker and Selden, *op. cit.*, pp. 239-40.
45. *Ibid.*, p. 240.
46. Smith and Best, *op. cit.*, p. 312.
47. *Ibid., p. 64.*
48. Jenny, *op. cit.*, p. 53.
49. Frohlich Herbert, 1975, "The Extraordinary Dielectric Properties of Biological Molecules and the Action of Enzymes,"*Proceedings of the National Academy of Science*, U.S.A., 72, pp.4211-15.
50. Smith and Best, *op. cit.*, p. 52.
51. *Ibid.*, p. 26.
52. *Ibid.*, p. 87.
53. Mishra, Jussal, Ludwig and many others.
54. Maman, Fabien, *The Role of Music in the Twenty-First Century*, Redondo Beach, California, Tama Do Press, 1997.
55. Charles Thornton, 1954, in Becker and Selden, *op. cit.*, p.56.
56. A. M. Sinyukhin, 1958, *Ibid.*, p. 61.
57. Dr. Robert Becker and many others have investigated this function of the reticular activating system extensively. For more information, please refer to Dr. Becker's book, *The Body Electric*, New York, Quill, 1985.
58. Matsumoto and Birch, *op. cit.*, pp. 9-13.
59. Harold Burr, *The Fields of Life*, New York, Ballantine Books, 1972.
60. Smith and Best, *op. cit.*, p. 55.
61. W.E. Burge, 1939, in Becker and Selden, *op. cit.*, p. 88.
62. Smith and Best, *op. cit.*, p. 30.
63. Popp, F.A., *Electromagnetic Bio-Information*, 2nd edition 1988, Munich, Urban & Schwarzenberg, 1988.
64. Li, K. H., "Physical Basis of Coherent Radiations from Biomolecules, "*Proceedings of the 1st International Symposium on Photon Emission from Biological Systems*, Wroclaw, Poland, January 24-26, 1986, pp. 63-95.
65. Smith and Best, *op. cit.*, pp. 38-9.
66. *Ibid.*, p. 222.
67. *Ibid.*, pp. 91-2.
68. McClintock, Barbara, 1983, in Briggs and Peat, *op. cit.*, p. 161.
69. Cairns, John,1988, *ibid.*, p. 161.
70. Science News, 1984 , Swicord, M.L. & Davis, C.C., 1983, *Bioelectromagnetics*, *4(1)*, 21-42.
71. Smith and Best, *op. cit.*, p. 142.
72. Keeton, W.T., 1979, "Avian Orientation and Navigation," *Brit. Birds*, *72*, pp.451-70.
73. R. Robin Baker, 1983, in Becker and Selden, *op. cit.*, pp. 254-5.
74. *Science*, June 1959.
75. Wever, R. A., 1985, "The Electromagnetic Environment and the Circadian Rhythms of Human Subjects," in Grandolfo, M., Michaelson, S.M. and Rindi, A. (eds.), *Static and E.L.F. Electromagnetic Fields: Biological Effects and Dosimetry*, New York, Plenum.
76. Perry, F. S., Reichmanis, M., Marino, A.A. and Becker, R.O., 1981, "Environmental Power-Frequency Magnetic Fields and Suicide," *Health Physics*, 41, pp. 267-77.
77. Dubrov, A.P., *The Geomagnetic Field & Life: Geomagnetobiology*, New York, Plenum, 1978.
78. Frank Brown and Rutger Wever in Becker and Selden, *op. cit.*, pp. 245-9 and Smith and Best, *op. cit.*
79. Schmitt, F. O., et al, eds. *Functional Linkage in Biomolecular Systems*, New York, Raven Press, 1975.

80. Becker and Selden, *op. cit.*, p. 319.
81. F. E. Cole and E. R. Graf, 1974, in Becker and Selden, *op. cit.*, pp. 258-9.
82. Lakhovsky, G., *The Secret of Life*, tr. Clement, M., London, Heinemann, 1939.
83. This research came from a brilliant ten year study that involved many participants from all around the world. Piccardi, G., *The Chemical Basis of Medical Climatology*, Springfield, Ill., C. C. Thomas, 1962.
84. Brown, F.A. *Biological Clocks*, Boston, Heath, 1962.
85. Bradley, D. A., Woodbury, M. A. and Brier, G. W., 1962,"Lunar Synodical Period and Widespread Precipitation," *Science*, 137, pp. 748-9.
86. Burr, H. S. and Northrop, F. S., 1935, "The Electromagnetic Field Theory," *Quarterly Review of Biology*, 10, pp. 322-33.
87. Ravitz, L. J.,1951, "Comparative Clinical and Electrocyclical Observations of Twin Brothers Concordant as to Schizophrenia," *Journal of Nervous and Mental Diseases*, 121, pp. 72-87.
88. Tromp, Solco, 1975, "Possible Geophysical Causes of Long Term Fluctuations in Blood Sedimentation Rate Patterns in the World," *Journal of Interdisciplinary Cycle Research*, 6(1), pp. 71-2.
89. Kollerstrom, N., *Astrochemistry*, Frome, Urania Trust, 1984.
90. Seymour, P.A.H., *Cosmic Magnetism*, Bristol:Adam Hilger.1986.
91. McGillion, F., *The Opening Eye*, London, Coventure, 1980.
92. Matsumoto and Birch, *op. cit.*, p. 192.

Countdown

1. Robert Fenwick, Academy of Celestial and Mundane Arts, Santa Cruz, California, Telephone: (831) 471-0388; Fax (831) 471-0688.
2. Vernon Mahabal, Director, Planetary Palmistry Institute, Oakland, California, Telephone: (510) 339-3765 and 1-(800) 221-0441

Appendices

1. Yan, Johnson, F., *DNA and the I Ching.*

2. Plichta, Peter, *God's Secret Formula.*

3. Dr. Caroline Bedell Thomas, 1946, in Becker and Selden, *op. cit.*, p. 221.

Bibliography

Alba, Victor, *The Horizon Concise History of Mexico*, New York: American Heritage Publishing, 1973.

Alexanderson, Olaf, *Living Water*, United Kingdom: Gateway Books, 1979.

Barefoot, Robert R. and Reich, Carl M.D., *The Calcium Factor*, Arizona: Bokar Consultants, 1992.

Beck, Barbara L., *The Aztecs*, New York: Franklin Watts, 1983.

Becker, Robert O. and Selden, Gary, *The Body Electric*, New York: Quill, 1985.

Berendt, Joachim-Ernst, *The World is Sound - Nada Brahma*, Rochester, Vermont: Destiny Books, 1983.

Braden, Gregg, *Awakening to Zero Point*, Bellevue, Washington: Radio Bookshop Press, 1993.

Bray, Warwick, *Everyday Life of the Aztecs*, New York: G.P. Putnam's Sons, 1968.

Brennan, Martin, *The Hidden Maya*, Santa Fe, New Mexico: Bear & Company Publishing, 1998.

Briggs, John and Peat, David F., *Turbulent Mirror*, New York: Harper & Row Publishers, 1971.

Caso, Alfonso, *The Aztecs, People of the Sun*, Oklahoma: University of Oklahoma Press, 1958.

Cook, Theodore Andrea, *The Curves of Life*, New York: Dover Publications, Inc., 1979

D'Adamo, Peter J., *Eat Right for Your Type*, G.P. New York: Putnam's Sons, 1996.

Ferris, Timothy, *The Whole Shebang*, New York: Simon & Shuster, 1997.

Ghyka, Matila, *The Geometry and Art of Life*, New York: Dover Publications, 1977.

Gleick, James, *Chaos*, New York: Penguin Books, 1987

Gomora, Xokonochtletl Antonio, *Juicio a Espana*, Mexico: Tlamatini, 1988.

Huntley, H.E., *The Divine Proportion*, New York: Dover Publications, 1970.

Infante, Fernado Dìaz, *La Estela de los Soles o Calendario Azteca*, Mexico: Panorama Editorial, 1987

Jenny, Hans, *Cymatics Volume II*, Basel, Switzerland: Basilius Press AG,1974.

Matsumoto, Kiiko and Birch, Stephen, *Hara Diagnosis: Reflections on the Sea*, Cambridge, Massachusetts: Paradigm Publications, 1988.

Meyer, Michael C. and Sherman, William L., *The Course of Mexican History*, New York: Oxford University Press, 1983.

Moctezuma, Eduardo Matos, *The Aztecs*, New York Rizzoli International Publications, 1989.

Moctezuma, Eduardo Matos, *Treasures of the Great Temple*, La Jolla, California: Alti Publishing, 1990.

Plichta, Peter, *God's Secret Formula*, Rockport, Massachusetts: Element Books Limited, 1977.

Schneider, Michael S., *A Beginner's Guide to Constructing the Universe*, New York: Harper Perennial, 1994.

Schonberger, Martin, *The I Ching and the Genetic Code*, New Mexico: Aurora Press, 1992.

Smith, Cyril W. and Best, Simon, *Electromagnetic Man*, London: J.M Dent & Sons Ltd., 1989.

Tompkins, Peter, *Mysteries of the Mexican Pyramids*, New York: Harper & Row,1976.

Townsend, Richard F, *The Aztecs*, New York: Thames and Hudson, 1992.

Yan, Johnson, F., *DNA and the I Ching*, Berkeley, California: North Atlantic Books, 1991.

Index

ORDER FORM

If you enjoyed *Day of Destiny*, please tell your friends.

Case and large quantities are available, call for pricing.

**Order by phone 24 hours a day 1-(800) 485-8095 or (415) 331-0230
Fax (415) 331-0231. On-line ordering: http://DayofDestiny.com**

Name: _____

Address: _____

City: _____ State: _____

Country: _____ Postal Code: _____

Phone: (_____) _____ Fax (_____) _____

Email: _____

☐ Please send me information on upcoming *Day of Destiny*
　 workshops and lectures.

☐ Please send me the free Trans-Hyperborean Institute of Science
　 Vibrational Medicine catalog and newsletter.
　 (Includes Cymatics books and videos.)

My Order:

_____ Copy(s) of *Day of Destiny*　　$14.95 each　　_____

Sales Tax, California residents only add 7.25%　　_____

Shipping - $4.00 first book, 1.00 each additional　　_____

　　　　　　　　　　　　　　　　　　TOTAL　_____

Payment:

☐ Check or Money order made payable to: T.H.I.S.

☐ Charge: Visa/Mastercard/American Express

Card: _____Expiration Date: _____

Name on the card: _____

Signature: _____

**Mail order to: T.H.I.S./Day of Destiny
P.O. Box 2344, Sausalito, CA 94966 USA.
Orders are shipped within a week of receipt.**

Please give us your feedback and suggestions on how we can improve future editions of *Day of Destiny*.

Would you like to become more involved with August 13, 1999? Visit the *Day of Destiny* website at http://DayofDestiny.com. You can participate in on-line discussions, read the newest information and find out what's happening with our world-wide community of friends who are following the Call.

Profits from *Day of Destiny* go to research and preserve the indigenous medicine of Mexico, and create opportunities to study the Nahuatl language.

Teopiltzin (which in Nahuatl means: "one who brings a message") is a non-profit organization that supports and promotes the study and practice of indigenous culture, traditions (oral & written) and sacred teachings. **Teopiltzin** was formed to give modern people opportunities to learn and benefit from indigenous traditions. We offer classes, workshops and ceremonies to help our world become aware of the power and necessity of the indigenous way of life. It is time for us as a culture to recognize our divine heritage – a heritage that is preserved in oral teachings from shamans, healers, medicine people, the grandparents and elders of native cultures. **Teopiltzin** gives you the opportunity to support these people and learn about their ways to benefit yourself and all our relations.

To learn more about **Teopiltzin** please visit the website: http://dayofdestiny.com/teopiltzin. Your financial contributions and volunteer support are used for study courses in Nahuatl, to research and preserve indigenous medicine and provide the opportunity for you to participate in ceremony and cultural studies. Please call to volunteer (415) 331-0231 and send a donation by check or money order payable to: **Teopiltzin**, P.O. Box 2344, Sausalito, CA USA. (receipts are provided by request.) Thank you for your support!